Writing Never Arrives Naked

Writing Never Arrives Naked

Early Aboriginal cultures of writing in Australia

Penny van Toorn

ABORIGINAL STUDIES PRESS

First published in 2006 by Aboriginal Studies Press
Reprinted 2021, 2023

© Penny van Toorn 2006

All rights reserved. No part of this book may be reproduced or transmitted in any form or by any means, electronic or mechanical, including photocopying, recording or by any information storage and retrieval system, without prior permission in writing from the publisher. The *Australian Copyright Act 1968* (the Act) allows a maximum of one chapter or 10 per cent of this book, whichever is the greater, to be photocopied by any educational institution for its education purposes provided that the educational institution (or body that administers it) has given a remuneration notice to Copyright Agency Limited (CAL) under the Act.

Aboriginal Studies Press
is the publishing arm of the
Australian Institute of Aboriginal
and Torres Strait Islander Studies.
GPO Box 553, Canberra, ACT 2601
Phone: (61 2) 6246 1183
Fax: (61 2) 6261 4288
Email: asp@aiatsis.gov.au
Web: www.aiatsis.gov.au/asp

National Library of Australia
Cataloguing-In-Publication data:

> Van Toorn, Penny, 1952– .
> Writing never arrives naked : early Aboriginal cultures of writing in Australia.
>
> Bibliography.
> Includes index.
> ISBN–13: 978 0 85575 544 X.
> ISBN–10: 0 85575 544 X.
>
> 1. Aboriginal Australian literature. 2. Australian literature — Aboriginal Australian authors. 3. Written communication — Australia. I. Title.
>
> A820.989915

Printed in Australia by Pirion Pty Ltd

 This project has been assisted by the Australian Government through the Australia Council, its arts funding and advisory body.

Contents

Illustrations	vi
Acknowledgments	viii
Introduction *Sites of writing*	1
1. Encountering the alphabet	8
2. Sky gods and stolen children	24
3. Bennelong's letter	53
4. Borderlands of Aboriginal writing	71
5. Textual battlegrounds in Van Diemen's Land	93
6. Literacy, land and power: the Coranderrk petitions	123
7. Hidden transcripts at Lake Condah Mission Station	152
8. Early writings by Aboriginal women	175
9. A book by any other name…?	206
Conclusion *The past is not another country*	224
Notes	231
Index	257

Illustrations

The Milbrodale Baiami.	50
Bennelong's letter.	55
Reproduced by permission of the National Library of Australia.	
Two Wiradjuri clubs.	77
Charlie Flannigan's drawings.	81
Reproduced by permission of the Museum Board of South Australia	
Batman treating with the Blacks.	85
Reproduced with permission of Rare Books, Fisher Library, University of Sydney	
James Dawson's facsimile of the Geelong deed.	88
Reproduced with permission of Rare Books, Fisher Library, University of Sydney	
William Barak at Coranderrk.	128
From the La Trobe Picture Collection, State Library of Victoria	
Petition from William Barak.	136
From the collection of Public Records Office Victoria, PROV, VPRS 3991, Unit 834, 75/12439	
Petition from William Barak to the Hon. JM Grant.	145
From the collection of Public Records Office Victoria, PROV, VPRS 1226/P, Unit 4, W2858 82x x1857	
Petition from Thomas Dunolly, 1884.	148
From the collection of the National Archives of Australia, NAA series B313/1, item no. 213, folio 30	

Letter from Maggie Mobourne to DN McLeod. *From the collection of the National Archives of Australia,* *NAA series B337, item 507, 1900*	168
Petition from Ernest Mobourne to Cabinet, 2 July 1907. *From the collection of Public Records Office Victoria,* *PROV, VPRS 3992, Unit 1056, A5318*	171–172
Petition from William Barak, scribed by Betsy Bamfield. *From the collection of the National Archives of Australia,* *NAA series B313, item 213, folio 30*	182
Postcards from Rebecca Maltilina to Dorothea Ruediger. *Photographs courtesy of the State Library of South Australia*	199

Acknowledgments

There is something very special about archival research, particularly when it involves handwritten documents. Every manuscript carries bodily traces of its author. We today touch the papers that they touched long ago. We read the marks made by their moving hands. Sometimes, weirdly, even photocopies evoke the bodily presence of the writer. The archival research on which this study is based would not have been possible without the help of staff at the Mitchell Library, the Fisher Library, the Australian Museum, the Public Records Office of Victoria, the National Archives of Australia (Victoria), the State Library of Victoria, Museum Victoria, the National Library and the South Australian Museum.

Many people generously contributed to this project. I am especially grateful to Victor Briggs at the Koorie Heritage Trust in Melbourne, and to Joy Murphy Wandin, Jim Wandin, Judy Wilson, Zeta Thomson, Margaret Briggs Wirrapunda and Irene Swindle at Coranderrk. My thanks go also to Kerry Paton, Gayle Harradine, Lionel Harradine, Gary Murray, Jeanette Crew, Doris Paton, Karen Jackson, Steve Ross, Dawn Lee and Elsie Greeno — all of whom offered valuable assistance, information, encouragement and advice.

For permission to publish a photograph of the Milbrodale Baiami, I thank Robert Leicester, Graeme Ward, Barry McTaggart and Victor Perry. My thanks go also to Niel Gunson and Eric Fuss for their assistance regarding the Rebecca Maltilina postcards.

I am also grateful to present and past colleagues at the University of Sydney, especially Wendy Brady, Dennis Foley, Ian Henderson, Geoff Williams, Helen Hewson, Helen Groth, Noel Rowe, Brigid Rooney, Bernadette Brennan, Judy Barbour, Simone Marshall, and all those who offered their comments in the English Department research seminars. On the conference circuit, I have received valuable advice and encouragement from Helen Tiffin, Helen Gilbert, Leigh Dale, Bill Ashcroft, Lyn McCredden, Deborah Bird Rose, Roland Boer, Gillian Cowlishaw, Gillian Whitlock, Kay Schaffer, Paul Eggert and Paul Taçon.

Research for this book was made possible by an Australian Research Council Discovery Grant.

Earlier versions of some of the chapters have been published in *Meanjin* vol. 55, no. 4 (1996); *Continuum* vol. 13, no. 3 (November 1999); *UTS Review* vol 7, no. 1 (2001); *Social Semiotics* vol. 11, no. 2 (2001); *Semeia* 88 (2001); *Telling Stories*, eds Bain Attwood and Fiona Magowan (Allen & Unwin, 2001); *The Cambridge Companion to Australian Literature*, ed. Elizabeth Webby (Cambridge University Press, 2000). I am grateful for permission to republish.

Pauline McGuire, my editor, has been a wise and patient adviser throughout the process of converting a series of articles and conference papers into a book. Many thanks go also to Gabrielle Lhuede and Rhonda Black at Aboriginal Studies Press. Finally, I wish to express my gratitude to Elizabeth Webby, without whose support this project would not have been possible, and to Ruby Langford Ginibi who makes me feel honoured by calling me 'tidda'.

Introduction

Sites of writing

In 1848, German explorer Ludwig Leichhardt attempted to cross the continent of Australia from east to west, but his entire party vanished without word or trace. Patrick White's novel *Voss* (1957) offered a fictional account of how the explorers lost contact with the European world. White proposed that it was Aboriginal people's superstitious fear and hostility towards written documents that effectively severed the explorers' last line of communication with home. As White tells it, when all hope fails and death is drawing near, Voss and his men put pen to paper to inform their loved ones of their fate and convey their last goodbyes. They enlist Dugald, one of their Aboriginal guides, to carry the letters back to the last white outpost. On the way, Dugald meets a band of Aboriginal men and women. He solemnly shows them the strange white sheets covered in rows of tangled black lines, and explains that the letters carry the white man's pain and sadness away.[1] A warrior jabs at the papers with his spear; a woman tastes the sealing wax and instantly splutters it out. The others examine the writing but see nothing but drawings of fern roots on the thin white sheets. Dugald, having failed to impress his newfound acquaintances, tears the letters to shreds, flings them into the air, and watches as 'the pieces of paper fluttered round him and settled on the grass, like a mob of cockatoos.' He abandons his role as letter-carrier, and treks away with the Aboriginal band towards a place of plentiful food.

Like many literary representations, White's account suggests that Indigenous Australians in the colonial period saw writing and books as alien and irrelevant or evil and potentially dangerous. This axiom of settler ideology was deeply rooted in Enlightenment cultural theory, 19th-century evolutionary biology and social Darwinism — modes of thought that in

Australia remained highly influential until well into the 20th century. In 1927, for example, the eminent anthropologist WB Spencer, Director of the National Museum of Victoria in Melbourne, asserted that:

> Australia is the present home and refuge of creatures, often crude and quaint, that have elsewhere passed away and given place to higher forms. This applies equally to the aboriginal [sic] as to the platypus and kangaroo. Just as the platypus, laying its eggs and feebly suckling its young, reveals a mammal in the making, so does the aboriginal show us, at least in broad outlines, what early man must have been like before he learned to read and write, domesticate animals, cultivate crops and use a metal tool. It has been possible to study in Australia human beings that still remain on the culture level of men of the Stone Age.[2]

Statements such as this make Indigenous literacy a contradiction in terms. The authority of science and the imaginative force of the arts have combined to create a perception that Aboriginal cultures are essentially oral, while literacy is the province of the settler society.

David Unaipon, whose *Native legends* was published in 1929, is generally believed to be Australia's first Aboriginal author.[3] Yet the history of Aboriginal writing might have various beginnings, depending on how we answer questions such as: What counts as 'writing'? What counts as authorship? and Who counts as Aboriginal? It's time to ask what the history of Aboriginal reading and writing would look like if we moved beyond Eurocentric concepts of authorship, included genres other than fiction and poetry, and situated reading and writing in specific cultural contexts.

By adjusting the theoretical lens through which Indigenous writing is perceived, a new history of Aboriginal writing comes into view. It becomes possible to see that when David Unaipon published his first book in 1929, Koori peoples in the Sydney region had been reading and authoring written texts for 140 years. Within a short time of the arrival of the First Fleet of British convicts and their minders in 1788, Aboriginal trade routes took printed objects and written papers into regions way beyond the frontier of white occupation, where they were exchanged as curiosities and, at times, assimilated into Indigenous graphic traditions and social life. In the 1830s and 1840s, Pallawah peoples in Van Diemen's Land (Tasmania) were generating subversive readings of the Bible, and writing sermons, a community newspaper, letters to colonial government authorities and a lengthy petition to Queen Victoria.[4] In the second half of the 19th century, members of the Kulin confederacy and other nations in Victoria were producing political documents in the form of letters and petitions, often in accordance with their traditional social protocols of oral communication. By 1901, when the independent colonies of New South Wales, Tasmania, Victoria, Queensland, South Australia and Western Australia federated to become the Commonwealth of Australia, Aboriginal men, women and children across the continent had written hundreds of letters and petitions to colonial officials in an effort to gain a measure of control over their lives. Members of this so-called Stone-Age race were also writing to each other, corresponding with white friends, assisting in the production of written translations of the Bible, reading and publishing their views in major newspapers, and preparing written submissions to official inquiries. Few had the leisure time to read novels and other book-length literary texts, and there are no known pre–20th century Indigenous-authored novels, plays or poems. Nonetheless, these early Aboriginal authors knew well how to tell stories and build compelling arguments in written English, and they were acutely aware that reading and writing were powerful political weapons. Humble as were the genres within which they worked, these authors deployed complex forms of language, narrative, political argument and self-construction, and they certainly used their reading skills to good advantage.

This book is a first attempt to tell the story — or a cluster of stories — of how the cultures of reading and writing introduced to Australia by the British in 1788 became entangled with the oldest living Indigenous cultures in the world. These are important stories. They extend and deepen knowledge of Indigenous Australian cultural and political history. They also cast new light on present-day Indigenous Australian literature and literacies, and address broader theoretical questions about reading and writing in intercultural contexts.

Chapter 1, 'Encountering the alphabet', identifies three distinct cultures of early Aboriginal literacy: those that were based on individual black–white collaborations, those that sprang up in traditional cultural settings without any European tutelage, and those that developed on missions and reserves. This chapter also critically evaluates the two main schools of theoretical thought on the question of how alphabetic literacy impacts upon so-called 'oral' Indigenous societies. On one side are those who believe the arrival of alphabetic script itself triggered radical cultural, political and epistemological changes. On the other side are those who stress the primary importance of contextual factors, such as the institutional and political settings within which literacy was introduced. As the chapter title indicates, I cast my lot with those who believe writing never operates alone as a force for change in Indigenous life-worlds. After briefly considering the crucial contextual variables — the clothing, as it were — of early Indigenous Australian writing, I attempt to resolve an intractable conundrum: if literacy *in itself* does not necessarily undermine traditional Indigenous cultures, why did those cultures so often break down when literacy was introduced? Here I confront the paradoxical fact that an erroneous theory can nonetheless be self-fulfilling.

In Chapter 2, 'Sky gods and stolen children', I examine the early colonists' late–18th century practice of taking Aboriginal children from their families and justifying such removals by promising them the benefits of literacy. During the early 19th century, Governor Macquarie institutionalised child removal. His annual 'Native feasts' at Parramatta were largely designed to lure Aboriginal parents into surrendering their children to the residential school he had established there. Aboriginal people came from hundreds of kilometres away to attend these feasts, but very few left their children at the school. In the 1820s and 1830s, other largely unsuccessful attempts to promulgate literacy among Aboriginal children were mounted at missions to the west and north of Sydney. This chapter connects the early history of the stolen generations with the early history of Aboriginal literacy, and suggests how Aboriginal societies in south-eastern Australia may have used their own narratives of Eaglehawk and Crow to make sense of the colonists' desire to take away their children and teach them to read. Of particular interest is Biraban, a stolen Awabakal child who grew up to be a spiritual leader of his people, while involved over many years in Biblical translation with Missionary Launcelot Threlkeld near Lake Macquarie, north of Sydney.

While the first Indigenous Australians to read were stolen children, the first Indigenous author was a stolen adult, Bennelong, a young Dharug man from Port Jackson (Sydney Harbour). Bennelong is one of the most widely known Indigenous names in Australia. There are numerous streets that carry his name, as does Bennelong Point where the Sydney Opera House now stands. What is not widely known is that Bennelong's letter of 1796 was the first piece of writing authored by an Indigenous Australian. The dictated letter is the central focus of Chapter 3. In 1789, Bennelong was captured by order of Arthur Phillip, the first governor of the colony of New South Wales. After escaping from captivity and wreaking revenge on the governor, Bennelong eventually made peace with Phillip and voluntarily accompanied him to England in 1792. He returned to Australia in 1795, and the following year dictated his letter to Lord Sydney's steward, who had cared for him in England during a period of serious illness. Bennelong was a consummate mimic, and an indefatigable entrepreneur. Close analysis and contextualisation of his letter suggest that although he used Governor Phillip's writings as discursive models, he also understood letter writing in terms of his own cultural norms of kin-based gift exchange and trade. As a tradable artefact, Bennelong's letter could potentially both fulfil his traditional Indigenous social obligations, and work in his favour in the gift economies of both British patronage and Aboriginal trade relations.

Chapter 4, 'Borderlands of Aboriginal writing', discusses three frontier moments in which Europeans and traditionally oriented Indigenous people assimilated each others' inscriptions into their own signifying systems: first, the production of a pair of carved wooden clubs in Wiradjuri country in central New South Wales in the mid-19th century; second, a set of drawings of writing produced by Charlie Flannigan, an Aboriginal prisoner in Fanny Bay Gaol in Darwin in the early 1890s; and third, John Batman's illegal treaty of 1835 with the Woiworung owners of the land where Melbourne now stands. I call these 'borderland' writings because they each cross the borders between categories of writing, showing that in frontier settings, Aboriginal people and colonists used each other's writing systems in accordance with their own desires and traditions of inscription, with little or no guidance or instruction as to how alphabetic characters would normally be created, deciphered and used in their culture of origin. These borderland writings show what happens when writing 'cross-dresses'; that is, when it is clothed in the ideology and institutionalised practices of a different culture. This chapter dismantles the categorical difference between pictographic, ideographic and phonographic scripts, and hence the associated distinction between savage, barbarian and civilised societies that was fundamental to colonialist ideology.

Chapters 5, 6 and 7 are devoted primarily to mission and reserve cultures. Chapter 5, 'Textual battlegrounds in Van Diemen's Land', examines the Bible in the Tasmanian wilderness, where it was incorporated into Indigenous rituals before being repatriated back into Christian liturgy. This chapter also explores the political dynamics of ventriloquism and refraction in the writings of two young Indigenous men virtually imprisoned on the windy, wave-battered rock known as Flinders Island during the 1830s.

Chapter 6, 'Land, literacy and power: the Coranderrk petitions', offers tangible evidence of an Indigenous reinvention of European literacy. As on other missions and reserves, it was the children at Coranderrk who first acquired alphabetic literacy and fluency in English, potent tools that could potentially shift power from the older, fully initiated men to the young of both sexes. Fissured and factional as it was, the Coranderrk community used alphabetic writing in accordance with their own traditional social protocols of communication.

On reserves and missions, *open* dissent by Aboriginal people brought trouble to both the governors and the governed. Aboriginal people's day-to-day survival depended largely on their ability to feign consent to their own subordination. Correspondingly, superintendents insisted their Aboriginal charges were content and well-behaved because their continued employment, funding and career advancement depended on this pretence. Chapter 7, 'Hidden transcripts at Lake Condah Mission Station', analyses the ways in which writing worked as a performative medium in Victoria from the mid-1870s to the early 20th century.

In Chapter 8 the focus shifts to Indigenous women's writing. There are conflicting arguments about the effects of colonialism on Indigenous women. Some see them as doubly oppressed on the basis of race and gender; others argue that women found niches and roles that allowed them a greater sense of self-worth and dignity than was possible for their menfolk. No Aboriginal woman ever authored a community petition. What roles, then, did Aboriginal women take up as readers and writers in colonial Australia? What social functions did their writing perform?

Chapter 9, 'A book by any other name…?', is concerned with Indigenous Australian transformations of the book, not only in frontier, patronage, and mission and reserve settings, but in present-day book cultures. Inspired by the work of Walter D Mignolo, I bring philological evidence to bear on the question of how Aboriginal people have perceived and used books — for many years the primary sign-carrying objects of those who occupy their lands.

Several of the chapters on Indigenous literacy in colonial times end with glances forward into the present. In the concluding chapter, I trace patterns of connection between today's Indigenous Australian literacy practices and the three cultures of literacy that developed in the colonial period.

Today, the most challenging question is perhaps this: what is to be gained by insisting that there is no such single thing as 'literacy', only 'literacies', when non-mainstream literacies seem to entrench disempowerment? If all literacies are equal in theory, how does it come about in practice that only certain varieties and standards of literacy prove empowering?

1

Encountering the alphabet

Broadly speaking, there are two schools of thought on what happened when Indigenous societies around the world encountered the cultures of literacy imported by Europe's imperial powers from late 15th century onwards. On one side are cultural historians and theorists such as Jack Goody, Walter J Ong and Marshall McLuhan who, beginning in the 1960s, argued that writing *in itself* has played a determining role in the biological and cultural advancement of humankind. Such ideas were initially articulated by Renaissance and Enlightenment philosophers, before acquiring authority in the late 19th century in the work of 'scientists' such as Edward Burnett Tylor, who took up the first Chair of Anthropology at Oxford University in 1895. In his influential book *Anthropology* (1881), Tylor had asserted that:

> The invention of writing was the great movement by which mankind rose from barbarism to civilization. How vast its effect was may be best measured by looking at the low condition of tribes still living without it, dependent on memory for their traditions and rules of life, and unable to amass knowledge as we do by keeping records of events, and storing up new observations for the use of future generations. Thus it is no doubt right to draw the line between barbarian and civilized where the art of writing comes in, for this gives permanence to history, law and science.[1]

Tylor's theories about 'primitive peoples' grew out of and fed back into field research carried out by correspondents in Australia and other parts of the British empire.[2] Like most anthropologists of his day, Tylor viewed writing as a primary criterion of civilisation, and looked to Indigenous Australians to see primitivity personified. Present-day theorists, such as

Ong and Goody, are far more aware than was Tylor of the complexity and sophistication of 'oral' cultures. They nonetheless follow his lead in believing writing to be an autonomous engine of cultural advancement. This 'autonomous' model, as it is often called, assumes that writing's impact is inherent in the nature of alphabetic script and 'literacy itself'.[3] In doing so, it takes insufficient account of contextual matters such as ideology, institutions and socio-political relations; in other words, it overlooks the effects of the specific circumstances and contexts in which writing and literacy enter Indigenous life-worlds. The autonomous model also remains blind to its own ethnocentricity, viewing modes of literacy that deviate from Western norms as a stage on the way to full literacy, as though the passage from Indigenous orality to European literacy were an invariable law of cultural evolution.

The central question addressed by adherents to the autonomous model is: how does alphabetic literacy shape the cultural, cognitive and socio-political history of human societies? The connection between literacy and cultural 'advancement' is embedded in the English language in terms such as 'illiterate' and 'pre-literate'. Words such as these keep alive the assumption that 'humankind is characterised by "a will to writing", that writing is a universal cultural goal, and that all cultures are somewhere along the road to writing.'[4] The autonomous model is thus central to grand, Eurocentric narratives of cultural progress.

The second, and in my view the more valid, way of understanding Indigenous literacy in Australia and other colonial settings derives from studies carried out by Brian Street, Ruth Finnegan, and other anthropologists and ethno-linguists.[5] Beginning in the 1980s, they challenged the idea that there is a single, canonical set of skills and practices that amount to literacy proper. While conceding that literacy is a necessary, but not sufficient, condition of certain kinds of change, they refuted the notion that literacy is *in itself* an autonomous force in human history. Instead, believing that writing and literacy are never practised in a vacuum, they focused on the impact of particular conceptions or ideologies of literacy, and on the specific purposes, means and institutions through which those conceptions were introduced and enforced. Their research indicated that there is no such singular thing as 'literacy itself', no single set of reading and writing practices that are inherently and invariably correct, but instead a multitude of ways to practise literacy. Literacy can therefore only be validly examined in context, at particular sites, rather than in abstract general terms.

Finnegan and others who shared her view dismantled the theoretical foundations of the orality/literacy divide. Instead of viewing orality and literacy as successive stages of cultural development, they highlighted the ongoing interplay between text and talk, and the multiplicity of reading and writing systems apart from the alphabet. Even within the empire of the alphabet, they urged that the focus should be on literacies in the plural, rather then a single normative literacy. Literacy is always culturally situated. Each act of reading and writing is carried out in a particular political and historical context in which the powerful decide which practices are to be counted as correct and normal, and which will be declared erroneous and insignificant.

The model holds that people's actual reading and writing practices are determined less by the nature of the particular script they use than by the political, social and institutional circumstances under which they have acquired and employed that script, as well as by the specific beliefs, attitudes, values and desires they bring to particular tasks of reading and writing. Hence their approach is referred to as 'the ideological model'. As James Collins and Richard Blot put it:

> Literate practices are not merely technical means transportable unchanged across socio-cultural contexts. They are specific practices manifested in different ways in differing contexts, whose meanings are more dependent on the processes by which they were acquired than on the specific skills applied.[6]

For those who adhere to the idea that literacy can only be understood within its specific cultural and political contexts, the key question is *not* How has literacy in itself shaped this or that society? but rather, How and why has this individual, or this group of people, at this particular point in their history, acquired, conceptualised, organised and used their particular reading and writing practices in the manner they have? It is this question that underlies each of the case studies presented in this book, and affords a rationale for the case-study approach itself.

o o o

Weighing up the pros and cons of these two models of literacy — the autonomous and the ideological — it may initially appear that colonial and post-colonial experiences offer little evidence to support the latter. In theory, according to the ideological model, literacy should not *necessarily* supersede Indigenous oral cultural traditions; however, in practice such 'replacement' seems very often to have been the case. If, as Street and others argue, literacy *in itself* does not change societies in consistent, predictable ways, why is it that in so many colonial contexts, traditional Indigenous worldviews, languages and modes of socio-political organisation have been seriously undermined by the introduction of literacy?

In addressing this question it is important to acknowledge at the outset that the 'loss' of Indigenous oral culture can be difficult to quantify. On the one hand, non-Indigenous people have failed to perceive the extent of Indigenous cultural loss and understand its dire ramifications. On the other, it is sometimes the case that 'losses' are actually adaptations or transformations of traditional Indigenous practices — transformations that are not recognised as such by non-Indigenous people, who underestimate the normal dynamism and exposure to otherness that so-called 'traditional' cultures are accustomed to. How can something as complex as cultural loss be measured? Where should the line be drawn between cultural loss and cultural transformation? Indigenous people the world over celebrate the survival of their cultures, as well as mourning what has been lost.

The chapters that follow offer evidence that, contrary to the predictions of the autonomous model, certain traditional orally grounded Indigenous Australian practices have survived the onset of literacy, and may in fact have been secured and reinforced through it. Traditionally based Indigenous practices of alphabetic literacy that emerged over 200 years ago in the late 18th century continued throughout the 19th and 20th centuries, and are still manifest in the authorial practices of Aboriginal writers today. The persistence of these practices suggests that they are not part of an insignificant, transitory adjustment process on a path that leads to 'literacy proper'. Instead, they are evidence that reading and writing have been reinvented, and that under certain conditions Aboriginal communities have been able to develop and adapt their own new and distinct cultures of literacy in a manner that perpetuates traditional, orally grounded social structures and values.

That said, there is no denying that in many parts of Australia important traditional Indigenous life-ways have not survived the introduction of literacy. Does such erosion attest to the destructive powers of literacy itself, as proponents of the autonomous model would have us believe? Or has cultural change been caused instead, as the ideological model suggests, by the impact of particular conceptions of literacy, and the ways in which they were enforced? Ideas about literacy can have serious, tangible, historical ramifications when they form a basis for action. Such has been the case with the autonomous model of literacy. Mistaken as it is, it looks like a self-fulfilling prophecy because it has formed the basis for assimilationist educational and cultural policies. But by examining diverse sites of writing, including 'untutored' engagements with alphabetic script, it becomes possible to see that, left to their own devices, Aboriginal people conceptualised and used alphabetic signs, paper and books in ways that differed radically from European norms.

Throughout the colonial period, and indeed until the 1980s, government policy-makers invariably assumed that literacy itself shaped societies — an assumption that went hand in hand with the belief that oral and literate cultures were successive, mutually exclusive stages in a single, unavoidable path of cultural evolution towards modernity. This mode of thinking has a long genealogy that extends at least as far back as the Renaissance. Western philosophers and ethnologists imagined that contemporary Indigenous societies were relics of a bygone age, and were thus similar to ancient pre-literate European societies. This positioning of Indigenous peoples as 'where Europeans once were' made the assimilation of Aboriginal people look like a historical shortcut, a mere speeding up of an allegedly natural, inevitable evolutionary process. In Australia, this belief justified the introduction of policies designed to transform Indigenous people, culturally and biologically, into whites. Colonial government and church authorities viewed literacy as a tool of assimilation, an effective means of hastening the 'inevitable' progress of 'primitive' peoples into the modern white Western world. Writing and literacy thus entered Indigenous Australian life-worlds most often as part of a colonialist Christian agenda.

What did Aboriginal people themselves make of writing and literacy, as these new texts and practices were integrated into their worldviews and day-to-day lives? At one extreme, in traditional Aboriginal societies, people assimilated writing and books into their own categories of objects and cultural practices. At the other extreme, in mission and reserve schools, people were taught to read and write in classrooms where they were required to participate in rituals such as copying lines and spelling out loud. In every one of the diverse contexts in which Aboriginal people engaged with the alphabetic script, reading and writing were imbued with attitudes, ideas and feelings. It was these contextual and ideological elements that primarily shaped Indigenous reading and writing in colonial Australia. The radical historical force lay not in writing or literacy per se, but in the colonists' firm belief that literacy would inevitably 'advance' Indigenous Australians, and in the means by which that belief was put into effect. The belief that literacy itself triggers certain kinds of changes is thus not only manifestly erroneous, it also obscures its own historical influence as a basis of the 'native policies' and assimilationist practices that shaped how most Indigenous peoples learned to read and write in the colonial period.

This paradox of the erroneous yet self-fulfilling prophecy explains why the autonomous model of literacy appears to have been borne out in practice in many colonial contexts. Indigenous peoples in Australia, North America and elsewhere are today living with the damaging legacies of the autonomous model of literacy, having seen their cultures undermined by missionaries and schoolteachers who prohibited traditional languages and ceremonies, and by welfare officers and assimilation policies that obstructed traditional oral channels of cultural transmission by separating children from their families. In Australia, as in many other parts of the colonised world, the autonomous model of literacy was institutionalised in ways that, paradoxically, annulled literacy's putative autonomy. In the regimented, poorly resourced, under-staffed mission and reserve schools that Aboriginal children attended, literacy did not in fact work as a historical force in its own right.

The chapters that follow offer evidence that it was not literacy in itself that set in train the cultural assimilation of Indigenous peoples into Euro-Australian society. It was not reading and writing per se that eroded traditional Indigenous cultures, but rather the particular circumstances under which Indigenous peoples acquired literacy and engaged with the material artefacts of literate Western culture.

What writing brings with it

Alphabetic literacy and written texts did not arrive in Indigenous Australian life-worlds naked and alone. Writing arrived, in fact, wearing several layers of clothing. Most important but least tangible were the ideologies that enveloped alphabetic script, books, and the practices of reading and writing. The nature of these ideological vestments depended on whether they were formed within Indigenous cultural settings, or through direct contact with the settler society, or both. If Indigenous Australians encountered alphabetic characters without white guidance or modelling, they assimilated them into their own understandings of the universe, perceiving and evaluating whatever novel graphic marks they saw in terms of their own traditional frames of reference, and conceiving them in ways potentially different from European ideas of writing. However, in settings where Indigenous Australians were schooled in European cultures of literacy, or were familiar with written texts through close acquaintance with whites, they may instead (or in addition) have adopted Western ideas about literacy and written texts.

Second, writing arrived in Indigenous life-worlds in the form of tangible objects that were part and parcel of the material culture and technology of the colonisers. Aboriginal people saw writing on objects as diverse as Bibles and flour-bags; not only on paper, but on things like coins, milestones and merchandise. The materiality of writing played an important part in Indigenous perceptions and uses of alphabetic script.

Third, writing almost invariably encoded a particular language: English. Except in South Australia, where the German missionaries knew very little English, and in isolated cases where missionaries recorded Indigenous languages on paper, Aboriginal people on missions and reserves encountered alphabetic writing as a code for the English language.[7] Literacy and English language acquisition were thus almost inextricable, and both were high on colonial government and mission agendas.

Fourth, writing was also invariably accompanied by meaning, whether encoded in the letters of the alphabetically written words and sentences, or ascribed to written documents on a different basis altogether. In the early 1790s, when Bennelong sat with Governor Phillip as he penned his official correspondence, or in the 1820s and 1830s when Biraban pored over the biblical verses that he and missionary Lancelot Threlkeld were translating, they did not engage with writing in general or writing in the abstract, but with particular words and sentences to which they ascribed particular meanings. These meanings must surely have played a role in shaping Aboriginal perceptions of writing.

Fifth, Aboriginal people did not engage with writing and literacy in a socio-political vacuum. Writing was carried into their world by individuals whose skin colour was the same as that of the people who shot them, sexually abused them, poisoned their water, ruined their hunting grounds, took away their children, and dispossessed them from their lands. Literacy and alphabetic script entered Indigenous life-worlds as part of a foreign invasion. Reading and writing were thus inherently political.

Sixth, and finally, Aboriginal people acquired literacy most often through formal schooling on missions and reserves. Their perceptions, attitudes and practices of literacy were shaped largely by these institutions. Writing and reading were, on the one hand, an onerous schoolroom task, part of the white man's agenda for 'lifting up the savage races'. But writing also proved to be a most valuable political weapon when Aboriginal people wished to level complaints against mission and reserve staff, or halt government plans to sell off their adopted homes. The government and church bodies that funded and administered reserves and missions were highly bureaucratic. If Aboriginal people had complaints, they were required to put them in writing. Consequently, the largest sources of 19th-century Aboriginal writing are government archives.

All these dimensions of literacy and written texts — the ideological, the material, the linguistic, the semantic, the socio-political and the institutional — must be taken into account in any attempt to read early Aboriginal writings adequately, and to understand the dynamics of Indigenous cultures of literacy in colonial Australia.

Literacy and the stolen generations

In the Sydney region, where the first British settlement was established in 1788, the first Indigenous Australians to read alphabetic script were the so-called orphaned children who, from 1889 onwards, were taken into the homes of white philanthropists and used as servants. From these very early days, the history of Aboriginal literacy cannot be separated from the broader experience of Aboriginal oppression and dispossession. The practice of child removal which began in the early years at Sydney Cove became firmly established on the missions and reserves that were set up in the 19th century during the protectionist era. In the 20th century, child removals continued under the assimilation and integration policies that operated into the 1970s. Today, Aboriginal children are still being removed from their families at much higher rates than non-Aboriginal children through the welfare and legal justice systems, a pattern consistent with that in Canada and the United States.

Schools — and empty promises of schooling — were part and parcel of the long history of separating Indigenous children from their families. In Australia, these children are known as 'the stolen generations'. In 1997, the separation of Aboriginal children from their families became a matter of public knowledge via *Bringing them home: report of the national inquiry into the separation of Aboriginal and Torres Strait Islander children from their families*. This 700-page report, which received intense media coverage and became a national bestseller, contains evidence that Aboriginal parents were deceived into relinquishing their children 'for their own educational good'.

It includes numerous testimonies by Aboriginal men and women who, as children, were literally torn from the arms of their families, under laws that, according to the Van Boven criteria, were genocidal.[8]

The deep and complex implication of Aboriginal literacy with racial oppression is a highly sensitive issue. Without at all denying the profound hurt and the ongoing suffering caused by the separation of Indigenous children from their families, it remains true to say that some Aboriginal families saw formal schooling as potentially empowering, and were genuinely keen to see their children educated, preferably in day schools where they were able to continue living with their families. Writing from a domestic placement in the town of Clare in South Australia, for example, Jessie Lindsay wrote to the Native Protector, asking him to:

> …see that my daughter Grace Power is sent to school at Point Pearce. I hear that she is working in a married person's cottage. I was asking why was it she is writing so badly as she writes to me from time to time & I don't see any improvement… I wish her my daughter to go to school as she is not 14 year of age yet… I wish her to go to school and look after her little sister… If she is not removed from that person's cottage I shall go down and take her away.[9]

Many associated schooling and literacy with child-stealing, however. In the early 1840s, Protector ES Parker reported that an Aboriginal leader in Victoria 'complained in his anger that the white fellow had stolen their country and that I was stealing their children by taking them away to live in huts, and work, and "read the book like whitefellows"'.[10] The issue here is not that literacy itself is inherently and inevitably pernicious. For Indigenous Australians, as for Native Americans and the First Nations, Métis and Inuit peoples of Canada whose children were removed from their families to be educated in residential schools, the problem lay not in literacy per se, but in the dehumanising circumstances and the harsh institutional settings in which literacy was imparted to their children.

If alphabetic literacy eroded Indigenous cultures, it was not due to the alphabet's allegedly inherent ability to reproduce speech in graphic form. Far more destructive were the separation of children from their families, and the methods, institutions and political circumstances under which literacy was imposed, usually hand in hand with the English language and a whole raft of English social values, Christian beliefs and cultural proprieties. As Aboriginal children practised writing and reading their lines, they were learning much more than penmanship, and much more than the association between letters and sounds. One can only speculate as to what was going on in their minds as their teachers instructed them to write:

> Captain Cook.
> Captain Cook.
> Captain Cook.
> Doing nothing is the hardest of work.
> Doing nothing is the hardest of work.
> Doing nothing is the hardest of work.

A whole page of each of these lines was penned in impeccable copperplate in 1896 by Jessie Lindsay's thirteen-year-old daughter, Grace Power, at the request of the South Australian Native Protector, who wished to disprove Jessie Lindsay's assertion that her daughter's writing was deteriorating.[11] Grace Power's copperplate, and the content of the lines, reflected well on the Protector's professional expertise as a builder of both literacy and moral fibre among his Aboriginal charges.

Another display of penmanship was produced in the early 1850s as a gift for Reverend Matthew Hale by a young Kaurna man at Poonindie Mission in South Australia:

> Whenever I take my walks abroad,
> How my poor I see.
> What shall I render to my God
> for all his gifts to me?
> > Not more than others I deserve,
> > yet God hath given me more;
> > for I have food while others starve,
> > or beg from door to door.
> The poor wild natives whom I meet,
> Half-naked I behold,
> > While I am clothed from head to feet
> > And covered from the cold.
> > While some poor wretches scarce can tell
> > Where they may lay their head,
> > I have a home within to dwell
> > And rest upon my bed.
> While others early learn to swear
> And curse and lie and steal,
> Lord, I am taught your name to fear

17

>   And do thy holy will.
>   And these thy favours day by day
>   To me above the rest,
>   Then let me love thee more than they
>   And try to serve thee best.[12]

These samples of early Aboriginal writing show that one can't just read and write: one has to read and write *something*. What then were those 'somethings' that Aboriginal people read and wrote in colonial times? And if reading and writing were implicated in the undermining of Indigenous oral cultures, precisely how and under what circumstances did that undermining occur?

When Aboriginal people adopted elements of colonial British literate culture, their traditional cultural beliefs and practices were not necessarily swept away. The archives contain ample evidence of oral traditions and ideographic writing systems coexisting with alphabetic literacy in various relationships of mutual entanglement that developed in an array of different contexts.

The prevailing popular perception, however, is that Aboriginal cultures have always been essentially oral, while European cultures are distinctively literate. Indeed, Aboriginal people themselves have rightly prided themselves on the power, richness and resilience of their oral cultures of song and storytelling. Labelling Aboriginal cultures as 'oral' and European cultures as 'literate' can be problematic, however. To deem Aboriginal cultures 'oral' is to reinforce a narrow Eurocentric definition of 'writing', a definition that excludes or demeans non-alphabetic graphic systems. Moreover, literacy comes to seem un-Aboriginal. Aboriginal literacy then appears to be a contradiction in terms, and can be gained, it may seem, only at the cost of Aboriginality. It was precisely this dangerous logic that colonial authorities used when they introduced literacy as an instrument of assimilation, long before assimilation policies were officially introduced in the 20th century.

Cultures of literacy

There is only one Roman alphabet, but many ways of practising literacy. Reading and writing are always shaped by micro-historical circumstances, and are invariably entangled with ideology, power struggles and institutional structures. Missions and reserves were not the only places where Indigenous Australians first engaged with reading and writing. At different times, in different parts of the continent, in different institutional and socio-political settings, Aboriginal people developed diverse cultures of literacy. Literacy did not spread uniformly across Indigenous Australian societies as a shadow moves over the land; nor did it move through a fixed succession of phases or stages in each locality. This book focuses mainly, but not exclusively, on the south-eastern colonies of New South Wales, Van Diemen's Land (Tasmania) and Victoria. By adopting a case-study approach, I attempt to do justice to the diversity of Indigenous cultures of reading and writing, while also recognising the extent to which people in different areas shared common patterns of political experience.

During the colonial period, that is, from 1788 to the early 20th century, three Indigenous Australian cultures of reading and writing emerged: individual black–white collaborations, traditionally oriented cultures, and mission and reserve cultures.

Individuals such as Bennelong and Biraban encountered European literacy through their personal relationships with non-Indigenous friends and patrons. Where such connections are documented or remembered, it becomes possible to imagine the circumstances and identify the kinds of written texts that these and other Indigenous people were exposed to. In these one-to-one social settings, Aboriginal people engaged with the practices and artefacts of European literate culture guided by their European associates. Writing and reading entered Aboriginal life-worlds clothed in the ideas and information supplied by white acquaintances, but always these alien elements were understood within Indigenous frames of reference.

On occasion, Indigenous Australians deciphered and used alphabetic writing and books in accordance with their own traditions of inscription and communication, with little or no modelling or guidance as to how written texts would normally be produced, deciphered and used in European cultures. In traditionally oriented contexts, Aboriginal people formed their own ideas about writing on the basis of their own scriptorial practices, their own categories of objects, and their own values and needs. In this sense, writing was from the outset perceived through Aboriginal frames of reference. Yet it entered Indigenous life-worlds embodied in particular material forms and social practices. The artefacts and tools of literacy took the form of tangible inscriptions of particular alphabetic and numeric characters on particular objects in particular social and cultural settings. Writing's uses are not self-evident; it has no inherent meanings or capabilities. In traditional settings, therefore, writing's value, meaning and manner of usage depended on how it was perceived by Aboriginal people using their own cultural objects and practices as points of reference. From the very first moment writing enters Indigenous people's awareness, it is clothed in Indigenous ideology. In traditionally oriented Indigenous cultures, tangible artefacts of writing, like other elements of material culture, are 'not what they were made to be [by whites] but what they have become' in Aboriginal eyes.[13]

When the first British settlers arrived on Australian shores in 1788, Aboriginal people were using several systems of graphic signification. These included the coded information engraved on message-sticks, tree trunks and rock surfaces, and the iconographic ground drawings that accompanied oral storytelling. Stylised maps and narratives were also engraved on sacred ritual objects, and Aboriginal people painted richly meaningful images and signs on rocks, bark, wooden artefacts, animal skins and human bodies. In addition, piercing, scarification and other inscriptions of the body were used to signify the wearer's intention, social status or level of religious initiation. Also important were the fleeting, intangible 'logograms written into the air'[14]: the ceremonial dance movements central to Indigenous religious practice, and the hundreds of readable hand signals and other body movements necessary for silent communication while hunting, for conveying information to people out of earshot, and for observing taboos against speaking the names of certain Dreaming ancestors and deceased people.[15] Not all modes of signification were practised in all parts of Australia. Indigenous cultures differed somewhat from region to region. Yet everywhere, whatever combination of signifying systems were used, Aboriginal people engaged in traditional communication and information storage practices that might broadly be called writing and reading.

Consequently, the arrival of the British in 1788 did not herald the beginning of a shift from orality to literacy for Indigenous Australians, but rather the beginning of an entanglement between two sets of reading and writing practices. From the outset, Indigenous Australians understood the alphabetic characters and material objects associated with English literacy in terms of the categories and practices of traditional Aboriginal culture.

On missions and reserves, Indigenous children and young adults learned to read and write in tightly regulated institutional environments, as part of the oppressive but 'elevating' apparatus of formal schooling, colonial governance and Christian proselytising. These sites of reading and writing were dynamic, complex intercultural zones where literacy became a powerful political practice and, if conditions were right, writing was carried out in traditionally oriented ways. On missions and reserves, European etiquettes and ideologies of writing were formally taught to Aboriginal people, but traditional Indigenous perceptions and social protocols of reading and writing sometimes continued. Aboriginal people on missions and reserves thus had a dual perception of literacy and its associated material culture. Although young people were formally schooled into literacy, much writing took place in secret, out of sight of mission and reserve staff, often at the behest of traditionally oriented elders who had not been schooled in the arts of writing and reading alphabetic script. On missions and reserves, European conventions cloaked practices of literacy based on Indigenous proprieties.

Missions and reserves were administered bureaucratically. Bureaucracies are a means of governance through writing. As well as insulating officials from the consequences of their decisions, the bureaucratic administration of Aboriginal people's lives had two other important effects. First, the bureaucratic system interpellated each Aboriginal person as an individual and a member of a particular race; second, bureaucratic governance induced the production of written documents by Aboriginal people themselves. The bureaucratic apparatus set up to administer the protection of Aboriginal people thus elicited a great deal of Aboriginal writing, especially when Aboriginal people saw how their letters and petitions could carry their complaints over the local reserve manager's head, and make their views known to higher authorities in the city. With regard to writing, colonial governance was thus not only repressive, it was also malignantly productive. It required Aboriginal people to produce written texts and to exercise individual agency. The bureaucratic system demanded, in other words, that Aboriginal people become authors in the European sense.

The places within which Aboriginal people did much of their writing in the 19th century had much in common with the institutions where Europe's vagabonds and paupers were confined and disciplined. To 'open up' the land for pastoralism and agriculture, colonial governments enclosed Aboriginal people on mission stations and government reserves. These were poorly funded, badly resourced and inadequately staffed. They were institutions in which Aboriginal people were subjected to tight regulation, strict discipline and close surveillance. Within these enclosures, some nuclear families were allowed to live together; others suffered the removal of their children to the dormitories. Aboriginal people whose subjectivity was formed through affiliations with places, kin and spiritual beings were each assigned a Christian name and a new individual identity in terms of their gender, age, marital status and degree of colour. Missions and reserves confined their Aboriginal residents not only spatially, but temporally. Aboriginal residents were locked into repetitive and monotonous daily, weekly and yearly routines. They lived their lives in narrow cells of time, in enclosed spaces that were subdivided into areas designated for work, schooling, Christian religious worship, leisure, sleep, and so forth. The activities and movements of each individual were meticulously recorded by white staff. The bureaucratic documentation that records and facilitates such regulation is chilling. Gridlines create rigid rows and columns that reflect the regimentation of people's lives, the confinement of each person's body in space, and the compartmentalisation of each person's life in blocks of time. Within these prison-like contexts, Aboriginal people preserved many traditional cultural elements in secret.

○ ○ ○

While these three categories may be useful tools for analytical purposes, it's important to recognise the extent to which they interpenetrated. In one way or another, tacitly or overtly, Aboriginal literacy in the colonial period was traditionally oriented. There is evidence to suggest that Biraban, for example, despite his close, fifteen-year collaboration with missionary Lancelot Threlkeld, interpreted the Bible in the light of his own traditional spiritual beliefs. At Coranderrk Reserve from the 1870s to the 1890s, the Aboriginal community generated letters and petitions to satisfy bureaucratic requirements, but did so in accordance with traditional land-based and kin-based protocols.

Literacy and agency

Many Aboriginal people were aware of the power and prestige attached to literacy in the colonial social order, and they produced a range of different texts, sometimes working collaboratively with each another and/or with whites. More damaging than literacy per se were the missionaries' and reserve managers' strict prohibitions against Aboriginal languages, ceremonial activities and access to the special sites where powerful stories and ancestor spirits were lodged in the land. Where no such restrictions were imposed, or could not be enforced, Aboriginal people adapted writing to their traditional protocols of communication, reinforcing rather than undermining their orally grounded, kin-based, place-based and gender-based social order.

This is not to say that writing is an unequivocal good, nor to deny the links between literacy, imperialist ideology and colonial governance. Modern Europe's imperial powers could not, in practical terms, have built and administered their trade and political empires without writing. Written materials such as logbooks, journals, annotated maps, letters, books and scientific records were crucial in sea and land exploration, and in the administration of trade, slavery, immigration, wars, and other dimensions of empire building and colonial governance. Writing, especially in educational institutions, carried English and other European languages around the world. As Albertine Gaur points out, 'A common script is a strong tool not only for unification but also for enforcing and…preserving political dominance.'[16] Writing was also a valuable means of morally laundering imperialism in the minds of the British populace at 'home' and the settler societies 'abroad'. Published ethnographies and phrenological studies propagated racial prejudice among Europeans, while colonial romances and travel writings made the winning of foreign lands and the ruling of 'natives' seem natural, excitingly heroic and morally legitimate.

Missionaries used the Bible as a weapon against Aboriginal religious beliefs and social customs. Yet the bringers of light found out the hard way that alphabetic writing, books and literacy per se could not in themselves transform 'primitive' heathens into modern, 'civilised' Christians. Aboriginal pupils proved themselves capable of deploying the Bible against the moral hypocrisy of their white teachers, and of making sense of biblical stories in terms of their own traditional values, laws and beliefs. Aboriginal writers and readers did not always use their literacy skills in predictable ways, because reading, writing and texts were not only enveloped in imported white ideologies, but invariably assimilated into Indigenous perceptions of its nature and usefulness. Alphabetic script fixed the important civilising, Christianising words, but did not necessarily limit their meanings or how they could be used. Literacy itself did not turn Aboriginal people into industrious, politically compliant, morally laudable Christians. Consequently, mission and reserve teachers and government inspectors monitored and controlled Aboriginal reading and writing practices. If literacy *in itself* had the inevitable impact described by Goody, Ong and other proponents of the autonomous model, there would have been no need for colonial officials to regulate its practice so strictly.

2

Sky gods and stolen children

Bringing them home is a heavy book, literally and metaphorically. The *Report of the national inquiry into the separation of Aboriginal and Torres Strait Islander children from their families* sits like a stone in the consciousness of many Australians. Indigenous communities have carried that weight alone for many decades. The inquiry gathered information from written records and scholarly research, and from 535 Aboriginal witnesses who testified at hearings held in every state and territory. Partly because the testimonies of living Aboriginal witnesses circulated widely in the media, public attention and debate have focused primarily on 20th-century experiences and policies of child removal. However, *Bringing them home* noted that Aboriginal children were first removed from their families in early colonial times.

The story of Aboriginal cultures of literacy in colonial Australia is closely bound up with the history of the first generations of stolen children, who were the first Indigenous Australians to be formally taught to read and write. From the earliest years of British settlement, Aboriginal children were taken into colonial households, where they were taught to read, write, and become 'useful'. The first recorded removal took place in 1789, less than sixteen months after First Fleet arrived at Sydney Cove. In a letter dated 9 April 1790, the colony's chaplain, Reverend Richard Johnson, mentioned that he had:

> …a native girl under my care. Have had her now about 11 months… Have taken some pains with Abaroo (about 15 years old) to instruct her in reading, & have no reason to complain of her improvement. She can likewise speak a little English & is useful in several things about our little Hutt [*sic*]. Have taught her the Lord's Prayer & C., and as she comes better to understand me, endeavour to instruct her respecting a Supreme Being, &c.[1]

Abaroo was not an orphan. In September 1790 she asked to return to live with her father, Maugoran, or alternatively with Bennelong's wife, Barangaroo. Her request was refused.[2] Her name was in fact not Abaroo; it was Boorong, which means 'star'. As well as reading English words on paper, Boorong read the world around her. She saw signs of impending doom written in lights on the black night sky. David Collins wrote: 'To the shooting of a star they attach a degree of importance, and once, on an occasion of this kind I saw the girl Boo-roong greatly agitated and prophesying much evil to befall all the white men and their habitation.'[3] Boorong's people believed planets, stars and constellations were actual ancestors and spirits, and that the same laws applied in the skyworld as in terrestrial regions.[4]

Boorong and others, such as Nanbaree who lived with the surgeon Dr John White, and Samuel Christian and Tristan who lived with Reverend Samuel Marsden, belonged to the clans upon whose traditional country the first British colony was established. The colonists viewed these children as orphans, despite being partially aware of the extended family networks within which parentless children would normally have been raised. The discourse justifying the removal of Aboriginal children 'for their own good' was in fact self-contradictory. On the one hand, it was claimed that Aboriginal children had to be taken into the colonists' households because there was no one to look after them in their own society; on the other, the colonists insisted that Aboriginal children had to be kept away from their families to avoid being dragged back into savagery by the primitive strength of their kinship ties.

Literacy was one of the principal benefits cited in colonial explanations of why Aboriginal children should be removed from their families 'for their own good'. The children's achievements in reading and writing were repeatedly invoked in debates over whether Aboriginal people were fully human, whether they possessed intellectual capabilities, whether they could be permanently civilised and Christianised, and whether they could 'advance' as a race. By bestowing the 'gift' of literacy on members of societies whose lands they had invaded, philanthropic individuals and organisations asserted a moral justification for their own presence in New South Wales. Reverend Samuel Marsden noted that Samuel Christian, 'My native boy, whom I have had now more than four years improves much; he is become useful in the family; can speak the English language very well; and has begun to read.'[5]

Marsden and his wife adopted another so-called orphan whom they renamed 'Tristan'. At the age of six, Tristan was able to read English and wait at table.[6] Together with Marsden's children, he attended William Crook's prestigious school (for white children) at Parramatta, living as a boarder in the school when it relocated to Sydney. Nonetheless, Mrs Marsden referred to her husband as Tristan's 'master'. Tristan left Sydney with the Marsden family bound for England in 1807, but absconded in Rio de Janeiro. He was eventually returned to Australia, but died shortly after coming home.[7] A *Sydney Gazette* correspondent cited Tristan's educational achievements as proof that 'the natives' possessed intelligence.[8] Marsden, however, like most other colonists, believed that while Aboriginal children had little trouble learning to read and write, deep-seated racial instincts surfaced at puberty, pulling them irresistibly back to their people. The real reason these adolescents were absconding, however, was not because of mysterious 'native instincts', but because they were approaching adulthood, and reasoned that they would not find a spouse in white society.

White patrons and teachers were very proud of their Aboriginal charges' achievements, partly because literacy helped bring 'these poor heathen...to the knowledge of Xtianity [sic].[9] For at least one Aboriginal pupil, however, reading was a source of shame, as Dawes records: 'Wurul. Wurulbadyaou bashful, I was ashamed. This was said to me by Patyegarang after the departure of some strangers, before whom I could scarce prevail on her to read 25th Sept 1791.'[10] Boorong likewise doubted the benefits of literacy. Six months after Johnson noted her improvement in reading, she left his household to marry within her own community.[11]

The Parramatta Native Institution

In an effort to alleviate precisely that problem, William Shelley, a former missionary with the London Missionary Society, proposed to Governor Macquarie in 1814 that a special school be established for the education, Christianisation and vocational training of Aboriginal children. William Shelley and his wife, Elizabeth, had fled to Sydney in 1800 after hostile Tongans had driven them and other missionaries from their island. Believing that cultural and environmental factors played a greater role than race or biology in human development, the Shelleys were aware that young, educated Aboriginal men and women were returning to their own communities to find a future spouse. Shelley therefore proposed that a 'native institution' be established to educate both girls and boys together, creating an elite, literate class of young Aboriginal men and women who would, it was hoped, see the advantages of marrying their 'class-mates,' and abandon their customary ways of choosing marriage partners from within the proper exogamous moiety groups. Shelley observed that 'the chief difficulty appeared...to be the Separation of the Children from their Parents, but I am informed that in many Cases this could be easily done.'[12]

This 'easy' process was initiated by Governor Macquarie sending word to Aboriginal communities in the Port Jackson region, inviting them to attend a feast on Wednesday, 28 December 1814 at the marketplace in Parramatta, where he would make an important 'personal communication' with them.[13] About sixty people turned up at this event, the first of Governor Macquarie's annual feasts, which were advertised in the *Sydney Gazette* as the 'Annual Assembling of the Chiefs and Native Tribes at Parramatta'. It was conjectured that more distant tribes stayed away, fearing that their children would be taken by physical force. In an attempt to win the trust and goodwill of the assembled 'guests', Governor Macquarie handed out blankets, and supplied copious quantities of food and drink. With his fellow members of the Native Institution Committee, he addressed the crowd, informing them of the advantages of allowing their children to be taken into the school. The people were warned, however, that if they surrendered their children, they must not attempt to remove them, but be satisfied with seeing them once a year at the annual Parramatta feasts. Four children were handed over, and on 18 January 1815, the Native Institution was officially opened.[14]

Six months later the institution's founder, William Shelley, passed away, leaving his widow to manage the school. Enrolment numbers remained low because as new children trickled into the school others died or absconded, including two boys captured in one of the murderous punitive expeditions ordered by Macquarie in 1816 to quell Aboriginal hostilities. Intended partly to recompense Aboriginal people for the takeover of their land, the Native Institution exacted its own exorbitant costs upon Aboriginal children and their families.[15] By 1817, most of the seventeen children who attended could read the Bible. Nonetheless, Aboriginal parents far and wide remained afraid of the 'men dressed in black' who tried to take their offspring away to the institution.[16] Literacy was no compensation for losing their children.

Governor Macquarie did his best to attract voluntary enrolments at the school by holding the annual feasts. These events also served broader diplomatic purposes. At the 1817 feast, the Aboriginal people formed a circle which Macquarie entered, and:

> ...passed round the whole of them, inquiring after, and making himself acquainted with the several tribes, their respective leaders and residences. His Excellency then assembled the chiefs by themselves, and confirmed them in the ranks of chieftains, to which their own tribes had exalted them, and conferred upon them badges of distinction; whereon were engraved their names as chiefs, and those of their tribes.'[17]

In this early bestowal of king-plates, Macquarie used these pieces of writing engraved on metal, which were to be worn on the body, as a means of endorsing, and perhaps co-opting, the authority of those he recognised as 'chiefs'.

Within a few years, word of these 'meetings of the tribes' was carried far and wide through the Aboriginal trade and communication networks that crisscrossed south-eastern Australia. In 1818 almost 300 Aboriginal people attended Macquarie's gathering, some walking to Sydney from over 160 kilometres north and south, and from beyond the Blue Mountains in the west.[18] Given the large distances travelled and the numbers of people who came, it is highly likely that intertribal meetings for trade, diplomatic and ceremonial purposes would have taken place in the Sydney hinterland in the days leading up to and following the governor's official feast day. An important by-product of Governor Macquarie's annual child-recruitment meetings was that they created new opportunities for cultural innovation and intertribal dissemination of ideas, stories, songs and ceremonies. These meetings for cultural exchange appear to have continued on a smaller scale after the Parramatta feasts were terminated in 1835. In October 1836, for example, James Backhouse encountered men from three tribes making their way to the Cowpastures to learn a new song: 'For an object of this kind, they often travel great distances.'[19]

After 1820, the feasts were no longer intended to recruit children to the school. Aboriginal attendance rose to 340 in 1821, many people coming great distances. That year, colonial officials attributed the increase to people's wish to farewell Governor Macquarie.[20] In 1825, the famous Wiradjuri warrior Windradyne, one of the main targets of the military killing squads who rode the Bathurst Plains in the early 1820s, caused a sensation by turning up at the feast with the word 'peace' written on a scrap of paper stuck in his straw hat.[21] Although Macquarie had left the colony in 1822, the feasts continued under governors Brisbane, Darling and Bourke until 1835. It was Macquarie, however, who established the tradition of bestowing food and drink, blankets, engraved metal king plates, and the 'gift' of literacy, in exchange for the custody of Aboriginal children.

Each year the Aboriginal children residing at the Native Institution displayed their art work, their writing, and their ability to read aloud. In 1819, Governor Macquarie was delighted to report that:

> The Adults now regularly attend the Annual Meeting of the Natives at Parramatta...on which occasion the Children at the Institution are paraded in presence of their Parents, read before them, and produce Specimens of their Progress in Education.[22]

While their families were most excited by the children's art, the Native Institution Committee 'were highly gratified with their progress in reading and writing'.[23] In 1819, almost a hundred white children from European schools and about twenty children from the Native Institution undertook the anniversary school examinations. To the delight of those who argued that Aboriginal people were susceptible to 'improvement', first prize was awarded to Colby's fourteen-year-old daughter, Maria, a pupil at the Native Institution.[24] (Colby had been captured at the same time as Bennelong by Governor Phillip.)

In her 1820 *Report on the literacy progress of the Aboriginal children in the Native Asylum, Parramatta*, Elizabeth Shelley noted that the children's capacity and inclination to learn varied considerably. In her mind, this variance could be explained in racial terms: 'I always found the half-caste children quicker and more tractable than the blacks.'[25] Nonetheless, in December that year, the *Sydney Gazette* report of the children's annual display at Parramatta rose to giddy heights of hyperbole:

> ...every heart must have fondly dilated with the glorious and humanizing conception of beholding so many...snatched from the wilds of barbarism, ignorance and misery. To every reflecting mind, the benignancy of the Institution must then have shone forth with all the resplendency so vast and glorious an object is capable of emitting and embracing; viz. the civilization and salvation of thousands of fellow creatures, at present involved in gross darkness.[26]

Three years later, JT Bigge issued a more sober report. He acknowledged that the children could read and write, and had learned the principles of Christianity, but he cautioned that, despite the 'natural capacities' of the children, 'it yet remains to be proved, whether the habits they acquire are permanent.'²⁷ His caution was well founded. Having completed their studies at the Native Institution, the boys and girls did not form pairs and get married as originally hoped by Macquarie and the Shelleys. Most returned to their families and communities, where their bookish classroom learning ceased to be relevant, and their marriage partners were chosen in traditional ways from the proper moiety groups. In 1823, the Native Institution was closed. The children were transferred initially to the Black Town settlement, and from there to the Male and Female Orphan Schools, where those who did not abscond received basic training in menial work, alongside white children. In 1826, the Black Town school was resurrected, but it never grew or flourished, and in 1833, the remaining three children, all girls, were conveyed to the Wellington Valley Mission of the Reverends William Watson and JCS Handt.²⁸

Private individuals continued to educate Aboriginal children in their homes. Reverend W Walker of Parramatta wrote of having two boys and a girl who 'have made very creditable progress in reading and writing, and are excellent house servants'.²⁹ Neither their schoolteachers nor these philanthropic individuals were in a position to teach Aboriginal people to read or write in their own languages. Noting in 1828 that Aboriginal children at Black Town and the National School at Windsor were making good progress in reading in English, Charles PN Wilton explained that:

> To attempt to give the 'adult' Natives in the neighbourhood of Port Jackson a written language of their own dialects, we consider, an unnecessary trouble, since their tribes are so greatly reduced in numbers, and at the same time understand the English language.'³⁰

Mac-quarra, Mukwara, Mokwarra, Macquarie

Wilton's claim that Aboriginal people understood the English language may have been correct, but it begged the question of whether they assigned the same meanings to English words as did the English. Little account was taken of the fact that certain English words and names were phonetically very similar to words and names in Aboriginal languages. While the colonists perceived their language to be very different from the Indigenous tongues, Aboriginal people were interpreting the meanings of English names and words on the basis of their resemblance to the sounds of names and words in their own languages. This fact is crucial in any attempt to reconstruct the ways in which Aboriginal people may have understood the words and actions of the colonists, particularly those of Governor Macquarie.

In the records of the early colonists, there is clear evidence of such word association. Lieutenant Ralph Clark noted that the Port Jackson Aboriginal people considered names very important and remembered them once they had been told them.[31] This observation was confirmed in an incident recounted by George Worgan, the surgeon from HMS *Sirius*. One day, Worgan was about to shoot a crow, but as he took aim an Eora man rushed forward and put his hand over the muzzle of the gun, crying out '*Bau Bau Bau Bau*' — meaning, as Worgan surmised, that he must not shoot the bird. In the Eora man's eyes, Worgan was about to commit the unlawful action of killing his own totem, the crow, the word for crow in the Eora's language being *worgan* or *worogan*.[32]

If the Eora man noticed how similar Worgan's name was to the Eora word for crow, what would the Aboriginal groups who attended or heard about Governor Macquarie's feasts have made of the resemblance between the name 'Macquarie' and the names Mak-quarra, Mokwarra and Mukwara, which in several Aboriginal languages mean 'Eaglehawk'? Would they have understood 'Macquarie' to mean 'Eaglehawk'? To Europeans, 'Eaglehawk' has connotations of power and fierce, predatory cruelty — a fitting title for anyone who attempts to steal Aboriginal children from their families, as a bird of prey might snatch and eat the chicks of other birds.

In many south-eastern Australian Aboriginal societies, however, the name 'Eaglehawk' carries a much larger and more complex body of meanings and functions. Eaglehawk and Crow — Mukwara and Worgan — occupy a central place in the mythology, ceremonial life and social organisation of Aboriginal societies across a vast region of central and western New South Wales, northern Victoria, southern Queensland and parts of South Australia.[33] Extensive as it is, this region remains well within the reach of Aboriginal communication and trade routes extending out from Sydney in the early 19th century when Macquarie was holding the annual 'meetings of the tribes' at Parramatta.

Lending credence to the idea that Aboriginal people knew Macquarie as Mukwara, or Eaglehawk, is the fact that his name was known among Aboriginal nations far and wide. Shortly before his departure from Australia in early 1822, he made a tour of regions to the south of Sydney. On the Illawarra coast he was welcomed by over a hundred Aboriginal people. While many were from the immediate vicinity, others hailed from as far away as Jervis Bay, 200 kilometres south of Sydney. Macquarie was delighted and flattered that the people knew who he was and pronounced his name distinctly.[34] This prior knowledge of Macquarie's name may well have been because the words Mak-quarra, Mokwarra, or Mukwara were already part of their own Yuin and Tharawal vocabularies, or those of their inland neighbours.

Eaglehawk and Crow — Mukwara and Worgan — are important ancestral beings in traditional Aboriginal songs, ceremonies and stories in many regions of south-eastern Australia. The central theme is the ongoing conflict between the mighty hunter, Eaglehawk, and the shrewd, opportunistic Crow. Sir Joseph Banks observed that 'a Crow in England tho in general sufficiently wary is I must say a fool to a New Holland crow.'[35] In *Eaglehawk and Crow* (1899), John Matthew explains:

> Before the earth was inhabited by the present existing race of black men, birds had possession of it. These birds had as much intelligence and wisdom as the blacks, nay, some say that they were altogether wiser and more skilful. The eaglehawk seems to have been the chief among the birds, and next to him in authority was the crow.[36]

Matthew's examination of the Eaglehawk and Crow stories draws heavily on R Brough Smyth's *The Aborigines of Victoria* (1878). Brough Smyth, who was Secretary of the Board for the Protection of Aborigines in Victoria from 1860 to 1876, maintained that Aboriginal societies in many parts of Victoria believed that:

> …the beings who created all things had severally the form of the Crow and the Eagle. There was continual war between these two beings, but peace was made at length. They agreed that the Murray [River] blacks should be divided into two classes — the Mak-quarra or Eaglehawk, and the Kil-parra or Crow.[37]

Although there are some variations between the social organisation of the Indigenous societies in south-eastern Australia, almost all are divided into two, four or eight patrilineal or matrilineal classes, or marriage-group categories. Eagle and Crow are prominent among the names of the moieties, classes and sub-sections on which traditional marriage and other social laws depend.[38] People belonging to the Eaglehawk moiety must marry Crow, and vice versa. In many of the stories, the relationship between Eaglehawk and Crow is antagonistic. Socially, however, people of the Eaglehawk and Crow classes live in a relation of mutual dependency which, if not maintained, leads to difficulties for both.[39]

The Eaglehawk and Crow stories serve as a reminder that Aboriginal people had their own culturally conditioned responses to and evaluations of white actions. Yet the stories offer no neat, unequivocal gauge of Aboriginal people's perceptions of Governor Macquarie's attempts to take their children away to be educated. In the many different narratives and songs about Eaglehawk and Crow, good and evil, correct and unlawful behaviour are not distributed consistently between Eaglehawk and Crow. Neither Eaglehawk nor Crow is invariably a hero or a villain. There is at least one story recorded both in Victoria and western New South Wales, however, in which Eaglehawk steals a baby from its mother.[40] He takes the baby up to his nest in the top of a tree, intending to eat it. Hearing the mother's cries, two 'heavenly men' called Buledji Brambimbul fly down from the sky and ask the woman why she is crying. 'My baby is up there and the eagle is going to eat it,' she tells them. Using a stone axe (a traditional Aboriginal tool, not a metal axe obtained from whites), the Brambimbul cut notches in the tree and climb up to the eagle's nest. They kill the eagle, return the baby to its mother, chop down the tree, and cut it up into fragments, which they gather into bags so that no gum trees will grow in that place ever again.[41]

Despite the manifold variants of the Eaglehawk and Crow stories, ethnologists have endeavoured to formulate comprehensive interpretations. In 1995, Johanna M Blows published a large selection of these stories in *Eagle and Crow*, advancing the Freudian hypothesis that they ultimately function as a form of psychodrama. Just under a century earlier, in 1899, John Matthew argued that the Eaglehawk and Crow stories were allegories of ancient interracial strife between a black-skinned race of Aboriginal people who first populated the Australian continent, and a brown-skinned race that invaded their lands and exterminated them. Matthew asked rhetorically:

> [I]s there any better explanation of the facts possible than that the eaglehawk and the crow represent two distinct races of men which once contested for the possession of Australia, the taller, more powerful and more fierce 'eaglehawk' race overcoming and in places exterminating the weaker, more scantily equipped sable 'crow'?[42]

Matthew failed to consider that if the Eaglehawk and Crow stories are indeed allegories of interracial strife, the conflicts they allude to may be those first unleashed in 1788 with the British invasion and armed occupation of Aboriginal lands. He is obviously aware of the ill-treatment of Aboriginal people, however at no point does he consider that violent struggles between

Eaglehawk and Crow may be renditions of post-colonial history, and he overlooks the fact that Macquarie's name is a cognate of Aboriginal words for Eaglehawk.[43]

Aboriginal interpretations of the Eaglehawk and Crow stories focus mainly on sexual and other social relationships, suggesting that the stories function primarily to preserve and transmit knowledge about proper, lawful social morality. If this is so, it is worthwhile trying to imagine what the hundreds or thousands of Aboriginal people who attended, or heard stories about, the Parramatta feasts made of Governor Macquarie's social morality. How would they have made sense of the fact that a man named Macquarie/ Mukwara/Mak-quarra/Mokwarra — Eaglehawk — had orchestrated a series of ceremonial gatherings designed *expressly* to lure parents into giving up their children, so they could violate traditional marriage laws, and be taught to write and read the white man's books?

Literacy and the Eaglehawk in Wiradjuri country

When the Black Town school was finally closed in 1833, the three remaining children were sent 350 kilometres north-west of Sydney to the Wellington Valley Mission in Wiradjuri country, on the far side of the Blue Mountains.[44] The Wiradjuri people had been fighting to defend their lands since the early 1820s when the fertile slopes west of the Blue Mountains became accessible from Sydney by road. Led by Windradyne in the Bathurst area, 'Old Bull' in the south, and 'Blucher' in the north, the Wiradjuri people fought a bloody war against land-hungry colonists whose claims were brutally enforced by the military. Governor Brisbane proclaimed martial law in the region between August and December 1824, during which time the military fought a war of extermination against the Wiradjuri, killing over 1000 men, women and children.[45]

Among the Wiradjuri people of the Wellington Valley, downriver from Bathurst, memories of this killing time remained fresh for many years, and would certainly still have been vivid in 1832 when Reverend William Watson and Reverend Johann Handt arrived to set up a mission, accompanied by a military detachment.[46] While the missionaries endeavoured to win people's trust by distributing food and treating the sick, William Watson had few qualms about forcibly removing Wiradjuri children from their families. In his journal for 29 August 1832, Watson made the following entry:

> We were visited today by a Black Native, his wife and a young child at the breast. I asked them to give me the child, the woman seemed

to feel all the mother kindling up in her bosom at the question, and clasping the infant tight to her breast cried 'Bayal Bayal (no no) why me give Pickininny?'[47]

While Watson and Handt were puzzled that Wiradjuri parents did not want to relinquish their children, they were sensitive and accommodating to Wiradjuri cultural needs when it suited their purposes. In their schooling of Wiradjuri children, they succeeded by teaching in a manner consistent with traditional Indigenous teaching methods. Adapting 'the Infant System', which had been developed in Britain to educate and regenerate the poor, they used music, body movements, games, visual props, stories and other oral teaching methods.[48] The Wiradjuri children evidently enjoyed these modes of learning. Using media other than the written word, the Infant System was found to be an effective preparation for the more formal modes of instruction in reading and writing that followed later. By 1839, Watson was able to record that:

> [T]he children taught to read at the Mission House are much attached to books, consider it a severe punishment to be deprived of them, and prefer the present of a new one to almost any thing else. While they are learning the Alphabet, and to spell, they feel no interest, and the work of instruction is tedious to both the teacher and the pupil; but when they have overcome these preliminary difficulties, and are able to read so as to understand, their attention becomes excited; they begin to feel a pleasure in the employment, and never appear to be wearied with it. The Aboriginal Natives are indeed capable of attaining to the knowledge of any thing in which they may be instructed.[49]

Despite these alleged pleasures of literacy, Reverend James Gunther, who had replaced Handt in 1837, was deeply troubled by Watson's child-recruitment methods. When touring about the region, he discovered that 'the Natives dread Mr Watson, on account of having taken children by force.'[50] Reading, writing, and Christianity were offered at an exorbitant price, which involved not only removing children from their families, but subjecting them to a life of regimentation, monotony and an unhealthy foreign diet. Even Reverend Gunther, accustomed to a life of discipline, found that 'there is so much sameness in the daily occurrences.'[51]

In 1837, when Gunther took over from Handt, there were three groups of Wiradjuri children at the Wellington Valley Mission. The missionaries vied with the elders and families to control the minds and bodies of these young people. One group consisted of teenage girls approaching marriageable age, whom the missionaries saw as too young to be married. A dozen uninitiated boys aged between nine and twelve years constituted a second group. Gunther was determined to wrest these boys from the influence of their elders. The boys lived in the Aboriginal camp, but would visit the mission each day for reading and moral edification. In June 1838, Gunther was delighted to find one boy, Cochrane, could read the words 'Let me not die in sin.'[52] Eight weeks later, however, when Gunther was seeking to break the power of the elders, he asked Cochrane, 'What need you these wicked fellows?' Cochrane's reply was: 'Why care you for the Governor? These old men our Governors, we must do as they say.'[53] The following year, when Gunther told the boys that the Bible forbade the cutting of cicatrices to signify mourning, Cochrane again challenged the authority of Gunther and the ethnocentricity of the Bible by asking: 'Where the Bible come from?' When Gunther answered 'From God, to be sure,' Cochrane demanded, 'To what country he sent it first, to England?'[54]

The third group of children at Wellington, most of whom were of mixed descent, had according to Watson been relinquished by their Wiradjuri parents, who wanted them to be educated. Within a year of Gunther's arrival, friction between the two men over the issue of child removals grew so intense that Watson and his wife left to establish a private mission at Apsley, the childless couple taking with them this youngest group of children. Gunther soon heard through the grapevine that Watson was still forcibly taking children from their parents. A crisis occurred in December 1839, when Watson tried to take a two-year-old child from her mother in the camp, claiming that the mother, Pol Plunkett, had sold the child to him. Watson attempted physically to snatch the child away, but her relations intervened, grabbing the child and running to Gunther's house for protection. Watson called the police; Gunther refused to hand over the child; Watson forced his way in and seized the child, leaving the mother and the other women 'screaming bitterly'.[55] From that time, Wiradjuri people called missionaries 'kidnappers'. They moved away from the Wellington Valley Mission, and hid when Gunther ventured into the bush to find them. It was at this point that Gunther discovered that Reverend Watson was known far and wide as 'the eaglehawk'.[56]

Peter Read and John Harris both imply that the Wiradjuri were using the name 'Eaglehawk' metaphorically to signal Watson's ruthless exercise of power. Yet if Wiradjuri culture remained as resilient as the missionaries' journals indicate, the name 'Eaglehawk' would also have had traditional associations as a classificatory and totemic name. In addition, the historical precedent set by the annual child recruitment feasts of Macquarie/Mukwara may also have contributed to the Wiradjuri practice of classifying all would-be child stealers as Eaglehawks.

Watson and Gunther were in no position to see these possibilities at the time. They showed little interest in learning about the culture they were trying to eradicate, except in so far as such knowledge could further their evangelical and assimilationist agendas. Prior to their split, for example, Watson and Gunther tried to accommodate traditional Wiradjuri social proprieties by conducting three separate outdoor church services each Sunday. The three services allowed people to attend church without infringing traditional avoidance laws, the restrictions on contact between certain categories of kin (such as mothers-in-law and sons-in law). In 1834, Watson completed a 2000-word Wiradjuri vocabulary, and translated the Lord's Prayer, the Apostles' Creed, and sections of the Bible and the Anglican liturgy into the Wiradjuri language.[57] In 1835, Watson began to teach Wiradjuri children to read both in their own language and in English, and conducted church services in Wiradjuri.[58] He also copied out all 10 000 words in *Johnson's portable dictionary*, and gave Wiradjuri equivalents for as many words as he could. Presumably, Wiradjuri people would have played a major role in this translation work, but Watson seems not to have acknowledged their contribution.

In 1836, Watson's journal records that when he read a passage from his Wiradjuri translation of the Scriptures, a number of people visiting from far away were so interested that they:

> ...came and sat down with me, one after another, and paid the greatest attention: they said they understood what I read. When I gave over reading, some of them said: 'Kurrandirung myengoo! Kurrandirung myengoo! — Book for black fellows! Book for black fellows![59]

Books translated into Indigenous languages at that time were usually designed to be read *to* Aboriginal people, rather than read *by* them. Literally and figuratively, the missionaries endeavoured to keep the meaning of the Scriptures in their own hands: they viewed understandings different from their own as *mis*-understandings. The missionaries wanted Aboriginal people to embrace the Bible as their own book of faith, but were wary of what the

Bible might say to people whose cultures were radically different to their own. Having translated the Bible into a language he did not know well, Watson himself would only have had a sketchy idea of how the scriptures were being understood by those who listened. The European cultural institution of reading aloud may have given him the illusion that he was in control, but reading aloud could not limit the meanings that Wiradjuri people attributed to the text, even though the words were carried from the page to their ears by his voice. The missionaries' Wiradjuri listeners would have understood the Bible in the context of their own traditional social values, their own cosmological order, and their own experiences of the violent, world-threatening history in which they were embroiled. The missionaries were trying to Europeanise the Wiradjuri's worldview by introducing them to the Bible; the Wiradjuri, meanwhile, were assimilating Christian doctrines and biblical stories, historical events and other new elements into their traditional understandings of the universe, including their own categories of sanctioned social relationships and their own traditional moral order. Such adjustments and innovations were necessary to make sense of what, in English at the time, was called 'colonisation'.

Watson, Handt and Gunther despaired at times that their teaching had made no impact on Wiradjuri spiritual life. Peter Read confirms this view, maintaining that while the Wiradjuri accepted the missionaries' physical protection and sustenance, they remained spiritually and intellectually 'untouched'.[60] Tony Swain argues, however, that a major religious innovation occurred at the Wellington Valley Mission: the emergence of Baiami, the Sky-God or All-Father.[61] The Wiradjuri may of course have worshipped Baiami from ancient times, long before the missionaries or ethnologists documented their spiritual life; nevertheless, the earliest written record of Baiami appears in Gunther's word list and journal where, in an optimistic moment, he writes: 'There is no doubt in my mind that the name Baiamai...refers to the Supreme Being; and the ideas held concerning Him by some of the more thoughtful Aborigines are a remnant of original traditions prevalent among the ancients of the Deity.'[62] Here, Gunther suggests that the Baiami tradition is a syncretic development, a practice emerging from interactions between Wiradjuri cosmology and the colonial Christian culture of the book.

In Gunther's word list, 'Baiamai' is defined as 'a great god; he lives in the east.'[63] Could this mean that the Baiami stories come from the direction of Sydney or Parramatta, or regions to the north of Sydney? In support of his argument that belief in Baiami emerged in colonial times, Swain cites Horatio Hale's observation that belief in the Sky-God had begun in the 1820s:

> When the missionaries first came to Wellington, the natives used to assemble once a year, in the month of February, to dance and sing a song in honour of Baiami. *This song was brought there from a distance by strange natives, who went about teaching it* [my emphasis]. Those who refused to join in the ceremony were supposed to incur the displeasure of the god.[64]

When the Wellington Valley Mission was established in 1832, the annual Parramatta 'meetings of the tribes' had been under way for eighteen years. Over the years, these annual events became a cultural, social, economic and, in all likelihood, a spiritual institution. They were usually held post-Christmas or in January, after which time people began the long walk back to their country. Could it be that the Wiradjuri people's Baiami ceremonies took place in February because it was then that the 'strange natives', or Wiradjuri travellers themselves, arrived back in Wiradjuri country after attending the annual meetings initiated by Macquarie/Mukwara?

Gunther argued that Baiami had three attributes of the Christian God: eternity, omniscience and goodness.[65] A fourth important attribute, however, links Baiami not only with the biblical God, but with the figure of Eaglehawk. Baiami's relationship with human beings is mediated through his son, Daramulun, the name also of Eaglehawk's son. While Eaglehawk, in some stories, is a stealer of children, in others it is his own son, Daramulun, who is killed by Crow, despite the fact that Eaglehawk is 'the chief amongst the birds'.[66] Parallels such as this led Emile Durkheim to hypothesise that 'a single sky-dwelling All-Father was an emergent transformation of one of the mythically paired birds that headed moieties.'[67]

Biraban and Threlkeld

If Aboriginal people associated Eaglehawk and Baiami with Jehovah, an important agent in this transformation may have been an Awakabal man named Biraban (c.1802–1842). Biraban was a stolen child who became known among white people as the Eagle Chief. For fifteen years he carried out biblical translations and linguistic work with Lancelot Threlkeld at Lake Macquarie Mission, 140 kilometres north of Sydney.

The Wellington missionaries' attempts to teach Wiradjuri children to read in their own language were not the first efforts to promote literacy in an Indigenous tongue. Lancelot Threlkeld had initiated such a scheme in 1824, when he was granted 4050 hectares at an ominously named site, Reid's Mistake, on the eastern shore of Lake Macquarie. Threlkeld was funded by the London Missionary Society to minister to the Awabakal, the people of Awaba, 'the plain surface'.[68] The society's representatives in Australia, Daniel Tyerman and George Bennett, believed that methods employed in the Society Islands, where people were taught in their own language, would best succeed with the Indigenous peoples of Australia. Threlkeld was therefore instructed to learn the local Awabakal language, establish a school, teach agriculture and carpentry, and propagate the gospel.

In his first four years at Reid's Mistake, however, Threlkeld's expenses were so large in relation to his negligible progress that, after protracted arguments over funding, the London Missionary Society dismissed him.[69] By this time, 1829, Threlkeld was passionately devoted to linguistic research and biblical translation. Having secured a modest level of private financial support for this work, he turned his indefatigable energies to setting up a new mission, Ebenezer, across the lake from Reid's Mistake, and from 1830, was granted a small salary from the New South Wales Government.

Not everyone shared his stubborn optimism or agreed with his modus operandi. Influential churchmen such as Samuel Marsden held that civilisation was a necessary prerequisite to meaningful study of the gospel. Threlkeld, by contrast, believed that the gospel, disseminated to Aboriginal people in their own languages, was the best basis for future civilisation. The civilisation of Aboriginal people was thus dependent on their involvement with a book: the Bible. Threlkeld's priorities were clear: 'First obtain the language, then preach the Gospel, then urge them from Gospel motives to be industrious.'[70] He strongly believed that imperialism was a legitimate means of disseminating Christianity and cultural advancement, maintaining that:

> [I]f the glorious light of the blessed Gospel of God our Saviour had never shed its divine lustre around the British Crown, or never penetrated the hearts of the people with its vivifying power, the aborigines of Albion's shores might still have remained in the state described by the eloquent Cicero...[who] says, 'Do not obtain your *slaves* from *Britain*, because they are *so stupid* and *utterly incapable of being taught* that they are *not fit* to form a part of the household of Atticus!'[71]

To his credit, Threlkeld fiercely opposed the phrenological view that Aboriginal people were innately unintelligent and incapable of instruction. To support his position he wrote memorable descriptions of his pupils inscribing 'on the soft paper-like bark of the tea-tree...the letters they had been taught to form'.[72] The ability to acquire literacy was, in British colonial eyes, proof of Aboriginal people's humanity and a sure sign of their capacity for 'improvement'. Threlkeld and others believed that Aboriginal literacy was a crucial indicator of Aboriginal intelligence. He asserted that on the mission:

> ...we had about a dozen youths learning to read and write the Roman Alphabet which they frequently cut with their hatchets in the bark of the trees, showing the march of intellect in the very bush, by those who were stigmatised as possessing no understanding and consequently were declared incapable of instruction!"[73]

Threlkeld insisted on the intellectual astuteness of the Awabakal people, even when it made his evangelical work more difficult. He reported, for example, that a young boy (re)named Billy Blue, when asked what he made of the account of the creation that had been read to him from Genesis, replied with deadly logic 'that he thought it was all gammon that master had told him about the Creation, for who was there who saw God create man?'[74]

Threlkeld raged against the hypocrisy of colonists who called themselves 'civilised', while committing or condoning 'atrocious acts of cruelty, which are but the sports of monsters boasting of superior intellect to that possessed by the wretched blacks!'.[75] Convinced that the Awabakal language was a window to its speakers' minds and souls, he thought of his linguistic research as a form of pro-Aboriginal Christian political activism. The complexity and refinement of the Awabakal language put paid to any idea that its speakers were mentally deficient or not fully human. Few Awabakal speakers were left, however, by the time Threlkeld's work was published, and his findings were of little use to missionaries working in other regions where different languages were spoken. A man of indefatigable zeal, Threlkeld nonetheless defended the value of his work as:

> ...a testimony against the contemptible notion entertained by too many who flatter themselves that they are of a higher order of created beings than the aborigines of this land, whom they represent as 'mere baboons, having no language but that in common with the brutes!';

and who say, further, that the blacks have 'an innate deficiency of intellect, and consequently are incapable of instruction.'[76]

Whether or not Threlkeld's learn-the-language-and-convert approach to Christian evangelism was effective, his *political* estimation of why it was important to appreciate the sophistication of Indigenous languages was perfectly valid:

> [I]t was maintained by many in the colony that the Blacks had no language at all but were only a race of the monkey tribe! This was a convenient assumption, for if it could be proved that the Aborigines of New South Wales were only a species of wild beasts, there could be no guilt attributed to those who shot them off or poisoned them as cumberers of the earth.[77]

Threlkeld was humbled when his linguistic blunders caused amusement among the Awabakal. Even his most patient teacher, Biraban, exclaimed, 'What for you so stupid, you very stupid fellow.'[78] One can only imagine what the Awabakal people made of Threlkeld's word-hunting expeditions, which he describes as follows:

> [K]nowledge of their language was obtained by providing natives with a fowling-piece and ammunition to shoot birds or other animals as came in the way. Whilst I with note book in hand, alphabetically paged, put down in order such words as could be obtained whilst walking and talking with them in the bush.[79]

It is a striking example of the ethnologist destroying the very world he endeavours to document and preserve.

In his studies of the Awabakal language and his translations of the Bible, Threlkeld was instructed by Biraban, whose name means 'Eaglehawk'.[80] As a boy, Biraban had been taken from his traditional Awabakal country to Sydney, where he was renamed Johnny McGill and kept at the military barracks as a personal servant to one of the officers. In that role he learned to speak English fluently.[81] As a young man, Biraban returned to his people and underwent his initiations, which involved a name change from We-pohng to Biraban.[82] In 1821, with two other Awabakal men, he accompanied Captain Frances Allman to establish the penal settlement at Port Macquarie. On this mission, Surgeon Cunningham noted how efficiently Biraban and his fellow trackers located and apprehended runaway convicts, remarking, 'Certainly three more powerful intelligent men he could not have selected.'[83]

2 ~ Sky gods and stolen children

Biraban evidently attended more than one of the annual Aboriginal conferences at Parramatta, and Governor Macquarie recognised him as a chief of the Awabakal people. At the 1830 gathering, Governor Darling presented Biraban with a king plate which read: 'Barabahn, or MacGill, Chief of the Tribe at Bartabah, on Lake Macquarie; a Reward for his assistance in reducing his Native Tongue to a written Language.'[84] By that time, Biraban was a clan-head, an Awabakal leader 'punctilious in observing his ceremonial observations'.[85] Threlkeld reported: 'Though he is acquainted with the doctrines of Christianity and all the comforts and advantages of civilization, it was impossible for him to overcome his attachment to the customs of his people, and he is always a leader in the corroborees and other assemblies.'[86]

Biraban's ceremonial responsibilities would have involved honouring his namesake, the eaglehawk, not only the living birds themselves, but the Eaglehawk Ancestors, spirit beings that emerged from the earth in the creation time, and whose inherent power was ritually activated by senior custodians of the Eaglehawk law, such as Biraban.[87] If Threlkeld's missions at Reid's Mistake or Ebenezer were on Biraban's clan estate, it is likely that, as clan-head, he would have been responsible for 'speaking for country', and serving as the main spokesperson for his clan in their dealings with outsiders such as Threlkeld.

Biraban is usually regarded as Threlkeld's helper, his 'principal informant'.[88] In fact, he was Threlkeld's indispensable teacher. Having cleared four hectares of heavy wooded land on the mission at Reid's Mistake, Biraban became involved in the colonists' culture of literacy, spending nearly two decades patiently instructing Threlkeld in the Awabakal language, and collaborating closely with him on his biblical translations. Ostensibly, it was through Threlkeld's patronage that Biraban encountered written texts. In reality, even Threlkeld, never an overly humble man, was equivocal about Biraban's role. In his *Australian reminiscences and papers*, Threlkeld frequently refers to Biraban as 'my black tutor', 'my valuable assistant in obtaining a knowledge of the language',[89] and 'the Black from whom I principally obtain the language'.[90] In a letter to his archdeacon in July 1829, Threlkeld cited Biraban's frequent absences from the mission as the main reason why the translation process of the Gospel of St Luke was proceeding so slowly: 'I am now as far as the 8th [chapter] of St Luke's Gospel, which gospel I hope to render into their language this year — But I am sometimes left for 6 weeks together, without a Black, especially the one who assists in the language.'⁹¹ This explanation implies that Biraban's contribution was indispensable, and that he actually deserved to be recognised as more than a 'tutor' or an 'informant'. Of the two, Biraban was, after all, the only one fluent in both English and Awabakal. He was Threlkeld's teacher, as well as his protégé, in a relationship of *mutual* patronage.

Threlkeld's letters to church and missionary officials, however, implicitly downplay Biraban's role by describing their translation work in the first person singular: 'I am at present engaged in a rough translation...'⁹² 'I have already translated...'⁹³ 'I have proceeded as far as the 14th Chapter of St Luke...'⁹⁴ In all likelihood, Threlkeld's use of 'I' rather than 'we' reflects not simply his egocentrism, but his need to emphasise his own industriousness so that crucial funding might continue flowing to the mission. Nonetheless, the result is that Biraban's agency as co-author of the Awabakal translation of Christian texts is obscured.

Threlkeld's understanding of how languages worked also led him to underrate Biraban's agency. Together, Biraban and Threlkeld completed an Awabakal translation of the Gospel of St Luke in 1831.⁹⁵ They went on to translate the Gospel of St Mark, a selection of prayers from *The book of common prayer*, and to compile an Awabakal spelling book and a reader containing selections from the Old Testament.⁹⁶ Threlkeld's way of describing his translation work with Biraban in his preface to the Awabakal Gospel of St Luke is worth examining:

> This translation of the Gospel of Luke into the language of the aborigines, was made by me with the assistance of the intelligent aboriginal, McGill... Thrice I wrote it, and he and I went through it sentence by sentence, and word for word, while I explained to him carefully the meaning as we proceeded. McGill spoke the English language fluently.⁹⁷

On the one hand, Threlkeld noted how difficult and time-consuming the translation process had proven to be; on the other, he viewed translation fundamentally as a process of linguistic repackaging, a recoding of fixed meanings that exist prior to being formulated in language. It is difficult to imagine that Threlkeld and Biraban's deliberations did not involve moments when it was obvious to both that there was no neat, exact fit between Awabakal and English. At such moments, Threlkeld may have glimpsed the possibility that the Awabakal gospel amounted to a transformation or a re-creation of the biblical text. Perhaps it was this alarming prospect that caused Threlkeld to cling tenaciously to the idea that languages are different sets of clothing for fixed, eternal meanings. A by-product of such a reaction, however, was that Biraban's interpretive initiatives and his creative contribution to the translation process were implicitly denied — that is, his authorial agency was denied.

As well as working with Threlkeld on the Awabakal language and translations, Biraban also assisted him as a court translator. Aboriginal people were prohibited from testifying in court because it was assumed they could not comprehend the significance of swearing an oath on the Bible to tell the truth. Biraban, however, while assisting Threlkeld at court, was questioned by Judge William Burton, and found to have a clear understanding both of what the oath meant and of biblical doctrines.[98]

The biblical translations of Biraban and Threlkeld were not published in book form in either man's lifetime. Governor Gipps cut off Threlkeld's salary in 1841, by which time it was clear that very few Awabakal people remained, and that the gospel translations were of little use outside Awabakal country. The results of Biraban and Threlkeld's collaboration appeared in print only much later, under Threlkeld's name alone, in *An Australian language: as spoken by the Awabakal* (1892), 're-arranged, condensed, and edited' by John Fraser. In that book, Biraban's contribution is most explicitly acknowledged in Threlkeld's two-page 'Reminiscences of Biraban', accompanied by a portrait in pencil by a member of the US Exploring Expedition of 1839.[99]

Was Biraban an author? I would say yes, but his authorial agency is contingent, disguised and refracted through Threlkeld's agenda. In the political context in which he engages with the medium of writing, Biraban's authority can seldom reveal itself. His transcribed utterances don't take the form of freestanding, purposeful acts of authorship. Biraban's descriptions of his life experiences, for example, are refracted through Threlkeld's linguistic samples. In *An Australian language*, the section headed 'Specimens of a Dialect of the Aborigines of New South Wales, being the first attempt to form their speech in to a written language' contains fragments of Biraban's announcement of the death of his child. This announcement is refracted through the illustration of a grammatical form:

Bo-un-to-a — the feminine pronoun, *she*.

Unne bountoa Patty ammoung kin-ba.
This she Patty with me.
This is Patty with me. [Patty was Biraban's wife.]

Ammoung katoa bountoa wa-nun.
Me with she move-will.
She will go with me.

Wonni bountoa tea unnung tatte ammoun-ba.
Child she to me there dead mine.
My child there is dead.[100]

Biraban is the author of these words that Threlkeld wrote down and translated without anything like an adequate comment on their grievous content. Fragments of the grim reality that Biraban and his people were living through are captured in print in these illustrations of grammatical principles. Biraban's authorial agency is conditional, and his message is refracted and translated; nonetheless, it is crucial to appreciate that Biraban chose to put his child's death on the written record when the opportunity arose.

Biraban's dream

Threlkeld was not especially interested in Awabakal spiritual and ceremonial life. His objective was to replace it with Christianity and a culture that revolved around the Bible. In his *Reminiscences*, however, he notes more than once that the name 'Biraban' means 'Eaglehawk' in English.[101] In popular culture today, 'Eaglehawk' seems a suitably romantic name for a Native American Hollywood hero. In Biraban's time too the name had heroic connotations. It certainly fired the imagination of Eliza Hamilton Dunlop, whose romantic poem 'The eagle chief' was published in the *Sydney Gazette* on 21 April 1842. Mrs Dunlop, the first Australian poet to attempt transliteration of Aboriginal songs, lived at Wollombi in Wonnarua country, which included or was adjacent to Biraban's Awabakal clan estate.[102] Her husband, David Dunlop, was the police magistrate and Protector of Aborigines in the region.[103] It is highly likely that an English-speaking Awabakal clan-head such as Biraban, whose traditional responsibilities included serving as a spokesperson for his people, would have had dealings with the region's Aboriginal Protector and his family. He almost certainly was the inspiration for Mrs Dunlop's poem.

Eliza Hamilton Dunlop was interested in Aboriginal thinking about the creative arts. In the *Sydney Morning Herald* of 11 October 1848, she asserted:

> There is a god of Poesy, Wallati, who composes music, and who, without temple, shrine, or statue, is as universally acknowledged as if his oracles were breathed by Belus or Osiris; he comes in dreams, and transports the favoured individual wrapped in visioned slumber to some bright warm hill, where he is inspired with the rare and supernatural gift.[104]

Although Biraban's creative agency was obscured by Threlkeld, Mrs Dunlop's remarks raise the possibility that, as well as being Threlkeld's loyal 'helper', Biraban was a visionary and spiritual leader in his own right. This spiritual leadership, and his importance as a visionary who mediated between Indigenous and Christian religions, perhaps grew out of a vivid dream he related to Threlkeld in 1836:

> The night before last, when coming hither, I slept on the other side of the Lake, I dreamed that I and my party of blacks were up in the Heavens; that we stood on a cloud: I looked round about in the Heavens; I said to the men that were with me, there *He* is; there is *He* who is called Jehovah; here he comes flying like fire with a great shining — this is *He* about whom the whites speak. He appeared to me like a man with clothing of fire, red like a flame. His arms were stretched out like the wings of a bird in the act of flying. He did not speak to us, but only looked earnestly at us as he was flying past. I said to the blacks with me, let us go down, lest he take us away; we descended on the top of a very high mountain like this pestle; (showing me one that was in the study) we came to the bottom, and just as we reached the level ground, I awoke. We often dream of this mountain, many blacks fancy themselves on the top when asleep.[105]

This written rendition of Biraban's dream-vision is not a verbatim transcript of the dreamer's oral account, even though, grammatically, it is written from the viewpoint of the dreamer. Biraban is undoubtedly the author of the story, but Threlkeld's presence is apparent in the parenthetical 'showing me one that was in the study'. Here, the pronoun 'me' refers to Threlkeld, whereas the 'I' who relates the dream is Biraban. The language and syntax are more formal and literary than orally delivered narratives usually are, and the account is in educated British English, not Aboriginal English. Written up by Threlkeld for inclusion in his 1836 report to the Lord Bishop of Australia, the story casts a favourable light on his own evangelical work.

None of this is to imply, however, that the story is fictitious. There is no reason to doubt that Biraban related the story that Threlkeld wrote down. As often occurs today, the white recorder of Aboriginal narratives does a bit of unauthorised editing. The story is still Biraban's and still authentic. Indeed, this story of an encounter with Jehovah as Eaglehawk could *only* be told by a man who had knowledge of both the Old Testament of the Bible and Awabakal sacred lore. Biraban was the only Indigenous man in the region who had such knowledge.

There are three biblical passages that may have served Biraban as points of reference in making sense of the catastrophic changes he had witnessed in his lifetime. Biraban was living in a world in the process of being destroyed. During the fifteen years he worked closely with Lancelot Threlkeld, he may have encountered Deuteronomy 28:49–51, which uses the image of an eagle when referring to destructive invaders from afar who wreak havoc on the local people and their world, in a manner comparable with the invasion of south-eastern Australia by the British:

> The Lord shall bring a nation against thee from far, from the end of the earth, as swift as the eagle flieth: a nation whose tongue thou shalt not understand. A nation of fierce countenance, which shall not regard the person of the old, nor show favour to the young. And he shall eat the fruit of thy cattle, and the fruit of thy land, until thou be destroyed…

Biraban may also have been familiar with Ezekiel 1:5–13, which contains an image of Jehovah in the form of four living creatures, including a man-god with the face and wings of an eagle. He may also have been familiar with Daniel 7:2–4. Daniel recalls his dream-vision of a similar figure, a being that was 'like a lion and had eagle's wings: I beheld till the wings thereof were plucked, and it was lifted up from the earth, and made stand upon the feet as a man, and a man's heart was given to it.' Any of these biblical images may have taken root in Biraban's mind to produce his dream.

Threlkeld's transcript of Biraban's words may not be the only record of Biraban's dream of Jehovah as Eaglehawk. At the head of a valley in Wonnarua country is a large rock shelter in which is painted a huge figure that closely resembles the flying Jehovah of Biraban's dream. Today, this painting is known as the Milbrodale Baiami. Biraban's account of his dream contains evidence that this extraordinary painting either inspired, or was based on, his dream-vision of Jehovah as Eaglehawk. In either case, the connection is extremely important, because it suggests that Biraban may have been assimilating biblical images of Jehovah into his own traditions of visual representation, which include the images of hybrid beings that were half human and half bird or animal.[106]

Bearing in mind that hybrid animal-human forms are common in Aboriginal art of the region, are the similarities between Biraban's dream and the Baiami painting too close to be coincidental? As in Biraban's dream, the painting represents a man who is also an eagle. Painted markings on the arms and penis indicate that this is a being of high degree.[107] As in Biraban's dream, the painted humanoid figure appears to be flying, and his eyes, which Biraban says 'looked earnestly at us' in his dream, are very large, bright and arresting.[108] As in Biraban's dream, the flying figure is painted 'red like a flame', red being the colour traditionally used to paint Baiami and a colour used by men only in Awabakal country.[109] Most importantly, the arms/wings of the bird-man-god are shaped like an eagle's, and are disproportionately long for a human being or any type of bird other than an eagle. The humanoid body is narrow (about 45 centimetres wide) and approximately two and a half metres tall, but the wingspan is extraordinarily wide (almost five metres at a guess). In their shape and size relative to the body, the wings are a highly accurate reproduction of the outstretched wings of a wedge-tailed eagle, complete with separated, slightly upturned feathers at the wing-tips, which look very much like the fingers of a human hand. There are also long wing feathers coming down from the upper arms.

These features make the Milbrodale Baiami different from other documented Aboriginal paintings of humans and eagles in the region.[110] If the Baiami painting at Milbrodale is indeed unique, is it valid to infer that it was the product of one man's imagination, rather than an element of a long-established, widely practised rock art tradition?

Threlkeld remarked on Biraban's artistic skills in the 1820s, so we may assume he was capable of painting the flying man-eagle that is the Milbrodale Baiami.[111] The Baiami cave, although some distance from Threlkeld's Ebenezer Mission, was well within the orbit of Biraban's travels, and was within the country of the Wonnarua nation, which included or was adjacent to Biraban's Awabakal clan. Given the nature of Biraban's dream, his knowledge of the Bible, his artistic abilities, his access and lawful association with the cave site, and his role as custodian of traditional sacred knowledge associated with Eaglehawk, there are grounds for arguing that this spectacular painting of the sky-god Baiami in the form of Eaglehawk

The rock shelter painting in Wonnarua country, known today as the Milbrodale Baiami.

and/or Jehovah may well have been painted by Biraban as a record of his dream. Another possibility is that the Milbrodale Baiami is an older painting that Biraban, as a senior custodian of the Eaglehawk ceremonies might have refreshed or repainted, and re-envisioned in his dream of Jehovah as Eaglehawk.

What we know about the dating of the painting does not preclude this possibility. In 1893, RH Mathews reported that the Baiami painting was already there when WG McAlpine, an early settler, arrived in the district around 1843. Biraban died in 1842, so the painting was in existence before he died. McAlpine stated, however, that when he arrived in the district the origins of the painting were unknown to the local Indigenous people.[112] This disavowal of knowledge could mean either that it had been painted very long before (and hence was not created by Biraban but might have inspired his dream), or that it was painted more recently (possibly within Biraban's lifetime) and the local people were simply keeping their spiritual knowledge secret.

Having assisted Threlkeld in developing an Awabakal reader that included sections of the Old Testament, Biraban would have been one of very few Aboriginal people to have been exposed to God as Jehovah, the God in the sky of the Old Testament, as distinct from Jesus, the God on Earth of the gospels which were the main focus of Threlkeld's biblical teaching.[113] The Milbrodale Baiami, however, shares features with images of Jesus Christ as well as Jehovah. Although the curved eagle's wings don't look at all like the arms of the crucified Christ, the plaque at the site (a recent addition) is headed 'Baiame — The Maker of All Things'. It includes a story told by the local Wonnarua people that could equally sum up the life of Jesus:

> After Baiami journeyed amongst the people, and having imparted to them the necessary knowledge, lore and ceremony for successful existence, he returned to the sky. Baiame stepped off at Mt Yengo, to the south. Hence its flattened summit.[114]

While Biraban's account of his dream invokes the images of the Old Testament Jehovah, the plaque tells a story consistent with the New Testament narratives of Jesus' life. Whether or not Biraban painted the Milbrodale Baiami, this extraordinary and arresting painting can be taken as evidence of the complex entanglement of traditional Aboriginal religion and book-based Christianity. Irrespective of whether Biraban's dream gave rise to the Milbrodale Baiami painting or was shaped by it —indeed, even if the dream and painting are not related — the eagle-like human form of both the Milbrodale Baiami and Jehovah in Biraban's dream invite the kinds of speculation that Durkheim made when he hypothesised that Baiami, the All-Father, was associated with the stories and ceremonies surrounding Eaglehawk.[115]

The rock shelter where the Milbrodale Baiami is located is not a secret site. It is open to the public, and has been described and photographed in several books. I visited the site in January 2004 and again in January 2005.[116] The large rock shelter that houses the painting gives a commanding view down the valley. Although the site is labelled as a Baiame site, it is clearly also a bird site. An eagle was circling as we first approached the site by car, and when we walked up to the rock shelter it was clear that the Baiami cave is inhabited by several kinds of birds. Swallows' nests cling to the roof of the cave; feathers, droppings, and footprints of large and small birds can be seen on the floor. Evidence of the ongoing presence of birds is everywhere. Yet the enormous painting of Baiami or Jehovah as Eaglehawk dominates the site. He hovers high up on the overhanging rock wall, gazing out at the valley and the sky. Seeing this awesome painting, and imagining Biraban's early life as a stolen child, it is not difficult to imagine why, in his dream of Jehovah as Eaglehawk, he said to his companions, 'Let us go down, lest he take us away.'

3

Bennelong's letter

The earliest piece of writing produced by an Aboriginal author is a letter dictated by Bennelong in August 1796. By that time, British colonists had been recording Aboriginal words in writing for over eight years, having commenced their ethnographic efforts even before they got off the boat. When the ships of the First Fleet initially anchored in Botany Bay on 20 January 1788, two senior officers recorded that Aboriginal warriors gathered on the shore, brandishing their spears, and shouting 'warra, warra'.[1]

Perceiving that these words and gestures 'could not be interpreted into invitations to land or expressions of welcome',[2] Governor Arthur Phillip sought a more suitable place to establish the colony, and on 26 January 1788 the colonists disembarked at Sydney Cove in Port Jackson, where there was fresh water and the 'Natives' seemed more friendly.[3]

Phillip and his officers recorded Aboriginal words and phrases in their letters, journals and notebooks, offering frequent, focused observations on the local culture. From November 1790, Lieutenant William Dawes studied the languages of Aboriginal people intently and systematically, making careful phonetic transcriptions, translations and lengthy word lists. When recording the Indigenous languages, these amateur ethnographers were scrupulous in their efforts to transcribe words and phrases as faithfully as they could. When it came to recording Aboriginal utterances in English, however, they lapsed into shameless ventriloquism. Watkin Tench's rendition of Bennelong's justification for assaulting a young woman, for example, transformed him into a villain of gothic romance: '"She is now," added he, "my property. I have ravished her by force from her tribe, and I will part with her to no person whatever until my vengeance shall be glutted."'[4]

A very different voice is heard in Bennelong's letter of 1796. Using a version of English that linguist Jakelin Troy has called 'the Sydney language',[5] Bennelong produced his letter by dictating it to a scribe whose identity is not specified in the records. The scribe appears to have recorded Bennelong's words verbatim, using English spellings of the day, without attempting to reproduce his pronunciation phonetically:

> Sidney Cove
> New South Wales Augst 29
> 1796
>
> Sir,
> I am very well. I hope you are very well. I live at
> the Governor's. I have every day dinner there. I have not
> my wife: another man took her away: we have
> had murry doings: he spear'd me in the back, but I
> better now: his name is now Carroway. all my friends
> alive & well. Not me go to England no more. I am at
> home now. I hope Sir you send me anything you please
> Sir. hope all are well in England. I hope Mrs Phillip
> very well. You nurse me Madam when I sick. You very
> good Madam: thank you Madam, & I hope you remember
> me Madam, not forget. I know you vey well Madam.
> Madam I want stockings. thank you Madam; send me two
> Pair stockings. You very good Madam. Thank you Madam.
> Sir, you give my duty to Ld Sydney. Thank you very
> good my Lord. very good: hope very well all family.
> very well. Sir, send me you please some Handkerchiefs
> for Pocket. you plese Sir send me some shoes: two
> pair you please Sir.
>
> Bannalong[6]

Unprecedented as it is, Bennelong's letter can't be regarded as an imprint of a pristine 'Aboriginal' voice. It is what Nicholas Thomas would call an 'entangled object', a product of intercultural engagement. Care is required, therefore, if we wish to avoid the twin dangers of, on the one hand, failing to perceive how Bennelong's letter is shaped by Indigenous customs and social values and, on the other hand, of making 'radical alterity out of partial or contingent difference'.[7] Bennelong used a range of discourses audible in the voice-scape and written genres he encountered in post-colonial Port Jackson. Just as Tench based his rendition of Bennelong's voice on gothic

The handwritten copy of Bennelong's original letter. **Reproduced by permission of the National Library of Australia.**

fiction, Bennelong drew on existing models of language, genre and social etiquette when orally composing his letter. To take on the role of author of a letter, he must have had some idea of what kinds of objects letters were, what kinds of work they could do, why people exchanged them, what kinds of topics they customarily raised, and the manner in which the recipients of his letter might expect to be addressed. How might he have formed these ideas?

In certain respects, Bennelong's letter conforms to British colonial epistolary norms. Like many a letter from the colonies, it offers polite greetings, snippets of news and requests for articles to be sent out from England. In other regards, it deviates markedly from polite late–18th century social decorum, most obviously by addressing several people in turn, alternating between familiar and formal registers, and asking bluntly and abruptly for specific gifts. Reading Bennelong's letter entirely in relation to British colonial epistolary norms would, however, be inappropriate: such an approach would deny the influence of Bennelong's own culture. Equally inappropriate would be any attempt to analyse the letter exclusively in relation to a discrete, timeless 'Aboriginal' cultural order: to do so would be to ignore the intercultural entanglement between the British and the Indigenous peoples of Port Jackson.

During the eight and a half years between the arrival of the first British settlers in January 1788 and the production of Bennelong's letter in August 1796, Bennelong was himself an important agent and medium of interaction between the British colonists and the Indigenous clans around Port Jackson. In terms of its language and socio-political functions, the letter is a product of the inter-cultural entanglement that Bennelong so vividly evokes when he mentions in the same breath his spearing and his regular dinners with the Governor. To understand the complex cultural and socio-political dynamics at work in Bennelong's letter, it is necessary to contextualise it micro-historically, both as a verbal text and a material object. First, I compare the letter to the genres of colonial bureaucratic writing to which Bennelong was probably exposed. Second, I examine the content and functions of the letter in relation to the patterns of gift exchange typical of both English patronage systems and Aboriginal kinship networks. Third, I suggest how Bennelong may have tried to use the letter as an object, as he himself had been used, in the broader trade networks that operated within and between Aboriginal and European societies. In each of these three contexts, Bennelong's authorial practices can be seen as a product of his individual agency working within the dynamic intercultural contact zone that emerged after 1788.

Mimicking Governor Phillip

Although Governor Phillip is neither addressed nor mentioned in Bennelong's letter, an understanding of the close relationship between the two is essential to any reconstruction of the context in which Bennelong's text was produced.[8] One of the orders issued to Governor Phillip by King George III was to 'open an intercourse with the natives…conciliate their affections...[and] report...in what manner our intercourse with these people may be turned to the advantage of the colony'.[9] To this end, Phillip had two 'Natives', Bennelong and Colby, captured in late November 1789 after a previous captive, Arabanoo, died of smallpox. Colby escaped within three weeks, after which Bennelong was shackled by his ankle to a minder and locked up at night in an upstairs room in Governor Phillip's house. Intensely curious, nonetheless, about the culture of his captors, Bennelong was a keen ethnologist who, according to Tench, 'acquired knowledge of both our manners and our culture'.[10] He escaped, in May 1790, having been in custody for six months. He kept his distance for several months, but was eventually reconciled with Phillip in October, after which time he and his people came and went freely from the settlement.

After their reconciliation, Bennelong spent a good deal of time voluntarily in Governor Phillip's presence. On occasion, Phillip wrote letters and reports with Bennelong at his side.[11] Hunter records in November 1790, for example, that 'Bennelong went into the [Governor's] house as usual, and, finding the Governor writing, sat down by him.'[12] Phillip lived in an era when Europeans viewed writing as a marker of civilisation. Since his stated intent was to befriend 'Natives' such as Bennelong, and furnish them 'with every thing that can tend to Civilize them',[13] it is logical to infer that he would deliberately have exposed Bennelong to the 'civilising' practice of writing, even if he did not attempt to teach him to read or write. Bennelong was well known as an accomplished mimic, however. While mimicry in some forms can be subversive, it is traditionally the main mode of learning in Aboriginal societies. Bennelong was also renowned as a keen observer of the colonists' culture. He would probably have noticed that Phillip, as governor of the colony, did a good deal of writing, and that writing was a elite activity practised by powerful men; convicts and other whites of low social standing rarely wrote. Bennelong's sense of social affiliation with Phillip was such that he exchanged one of his five names with him, so that Phillip was called 'Woolewarre', and Bennelong became 'Governor'. Given this convergence of beliefs, observations, intentions, social affiliations, and opportunities it is highly likely that Governor Phillip was the primary means through which Bennelong formed his ideas about reading and writing in general, and about the practice of exchanging letters in particular. Phillip doubtless learned many things from Bennelong, but with regard to the reading and writing of alphabetic script they related as patron and protégé.

Many of Governor Phillip's letters have not survived;[14] those that have, however, provide evidence to suggest that they served as models for Bennelong. While there are no records of Bennelong being taught to read or write, it is possible that Phillip may have explained to Bennelong what he was doing at his desk, and read sections of his letters to Bennelong as they sat together where Phillip did his paperwork. Phillip wrote three kinds of letters that may have had a bearing on Bennelong's letter. First, as governor of a convict colony, Phillip was required to write reports to the British Home Secretary responsible for prisons, Lord Sydney, and, after 1790, Lord Grenville. Although much longer and broader in scope than Bennelong's letter, these official dispatches may have led Bennelong to believe that one of the functions of letters was report on the writer's activities and other happenings in the colony; hence, his inclusion of the news about his dinners with the Governor, the loss of his wife, his spearing, the health of his friends and his intention not to leave his home again. No doubt Bennelong would have recognised that bringing news was an important activity in English society as well as in his own society.

Phillip also maintained a personal correspondence with Lord Sydney, who was his friend and patron as well as his superior in the government hierarchy. These letters are minor masterpieces of tonal subtlety and control. They invoke Phillip's warm personal friendship with Lord Sydney, while also conveying his profound respect and gratitude for the patronage of this immensely powerful nobleman. Phillip included specific greetings to Lord Sydney's wife and children, whom he called by name. In this regard, the letters speak indirectly to people other than the nominal addressee. Bennelong's letter does likewise, but in his case everyone is addressed directly as 'you', after an initial, indirect third-person greeting. At the beginning of Bennelong's letter, the word 'you' refers to Mr Phillips, Lord Sydney's steward, the letter's nominal addressee, of whom he requests 'anything you please'. Further down, Bennelong mentions Mrs Phillips, and turns to address her, asking her to send him two pairs of stockings. He then refers to Lord Sydney, to whom he directs his good wishes and thanks for an unspecified gift or favour that has either been received or is anticipated. Finally, Bennelong returns to addressing Mr Phillips, asking him to send him some handkerchiefs and two pairs of shoes. In Bennelong's letter, the word 'you' refers not to a single interlocutor, but in turn applies to Mr Phillips, Mrs Phillips, Lord Sydney, and again Mr Phillips. Bennelong proceeds as though everyone he speaks *about* is in each other's physical proximity, and can thus be spoken *to* in a single letter. Perhaps he had seen people passing letters around for others to read, and decided to address each person he thought likely to read his letter. Another possibility is that Phillip read out to Bennelong some of his own letters to Lord Sydney, and that Bennelong was imitating Phillip's practice of sending his polite greetings and other little messages to various members of Lord Sydney's family.[15]

The fact that Bennelong's greetings get tangled up with requests for clothing and shoes can perhaps be explained by looking at a third type of letter regularly written by Governor Phillip: his requisition orders to Evan Nepean, Lord Sydney's under-secretary at the Home Office.[16] Nepean's job was to arrange the supplies and provisions for British Colonies around the world.[17] Phillip regularly made written requests for provisions and stores, using lists compiled by his commissary, Andrew Miller. Part of what makes Bennelong's letter seem unusual is that he does not request just a single gift, but specifies that he wants two pairs of shoes, two pairs of stockings and some handkerchiefs. In this regard, Bennelong's letter resembles Phillip's requisitions, in which clothing, shoes and other goods were routinely ordered in the plural, including 'Long Frocks and Strong Jackets for the Natives', and other 'articles for traffik' with the clans in the region of Port Jackson.[18] A striking aspect of Bennelong's letter is that his requests for goods are dropped abruptly into messages of personal greeting and snippets of news, as though he were combining in a single piece of writing several epistolary genres that, in Phillip's letters, remained largely separate and distinct. Had Arthur Phillip read Bennelong's letter, he may have seen elements of his own reports, letters and requisitions intermingled and 'writ strange'.

Placing strangers

When analysing the influences Governor Phillip may have had on Bennelong, it is important to remember that Bennelong's mind was not a blank page. Whatever he learned from Phillip, he would have utilised in accordance with his own society's codes of conduct, and understood in terms of the larger cosmological order that shaped his people's sense of propriety. Bennelong integrated Governor Phillip into his moral and social universe by adopting him into his kinship network. As Hunter and others noted, Bennelong 'sits at table with the Governor, whom he calls "Beanga", or father; and the Governor calls him "Dooroow", or son.'[19] Bennelong also referred to the Judge, David Collins, and the Commissary, Andrew Miller as 'Babunna' or 'brother.'[20]

In Bennelong's culture, as in Aboriginal communities today, kinship terms such as father, mother, auntie, uncle, son and daughter are used not only to identify people related 'by blood', but also to bring strangers into 'the domain of sanctioned human relationships'.[21] Specific codes of behaviour, including the giving and receiving of gifts, are required in every kinship relationship. By classifying Governor Phillip as his father, Bennelong was endeavouring to make clear the mutual rights and reciprocal obligations that should pertain between them. Their father–son relationship enabled both Bennelong and Phillip to know exactly where they stood and how they should behave, not only in relation to each other, but towards their respective family members and other associates.

Governor Phillip had his own professional uses for his *beanga–dooroow* relationship with Bennelong. At a whale feast in early September 1790, Phillip invoked the connection in an attempt to re-establish amicable relations with Bennelong after his escape the previous May. He may also have been trying more broadly to regulate his relationship with the Aboriginal clans around Sydney Harbour. John Hunter recorded that 'The Governor stood up in the boat and asked in their language where Ba-na-lang [Bennelong] was; Ba-na-lang answered, I am here; the governor then said, I am the governor your father: (a name he wished the Governor to be known by when he lived with him).'[22] Phillip was not playing great white chief to an amorphous black hoard. By hailing Bennelong and publicly proclaiming their father–son relationship, Phillip not only located Bennelong in the crowd, but implicitly located himself in relation to every other member of Bennelong's clan present at the feast. As Bennelong used the Governor as a fixed point of social reference in his dealings with the British, Phillip invoked his father–son relationship in an effort to regulate his relations with Bennelong's people. This process of social positioning may have been facilitated by the fact that Governor Phillip had a missing front tooth, which members of the local Aboriginal societies would have interpreted as a sign that he had been ceremonially initiated into manhood.

On the day of the whale feast, however, Phillip's plan for a public reconciliation with Bennelong went horribly awry. Phillip was speared in the shoulder by a man named Willemering. Collins insisted that Bennelong played 'no culpable part' in the spearing, and Bennelong later told Phillip that he had given Willemering a beating.[23] In the moments when Willemering was taking aim at Phillip, however, Bennelong neither protested nor physically intervened, leading some historians to infer that he had orchestrated Phillip's spearing as 'pay-back' for his capture and imprisonment.[24] According to Bennelong's biographer, Keith Vincent Smith, Willemering was a '*koradgee*', or clever-man, from Gurugal country to the north around Broken Bay, who had come to Port Jackson at Bennelong's behest to carry out the ritual spearing.[25] Vincent Smith argues that in Bennelong's eyes, 'atonement was necessary before he could resume friendly dialogue once more with Phillip.'[26] Phillip chose to interpret the spearing as a misunderstanding, and ordered that no retaliation or punishment be administered.

After Phillip's reconciliation with Bennelong, the high level of trust between the two men is reflected in the fact that, in December 1792, Bennelong and a younger man named Yemmerrawanie accompanied Phillip to England on the *Atlantic*, along with four kangaroos, and other fauna and cultural curiosities peculiar to New Holland.[27] When they arrived five and a half months later, Bennelong and Yemmerrawanie were presented to King George III, in accordance with precedents set by Native dignitaries from the Pacific and North America. Bennelong at first enjoyed his stay in London, where he dressed in fancy clothes and learned to box, skate, smoke and drink.[28] But by the end of their first year in England, he and Yemmerrawanie were ill and homesick. Yemmerrawanie died in May 1794, leaving Bennelong alone.

Little is known of Bennelong's time in England. His bills for board and lodgings indicate that he and Yemmerrawanie lived for a time in London, before taking up lodgings at the house of a Mr Edward Kent, in the village of Eltham near Lord Sydney's estate, Frognall Manor.[29] Mr Phillips, the main addressee of Bennelong's letter, was Lord Sydney's steward at Frognall, in which role he may have been responsible only for ensuring that Bennelong was well looked after by Mr Kent. Yet Bennelong's letter suggests that during his illness he became close to Mr and Mrs Phillips, whether or not they nursed him back to health in their own home.[30] In either case, two things are clear: first, that Bennelong was very grateful to Mr and Mrs Phillips and, second, that Mr Phillips' responsibility for Bennelong would most likely have been brokered by Governor Phillip through his patron, Lord Sydney. Bennelong was looked after by Lord Sydney's steward, Mr Phillips, because he was the protégé of Lord Sydney's protégé, Governor Arthur Phillip.

Bennelong opens his letter by announcing that he is well, and expressing his hope that Mr Phillips is likewise in good health: 'Dear Sir, I am very well. I hope you are very well.' Such remarks are not a traditional Aboriginal mode of greeting, so it appears Bennelong had noticed that polite greetings in the form of questions and statements about health were a type of ceremonial word exchange, and thus a powerful bonding agent in British society. Given that he was gravely ill when he last saw Mr and Mrs Phillips, however, his remarks about health may not have been merely a polite formality. Similarly, Bennelong's announcement that his wife has been stolen away, and that he dines daily with the Governor (Hunter), may be read not simply as news, but as a mode of social positioning, a way of informing Mr and Mrs Phillips that as an unmarried man closely associated with the Governor, he should appropriately receive their patronage in the form of gifts. When addressing Mr and Mrs Phillips, Bennelong does not use familial terms as he did with Governor Phillip, yet elements of his letter implicitly position his English carers in a quasi-familial relationship with him.

Again, Governor Arthur Phillip was his orientation point. By the time Bennelong sailed for England with Phillip in December 1792, they had been calling each other father and son for some time. What would Bennelong have made of the fact that an arrangement made by his *beanga*, Phillip, led to him being looked after by a man and woman named Phillips? Would he have reasoned that his *beanga* was related, directly or otherwise, to Mr and Mrs Phillips? If so, Bennelong may have located himself as son or nephew of Mr and Mrs Phillips, in which case the apparently gauche requests for clothing, shoes and handkerchiefs that he makes in his letter could be understood as part of a customary Dharug practice of gift exchange between kin. A crucial element of Aboriginal kinship systems is the obligation to give and receive gifts from particular kinfolk. Giving and receiving binds clans together, particularly on occasions such as marriages and inter-group meetings when gifts are exchanged ceremonially for diplomatic reasons. Through cycles of giving and receiving, people are constantly creating and discharging obligations to members of their extensive kinship networks and to trading partners further afield.

Bennelong's letter addresses Mrs and Mrs Phillips and Lord Sydney in a tone that, to European ears, shifts awkwardly between intimacy and respectful formality. On the one hand, Bennelong addresses them formally in the English manner as 'Sir' and 'Madam'; on the other, he explicitly asks Mr and Mrs Phillips for gifts, as though they were his parents or his uncle and aunt. This instability makes Bennelong's requests for clothing and shoes seem, by English standards, to be gauche attempts to secure favours from distant acquaintances. Yet Troy maintains that Bennelong was 'a linguistic virtuoso', and that in early colonial times Aboriginal people in the Sydney region used different kinds of language in accordance with the nature of their relationship with the person they were addressing.[31] What kind of (English) language would Bennelong have used when addressing people with whom his relationship was not clear and could be construed in different ways, depending on the cultural perspective adopted? Attempting to negotiate his relationship within two overlapping social orders, Bennelong refers to Mr and Mrs Phillips formally as 'Sir' and 'Madam', as polite English manners required, yet his requests clearly also invoke the kind of close familial relationship he had with his *beanga*, Governor Phillip.

Asking openly for things does not *in itself* make Bennelong's letter seem awkward and tactless. The appearance of awkwardness stems from the contrast between his formal manner of address and his blunt way of asking Mr and Mrs Phillips to look after his needs, as though they were his close family members. Bennelong faced the challenge of translating kin-based and place-based codes of oral communication into modes of written address to faraway foreigners who had once been close. The task must have been all the more difficult given that he was dictating his letter to a scribe, speaking his message out loud with little opportunity for reflection or revision, to people who were way out of earshot, yet whose kindness seems to have remained vividly present in his memory.

The instability of Bennelong's tone shows his struggle to negotiate a position in two social orders simultaneously. His mixture of formality and familial intimacy reflects the entanglement of his own kin-based cultural norms with the European-style patronage network that existed between Lord Sydney, Governor Phillip, Mr and Mrs Phillips, and himself. These two social orders were quite different, yet in many ways very similar — a circumstance that multiplied the danger of committing improprieties in cross-cultural communication.

Kin-based Indigenous relationships resemble European patronage systems in that both are based on exchange and mutual obligation. Patronage systems are in fact quasi-kinship relationships, the English word 'patron' deriving from 'pater', the Latin word for father. Lord Sydney and Arthur Phillip were certainly connected as patron and protégé. Phillip visited Lord Sydney at Frognall Manor in the mid-1780s.[32] Lord Sydney took a lively interest in Phillip's career, and offered him the position of first governor of New South Wales, just as he installed his eldest son in the position of junior under-secretary to Evan Nepean in the Home Office.[33] Between October 1786, when Lord Sydney put the royal seal on Phillip's commission, and May

1787, when Phillip sailed for New South Wales, the governor-designate became well acquainted with Lord Sydney's family at Frognall.[34] Hence, the likelihood that it was through Lord Sydney's close relationship with Arthur Phillip that Mr and Mrs Phillips' care of Bennelong was arranged. Hence also the likelihood that differences, disguised as similarities, between Dharug and English codes of proper social behaviour made Bennelong's manner of addressing Mr and Mrs Phillips seem erratic and impertinent.

Complicating the question of how Bennelong located himself socially in relation to Mrs and Mrs Phillips is an observation made by Tench in 1789. Tench recorded that Bennelong referred to a pair of candle snuffers as: 'Nuffer for candle (the S is a letter which they cannot pronounce, having no sound in their language similar to it. When bidden to pronounce sun, they always say 'tun'; salt, 'talt'; and so of all words wherein it occurs)'.[35]

If 's' was not a meaningful sound in Bennelong's language, he may not have distinguished between the names 'Phillip' and 'Phillips'. In fact, the only time the name 'Phillips' appears in Bennelong's letter it is written *without* the final 's', making it the same name as that of Bennelong's adopted father, Governor Arthur Phillip, the source of many gifts.

Bennelong was an accomplished mimic, however. Between 1789, when Tench made this observation, and 1796, when Bennelong dictated his letter, Bennelong would probably have learned to pronounce the 's' sound, and to differentiate clearly between the two names. Looking at his letter as a whole, it seems he had no trouble pronouncing the 's' in other words, although the scribe might have silently corrected recognisable aberrations.

Muddying the waters further is the fact that the manuscript copy of Bennelong's letter, housed in the National Library in Canberra, is not the original transcript of the words Bennelong dictated in 1796. The whereabouts of the original transcript — if it still exists — are unknown. Perhaps the final 's' in 'Phillips' fell off in the process of reproducing the letter — not because Bennelong couldn't pronounce it, but because the copyist simply ran out of room at the end of the line.[36] It is difficult to imagine that during the time Bennelong was nursed by Mr and Mrs Phillips he would not have established how, if at all, they were related to Arthur Phillip. His treatment of Mr and Mrs Phillips as family may have been based on the way they nursed him through his illness, rather than on any perceived kinship tie with Bennelong's *'beanga'*.

A human curiosity

Bennelong departed England in February 1795, arriving in Sydney in September. He had been away from his kin and country for almost three years. As his letter states, he returned to find his wife, Go-roo-bar-roo-boo-lo, living with Carroway. A petticoat, jacket and hat lured her back briefly, but these gifts were soon gone and she went back to Carroway, reducing Bennelong's social status to that of an unmarried man.[37] Having been celibate during the entire time he was away, Bennelong assaulted Boo-rre-a, the wife of Bennelong's old rival, Colby, who asked him sarcastically 'if he meant that kind of conduct to be a specimen of English manners', and pressed his point by giving Bennelong a beating.[38] Bennelong's absence from Port Jackson appears to have enhanced his notoriety among his own people and English colonial society, but rendered his social status precarious and uncertain. Governor Phillip was no longer at hand to present him with gifts he could use to elevate his standing among his people. It was in this context that, in late August 1796, almost a year after his return, Bennelong dictated his letter to Mr Phillips, with its requests for clothing, handkerchiefs and shoes.

In her study of cross-cultural exchange at Port Jackson, Isabel McBryde notes:

> Traditions of reciprocity in the conduct of relationships of all kinds were strong, and the re-distribution of valued goods played a significant role in social, political and ceremonial life. At both the individual and group level it was important for the acquisition and maintenance of status, hence power… To default in exchange obligations was a serious offence.[39]

In the Sydney region, Aboriginal people were keen to acquire functional implements such as hatchets, knives and fishhooks; however, there was also a lively trade in cultural curiosities among Europeans and Aboriginal people alike. The colonists saw spears, shields, clubs and other artefacts as curiosities, strange rarities to sell, or hoard and display. Conversely, the Indigenous peoples of Port Jackson valued European clothing and hats as exotic tradable curiosities rather than for their practical utility. In both societies, 'goods from distant localities acquired great prestige which enhanced that of the giver'.[40]

According to McBryde, in the early years of the colony at Port Jackson, Bennelong and his kin dominated trade transactions. During this period, the Governor and his senior officers, to whom Bennelong had ready access, tried to maintain control of trade negotiations.[41] It was crucial to the colony's survival that proper protocols and equivalencies of value be established in order to stabilise essential diplomatic and trade relations with the local clans. Only when protocols and equivalencies of value for essential provisions had been clearly set in place were other officers and members of the civil, military and naval detachments permitted to begin bartering.

After the spearing of Governor Phillip in September 1790, Bennelong emerged 'with the advantage' in the diplomatic gift exchanges that helped restore trust between the British and the Port Jackson clans.[42] From Bennelong's point of view, these gifts were not mere bribes, but rather a means of discharging debts, remedying grievances, or perhaps even compensating for loss of land and resources. The journals of Phillip and his officers record a constant exchange of gifts and favours between colonists and Aboriginal people, with Bennelong one of the main recipients. Bennelong, however, did not hoard the goods he received, or parade them as personal status symbols. According to Hunter, Bennelong traded away most of them:

> Of all the cloaths and the multiplicity of other articles which had been given to Bennelong, very little now remained in his possession; his shield, and most of his cloaths, were, by his own account, sent a great distance off; but whether he had lost them, or given them away, was uncertain.[43]

Hunter explains Bennelong's actions in terms of the 'feckless savage' stereotype, implying that Bennelong carelessly mislaid his possessions, or absent-mindedly gave them away. Feeding into and growing out of this stereotype, is the mistaken assumption that Aboriginal people saw no use for *things*. A more likely explanation of Bennelong's behaviour is that he was using the gifts to elevate his position within his own expanding networks of trade and exchange.

In Aboriginal trade networks, European goods were in high demand because they enhanced the status of the receiver when s/he, in turn, became a giver.[44] As Bennelong fed the Governor's gifts into Aboriginal trade networks, his importance as a conduit between two vast exchange systems would certainly have enhanced his social status. The timing of Bennelong's letter can perhaps be explained in relation to his fortunes as a trader. When he returned to Sydney in September 1795, his main source of gifts was gone. Phillip had sent some money for Bennelong, in return for which Bennelong conveyed his best wishes via Henry Waterhouse's letter of 24 October 1795 to Phillip.[45] Over time, however, Bennelong's relationships, both with the officers at the settlement and with the local Aboriginal community, became increasingly strained. He offended his kinsmen by using his English manners and clothing to aggrandise himself, and his frequent returns to the bush dismayed the colonists, who saw it as a sign that he was regressing to a state of savagery. A decline in the colonists' demand for his services as a mediator and translator meant that he would have received fewer gifts of clothing and goods by way of payment. When leaving England, however, Bennelong had had the forethought to bring 'a rich wardrobe' with him.[46] If he traded and gifted these clothes away over a period of several months, and replenished his supply at a somewhat slower rate, it may explain why Bennelong did not request clothing, handkerchiefs and shoes from Mr and Mrs Phillips until he had been home for just under a year, when his supply finally ran out. Bennelong's letter may have been motivated not only by his wish to maintain his quasi-kinship ties with his carers in England, but by his need to obtain tradable goods to restore his social standing among the Port Jackson clans.

During the times when Bennelong had sat with Governor Phillip at his desk, he may have perceived that written texts, as sets of meaningful marks inscribed on portable objects, were comparable in certain respects to message-sticks. Letters were also *things*, however, and as such could serve additional purposes: letters were objects to be exchanged, like diplomatic gifts and trade goods. Bennelong may have noticed, for example, that Phillip's written requests for supplies invariably got results. The letters left Sydney Cove on the same ships that bore away Aboriginal trade goods such as spears, shields and clubs to be sold in Europe to merchants and collectors. Replies to Phillip's letters arrived on ships that brought hatchets, knives, clothing, food, and other trade goods and diplomatic gifts that passed into the hands of the Aboriginal peoples of Port Jackson.

Letters are a means of asking for things. They are also themselves *things*, objects to be exchanged, like diplomatic gifts or trade goods. When a person receives a personal letter they owe the sender one in return. By replying, one discharges this debt, and creates a new obligation for the original sender to reply. Given his familiarity with gift exchange cycles traditional to his own culture, Bennelong may have viewed his letter to Mr and Mrs Phillips and Lord Sydney as a gift that would both discharge his debt to them for their hospitality, and trigger a reciprocal act of giving in return for his letter-gift. Unlike a non-verbal artefact, Bennelong's letter could *explicitly* invoke and restore his relationship with Mr and Mrs Phillips and Lord Sydney. It could also stipulate exactly what Bennelong wanted in exchange for his letter-gift, and for the greetings, good wishes and news it carried to its recipients. In this sense the letter stipulates its price, in barter rather than monetary terms.

It may not be far-fetched to suggest that if Bennelong saw letters as things that could be exchanged for other things, he also reasoned that by writing to three people in a single letter he would be situating all of them in a relation of obligation to himself. Far from being a mistake, Bennelong's practice of addressing three people in one letter may have been a cross-cultural entrepreneurial manoeuvre, an innovative means of obtaining multiple gifts for a single, news-carrying, kinship-affirming object. Albeit on a small scale, Bennelong's attempt to gain three gifts in exchange for a single manuscript takes advantage of the same multiplier effect that makes writing for publication potentially profitable.

There is no record of whether Mr Phillips received Bennelong's letter. It may seem that Bennelong conforms to the racist stereotype of the 'cheeky native' by daring to assume his letter was a fair exchange for two pairs of stockings, two pairs of shoes and some handkerchiefs. As McBryde notes, however, 'perceptions of value are neither absolute nor universal'.[47] Many recorded exchanges look inequitable because they involved goods with radically different kinds of value, or because of misperceptions of how items were valued in other cultures. Little is known of how traditional Aboriginal societies valued books, paper and other objects that carried alphabetic writing. Parts of books and other printed materials were occasionally found in Aboriginal camps far from the frontier.[48] Some were used for trade and ceremonial purposes, as we'll see in chapters 4 and 5.

In the early years of British settlement, it was difficult for Governor Phillip and his successors to control the trade in cultural curiosities that flourished around Port Jackson. Convicts and free settlers simply picked up Aboriginal tools, weapons and artefacts — anything they thought they could sell to the officers and crews of the transport ships, who in turn sold them on to collectors in England and Europe. Governor Phillip understood the potentially serious economic and political consequences of colonists helping themselves to cultural curiosities; nonetheless, his own officers were keen traders and collectors.[49] At the same time, Phillip himself sent natural history specimens such as birds and skins to Lord Sydney's daughters. He even sent a large stuffed kangaroo to another of his patrons, Sir Joseph Banks.[50] His crowning achievement as a purveyor of objects rare and strange, however, was Bennelong, who embodied the attributes of both a cultural curiosity and a scientific specimen.

Although Bennelong appears to have travelled voluntarily to England with Phillip, one wonders whether he had any idea of what he was in for. Politically, he would have been rendered entirely impotent, like an exhibit, an amusing pet of the kind Joseph Banks described in his musings about Tupaia, a Pacific Islander:

> I do not know why I may not keep him as a curiosity, as well as some of my neighbours do lions and tygers at larger expense than he will ever probably put me to; the amusement I shall have in his future conversation and the benefit he will be of to this ship...will I think fully repay me.[51]

Bennelong's position as a human curiosity is captured vividly in a famous portrait included in the first volume of David Collins' *Account of the English colony in New South Wales* (1798).[52] Bennelong appears in profile, from the chest up, in an oval portrait, his hair groomed and his face composed and cleanly shaven. Surrounding the portrait is an arrangement of Aboriginal spears, shields, stone axes, clubs and spear-throwers.[53] Bennelong appears as a civilised savage, his waistcoat, jacket, bow tie and ruffled white shirt creating a frisson through their contrast with the weapons and tools that symbolise savage primitivism.

What had Bennelong been led to expect he would gain by visiting England? How did he summon the courage to spend months on a boat sailing halfway around the world, an action comparable today to befriending aliens who arrive by spaceship and accompanying them back to Mars? If he was angry at being captured and locked up by Phillip in 1789, how would he have felt about being paraded and lionised in London and then, when his novelty value declined, consigned to lodgings in the wet, cold obscurity of Eltham, where his kinsman died, and he himself fell gravely ill? In 1790, there had been diplomatic gifts to heal his rift with Governor Phillip. In 1796, when he wrote his letter to Mr and Mrs Phillips, was he asking for shoes, stockings, and handkerchiefs as a form of paltry compensation for everything he had lost during his long absence from his kin and homeland?

○ ○ ○

Did Mr and Mrs Phillips ever receive Bennelong's letter? Did they send him the goods he asked for in this letter-gift? If he could have seen into the future, what would he have made of the fact that, today, the whereabouts of the original transcript of his spoken words is unknown, but a copy of the letter is housed in a national sacred place, the National Library of Australia? What would he think of the politics of locking his letter away as a curiosity or specimen, just as he was? How would he respond to the fact that his letter's physical location and monetary value places it largely beyond the reach of his descendants? How many suits of clothes and pairs of shoes could his letter buy today? When Bennelong saw his letter as a potentially valuable commodity, was he indeed wrong, or was he 200 years ahead of his time?

4

Borderlands of Aboriginal writing

Western understandings of the development of writing and literacy have long been dominated by a narrative of evolutionary progress. This narrative locates the primitive beginnings of writing in a pictographic stage, which advances to an ideographic stage before crossing the final threshold into 'writing proper', epitomised by the alphabet, a phonographic script or code for spoken words. Different cultures were thought to be located at different stages in a universal human journey towards 'writing proper'. While Indigenous peoples were said to be fixed at the primitive pictographic stage, and oriental cultures at the ideographic stage, Europeans were supposed to have led the way forward by inventing the alphabet. As Rousseau put it in his *Essai sur l'origine des langues*:

> These three ways of writing correspond almost exactly to three different stages according to which one can consider men gathered into a nation. The depicting of objects is appropriate to a savage people; signs of words and of propositions, to a barbaric people; and the alphabet to civilized people.[1]

In recent times this model has attracted criticism from several quarters.[2] Critics have pointed to its Eurocentricity, its failure to appreciate that 'writing is not adequately thought of as the transcription of speech'.[3] In several disciplines there is growing interest in forms of 'writing before the letter' and modes of 'non-literate' reading. Concepts of writing and reading are now being expanded to accommodate non-Western, non-phonographic modes of graphic communication and decipherment.

At the same time, the Eurocentric evolutionary narrative continues to dominate popular concepts of writing, and has been rearticulated by Walter

J Ong and others, who privilege the alphabet as writing proper because 'it is a representation of utterance'.[4] While stressing the sophistication and functionality of what he calls oral societies, Ong has drawn a sharp line between phonographic scripts epitomised by the alphabet, and non-phonographic 'quasi-writings' such as ideographs and pictographs. By using a system of visible marks that represent words as sounds, the writer of text in alphabetic script can determine 'the exact words that the reader would generate from the text'.[5] By contrast, ideographs and pictographs can be translated only loosely and indirectly into spoken words. How they are verbalised depends on who is reading them, and under what circumstances. Consequently, according to Ong, these non-alphabetic signifying systems only function efficiently if the communicating parties are both immersed in the same life-world, dealing in stable cultural settings with restricted subjects in a limited range of circumstances that determine in advance what the symbols might 'say'.[6] While recognising that many words are not spelled phonetically, and that even the tightest contextual controls can never entirely expunge ambiguity from written texts, Ong wants to retain the categorical distinction between 'writing proper', which functions as a visual code for sounded utterance, and other visual sign systems which have no necessary relation to sound.

My concern here is not to side with Ong or his opponents, but to point to a type of essentialism that enters both sides of the debate whenever any sign system is seen to have any intrinsic, fixed way of working. The problem is not so much that non-phonographic scripts are excluded from the realm of writing, although such exclusions have been a pernicious component of European ethnocentrism, as we saw earlier when authorities such as EB Tylor and Baldwin Spencer classified Indigenous Australians as primitive on the grounds that they lacked recognisable forms of writing. Such exclusions are based on a more fundamental conceptual error: the assumption that any sign system is itself *inherently* phonographic, ideographic or pictographic. This assumption leaves out of account the fact that reading practices are neither automatically activated by scripts themselves, nor determined for all time by conventions prevailing in a script's original cultural context. Visual sign systems have no intrinsic means by which they mean: all are potentially subject to multiple, mutable, contextually determined modes of reading. It is this ideological and cultural clothing that determines whether, in any given context, a sign will operate phonographically, pictographically or ideographically.

This dynamic potential is perhaps most fully realised when signs move across borders between cultures, or move between disparate intracultural contexts of reading. By examining the changing ways in which scripts work as they move between different cultures, it becomes possible to observe that the defining characteristic of any script — its capacity to 'be' phonographic, ideographic or pictographic — is not intrinsic to it, but held in place by culturally and historically specific conventions of reading. The difference between categories of scripts, or between what Ong would call 'writing' and 'non-writing', depends on who is reading, and according to what conventions. Whether a given set of graphic signs functions as a code for spoken words, or as a picture or a concept, depends on what readers 'make' of that sign. That is to say, writing is as reading does.

With this idea in mind, it becomes obvious that when signs move back and forth between different cultures the ways in which they are read may change radically. In cross-cultural transactions between 'non-literate' and 'literate' societies, alphabetic characters may function in ways that have nothing to do with the sound-values ascribed to the letters by Europeans. Alphabetic characters can be read as non-phonographic signs. A given combination of letters may move in and out of a phonographic phase, or operate simultaneously as an ideograph, a pictograph and/or a phonograph. Conversely, it is theoretically possible that a mark which begins its life as an ideograph or pictograph may, in certain contexts, be read as a word or a name, as though it were an alphabetically written word, despite the fact that the mark contains nothing that can be recognised as an alphabetic character. No visual signifying system is inherently or inevitably phonographic, ideographic or pictographic. The way an alphabetic character (or any other kind of a sign) is made meaningful depends usually — but not *necessarily* — on the rules set down by the elites in its culture of origin.

This chapter focuses on a three frontier cultures of literacy, three spaces of exchange, entanglement, and transformation between Aboriginal and European signifying practices. In these borderland zones it becomes possible to see writing in the process of being re-clothed or cross-dressed. The nature and function of visual signs are altered, along with the technologies and media through which they are transmitted. In this frontier zone, writing can precede literacy, and the line between what Ong would call writing and non-writing becomes overtly contingent and unstable. On the borderland between cultures, it becomes obvious that Aboriginal uses of alphabetic script do not begin only after they have been formally schooled into using the alphabet in the conventional European mode as a phonemic script for spoken words. What I want to suggest instead is that, in frontier settings, Aboriginal involvement in the making of European-style documents and the use of alphabetic script begins, in a sense, *before* literacy, in a double movement in which, on one side, traditional Aboriginal ideographs are transcribed onto European documents and made to serve as signatures, while on the other side, Aboriginal people appropriate alphabetic and numerical characters and put them to work in ways that have little to do with European conventions of phonographic writing and reading. Both these movements occur prior to formal schooling in European reading and writing practices. To illustrate this double movement, I'll attempt a provisional reading of two clubs carved in the 1860s in Wiradjuri country, then discuss Charlie Flannigan's prison-cell 'drawings of writing' in the early 1890s, and finally revisit the 'signing' of the Batman treaty in the Port Phillip District in 1835.

Writing before literacy: Wiradjuri clubs

Some Indigenous Australians didn't wait to be taught how to write. Instead, they appropriated alphabetic characters by carving them into wooden objects such as clubs, boomerangs, spear-throwers and shields. It is difficult to know how widespread this practice was during the 19th century. Very few alphabetically inscribed objects from that period have been preserved in museums because most collectors of Indigenous artefacts were trying to preserve what they thought were pure, uncontaminated 'primitive cultures'.

To understand how Aboriginal people used alphabetic characters non-phonographically, it's necessary to keep in mind the *materiality* of writing — its manifestation in the form of objects — and undo some of the highly abstract ways of thinking about the alphabet that, for most people in modern Western societies, begins when their kindergarten teacher writes up the letters of the alphabet on the blackboard, and coaxes the class to recite 'A is for apple, B is for ball, C is for cat...' Beyond the frontier of white occupation, Aboriginal people would not have encountered alphabetic writing in the abstract, nor seen alphabetic characters physically sequestered on specially prepared surfaces such as blackboards or paper. Nor would their seeing of alphabetic characters have been mediated by known phonemic principles that tied particular sounds to particular letters. Instead, in frontier settings, and even more so beyond the frontier, they would have encountered writing primarily as 'stuff', not separated from the objects that carried it. Before attending schools or engaging with the principles of European literacy, Aboriginal people would have seen alphabetic writing at large, out in the world, doing its work alongside numerical and other symbols, in a range of different graphic styles and notational systems. This variety of graphic styles reflected both the diversity of European technologies in use at that time, and the practice of branding merchandise with distinctive lettering on labels and signs. Indigenous Australians would have seen alphabetic characters stencilled, chiselled, stamped, printed or handwritten (in the foreign language of English), on objects such as coins, ships, milestones, rifles, metal tools, packing crates, flour bags, barrels, china, pocket watches, wool bales and signs, as well as in newspapers, books, handbills and handwritten documents. Sometimes interspersed with numerals, they were always on tangible objects that formed part of the alien material culture of the settler society. Together with traditional Indigenous oral and scriptorial practices, these objects and the distinctive lettering styles used on them would have shaped Aboriginal people's understandings of the nature and functions of alphabetic script. It's necessary to keep this material aspect of writing in mind when trying to attribute meaning to the inscriptions on the two Wiradjuri clubs made near Wagga Wagga in the 1860s.

In my attempts to read these clubs, I am in a similar position to Aboriginal people when they were initially faced with alphabetic script without having been formally schooled. Looking at 'Club A' from bottom to top (see p. 77), we see what Paul Taçon interprets as traditional clan-markings at the narrow end.[7] Above these markings is a blank space, above which is a traditional, deeply incised, relatively regular cross-hatch pattern. At a certain point, however, the regularity of the cross-hatch pattern begins to break up, leaving gaps and lines of irregular length but consistent diagonal directionality. There is no clear demarcation dividing the regular pattern from the disrupted pattern. The former seems rather to merge into the latter. In the disrupted section, zigzag lines and marks resembling Xs and Vs progressively confuse the basic cross-hatch pattern, as though the carver had begun to notice the similarity between the traditional cross-hatch marks and some of the symbols inscribed on the goods and chattels of the white man. At the top of the transitional section is a deeply carved line, and above that the carver begins experimentally to reproduce shapes that are recognisable as alphabetic characters. Above those letters, dividing them off from the head of the club, is another deeply carved line. Read from bottom to top, the club can be understood as a record of a transition from traditional to non-traditional practice.

Three features of the alphabetic characters on Club A warrant close attention. First, all the letters are configurations of straight diagonal lines. There are no curved letters, and no non-diagonal straight lines. Every one of the alphabetic characters is congruent with the straight-line diagonals the carver was using to produce the traditional cross-hatching on the lower section of the club. It was perhaps this coincidental congruence that inspired or licensed the carver to begin experimentally reproducing selected alphabetic characters.

The second thing to notice on Club A is that all the letters, with the possible exception of the 'N', are also Roman numerals. The symbol next to the 'X' is as likely to be an upside down V as an incomplete capital A, given that the Aboriginal carver may not have been familiar with Western conventions of letter-orientation. The 'N' may be an inaccurate reproduction of M, the Roman numeral for 1000.[8] The carver has reproduced only those Roman numerals that are congruent with the traditional diagonal straight-line pattern on the lower section of the club. The Roman numerals with curves or non-diagonal straight lines, such as C, D, and L, have not been reproduced on the club, perhaps because they are not congruent with the traditional cross-hatch pattern. Aboriginal people may have seen Roman numerals on round objects such as pocket watches and clocks, and this might explain the inconsistent orientation of many Aboriginal inscriptions. If Aboriginal carvers were copying symbols arranged around the rim of a watch-face or a coin, it would have been difficult to know which way was up. The possibility that the 'V', 'M' and 'X' on this club are imitating Roman numerals serves as a reminder of those sites in Western manuscript and print cultures where alphabetic characters function ideographically as symbols conveying a concept, rather than phonographically as elements in a visual code for sounded words.

The third important feature of the characters on Club A is that they all have serifs, as Roman numerals almost invariably do, or did at that time. The prevalence of serifs suggests that the letters were copied from carved, stamped, stencilled or printed inscriptions of the kind found on milestones, coins, pocket watches, crates or merchandise. Serifs are little things, but their significance is potentially great. When Europeans copy by hand a quote from a printed source, they do not normally try to imitate the printed typeface. Under ordinary circumstances, the typeface is irrelevant; all that

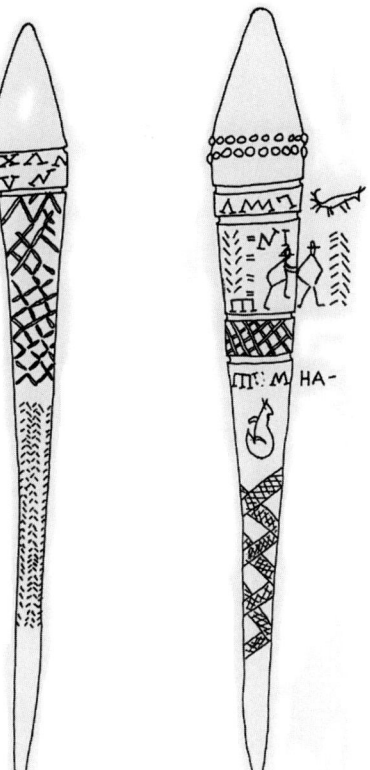

Wiradjuri clubs as sketched by the author. 'Club A' on left and 'Club B' right. The original artefacts are in the collection of the Australian Museum, Sydney.

counts is the phonemic value of the letters. Yet when Aboriginal people initially encountered alphabetic characters, they would have had no way of knowing which features of the characters 'carried' meaning (in the eyes of literate Europeans), and which did not. Indigenous Australians in frontier settings are unlikely to have known, for instance, whether M, W, V, N, and Z had to have a specific orientation and a specific number of zigs and zags, or whether these letters were simply bits of zigzag pattern of arbitrary length and orientation. Nor would they have known whether or not a given letter in two different typefaces, or in upper and lower case, amounted to two different letters or two ways of writing the same letter. Even if they knew that literate Europeans assigned particular sounds to particular characters, they would have had no principle upon which to distinguish the sounded parts of letters from the incidental, non-phonemic elements such as serifs. If the first typeface an Aboriginal person had ever encountered happened to be Roman type, they might reasonably deduce that serifs were a crucial, indispensable feature of the white man's signs.

77

In fact, serifs have turned out to be a telltale sign that Aboriginal inscriptions are reproductions of alphabetic or Roman numeric characters. It is theoretically possible that Aboriginal inscriptions resemble these characters purely by coincidence. Sometimes an inscription is worn or ill-defined, making it difficult to decide whether its resemblance to an alphabetical character is intentional, or simply a meaningless cross-cultural, coincidental resemblance of marks. Serifs often provide the key. Since they were not traditional to Aboriginal cultures, serifs are a fairly reliable sign that an otherwise ambiguous motif has been copied from a stencilled, stamped or printed model.

All but two of the characters on Wiradjuri 'Club B' had serifs. The handle end of Club B has shallow carved bands of cross-hatching which, as with Club A, is a traditional design.[9] Above is the figure of a kangaroo or wallaby and five letters, three with serifs, two without. Next is a band of deeply incised cross-hatching, bounded at the top and bottom by deeply carved horizontal lines. Above that again is a section that includes traditional and non-traditional elements: diagonal notches that traditionally identify the clan-group, alongside a figurative carving of two men with hats in a possible conflict situation, and some alphabetic characters. In the next section is a group of letters and the figure of a dog, and finally at the business end of the club are two bands of iron nails, the heads protruding a few millimetres either for decorative purposes or to give the club a bit of extra clout.

At this point I can only speculate about the functions of the alphabetic characters inscribed on this club. One possibility is that the letters functioned as power symbols, helping the club do its work effectively. Another is that the letters were inscribed to enhance the exchange value of the clubs, or to mark their status as potential merchandise. Taçon has noted that wooden objects such as boomerangs, shields, clubs and spear-throwers were usually inscribed with abstract geometrical motifs and patterns prior to European contact.[10] Figurative images of people, animals and so forth were typically found in rock shelters rather than on portable objects. In central New South Wales, figurative images did not appear on wooden objects until the mid-19th century, when such items began to be made for trading with non-Aboriginal people. When alphabetic characters appear alongside figurative images on portable objects, it may not be far-fetched to see both kinds of inscriptions as attempts to attract potential buyers. Alphabetic characters might, in such cases, work as exemplars of 'the white man's signs', in much the same way as Taiwanese-made merchandise carries American baseball or football team logos in order to say 'buy me, I'm yours' to Westernised customers.

Where Aboriginal carvers were incising alphabetic characters on clubs and other objects to enhance their exchange value, the characters' respective sound-values, along with the European reading conventions that reproduced them, would have been entirely irrelevant. Two nice paradoxes emerge here. The first is that Aboriginal people, including Bennelong and the carver of the Wiradjuri clubs, may have been writing for material gain or monetary profit without ever entering that state of knowledge Europeans call literacy. The second paradox is that as modern Western consumer culture increasingly incorporates alphabetic characters into brand logos and high-tech advertising graphics, sectors of the 'most advanced' societies are moving towards a non-phonographic space previously associated with cultures that the West deemed 'primitive', 'backward' and 'other'.

Drawing writing: Charlie Flannigan

In medieval European manuscript cultures, documents were often reproduced by copyists who were neither able to read nor to independently compose written texts. These copyists engaged with the visual and aesthetic aspects of alphabetic characters rather than with their sound-values. As print replaced hand-copying as the primary means of textual reproduction, the visual and aesthetic dimensions of alphabetic script lost their traditional mnemonic and spiritual raison d'être, and reading became in most contexts a matter of gulping down typographically uniform eye-bites rather than devoutly sounding words out, or savouring the memorable beauty of letters and the layout of individual pages. The careful page designs and ornamental lettering styles devised by William Blake, William Morris and Ezra Pound in the 19th and early 20th centuries were in part an effort to resensitise readers to the aesthetic and semiotic potential of the visual dimension of written and printed words.[11]

Two years after William Morris established the Kelmscott Press in London, a young Aboriginal prisoner in Darwin's Fanny Bay Gaol was engaging with the visual and aesthetic values of alphabetic characters in a series of pencil drawings on government-issue paper. Charlie Flannigan (also known as Charlie McManus) had spent most of his working life as a stockman and station hand in western Queensland and the Northern Territory. In September 1892 while working on Auvergne Station in the Northern Territory he killed the acting manager after a dispute over a card game. Flannigan gave himself up to the police, and was held in Darwin's Fanny Bay Gaol for several months awaiting trial. He was found guilty of murder and was hanged in July 1893 at the gaol. His drawings were all created while he was in prison.[12] They are presently held at the Museum of South Australia. Again and again he draws his home country, the land and the buildings of Wave Hill Station and Victoria River Downs, and himself or another stockman on a horse.

Andrew Sayers suggests that Flannigan had probably had some schooling, which means in this context that he had had some training in the reading conventions that make writing intelligible as a code for the sound of English language words. As evidence of Flannigan's literacy, Sayers points to the fact that 'his drawings sometimes incorporate words'.[13] Looking at these words, however, we see two distinct kinds of writing: cursive script where Flannigan uses writing as a phonemic code, and ornamental lettering where he engages primarily with the visual and aesthetic values of the letters. A curious discrepancy exists between his tentative handling of cursive script and his confident use of ornamental lettering. It is possible that he used cursive script when composing written words for himself, and ornamental letters when he was copying from an existing text. On one drawing, Flannigan practised writing his own name in the manner of a signature, knowing perhaps that artists did so in the white man's culture.

Being able to reproduce even ornate forms of lettering does not necessarily mean one can read or compose written texts independently. One does not need to be literate in the sense of being able to decipher written words phonetically to be able to engage with the visual values of alphabetic characters. Like some medieval copyists, Charlie Flannigan may have been writing by sight rather than by sound and the learned rules of spelling. In his drawing of Wave (Hill) Station, he is clearly concerned to reproduce a special style of lettering, but instead of setting down the letters according to the way the word sounds he makes the copyist's common error of looping back to repeat a sequence of letters he has already reproduced.

Flannigan evidently copied ornate forms of lettering from popular illustrated journals such as *Punch*. In these, his alphabetic characters function in a manner that has little to do with their sound-values. He is engaging with writing not as a code for utterance but as a set of aesthetically pleasing visual patterns and configurations of lines. His lettering invites the eye to scan a spatial design rather than a linear sequence of written phonemes. Whether or not Flannigan was functionally literate, he seems here to be *drawing* writing rather than inscribing letters on the basis of their sound-values. In this regard, Flannigan's use of alphabetic characters foregrounds the principle that the alphabet is not *inherently* a phonographic code. Charlie Flannigan's drawings show that meaningful graphic patterns can be seen in written language, irrespective of whether or not the letters are intelligible on the basis of their sound-values.

Charlie Flannigan's drawing of Wave Hill Station (top), and another where he uses letters for an ornamental rather than phonemic purpose. **Museum Board of South Australia.**

Dendroglyph signatures: the Batman treaty

Questions such as What counts as writing? and What counts as authorship? are not merely academic. In colonial Australia, these questions where politically and legally crucial. On 6 June 1835 on the banks of Merri Creek, where the Melbourne suburb of Northcote is now located, eight clan-heads of what was erroneously called the Dutigallar tribe allegedly signed a treaty with John Batman.[14] The treaty applied to two tracts of land totalling approximately 243 000 hectares, and offered blankets, knives, mirrors, tomahawks, scissors, clothing and flour in return. To effect the conveyance, the Indigenous 'chiefs' were said to have signed the deeds and placed some soil in John Batman's hand. As far as Batman was concerned, the elders were observing the archaic European ritual of enfeoffment. In their own cultural terms, they were probably performing the Tanderrum ceremony, which bestowed hospitality, affirmed allegiance and allowed mutual sharing of resources, without transferring ownership of land.[15]

It is difficult to know precisely what the Woiworung leaders made of Batman's ceremony of signatures and soil. Wurundjeri elder William Barak, who was present as a boy at the treaty signing, spoke neither of the documents nor the signatures when recalling the event in old age.[16] Despite the treaty deeds' assertion that the terms of the purchase had been 'fully and properly interpreted and explained to the said Chiefs', Batman's rival, John Pascoe Fawkner, had serious doubts. He rightly argued that the Aboriginal signatories could not possibly have grasped the treaty's implication:

> ...it was not read over to them; it was not interpreted to them or explained, for these reasons; not one of the Sydney blacks knew the language of the men of this colony; not one of the Sydney blacks could read, except Bullett, and he only learnt words of one syllable... and any man of sense must know that to translate a deed to any one of a different tongue or language requires a real knowledge of both languages, and these Sydney blacks could not read, much less translate writing.[17]

Anticipating criticism on several points, Batman introduced his treaties into official channels in ways calculated to emphasise their moral integrity and legal validity. Potential discrepancies exist, however, in the three accounts of how the treaty was signed. The process as recorded on the deeds themselves differs from that recounted in Batman's journal, and a different version again is offered in Batman's report to Governor Arthur.

The treaty deeds state that 'We…the Chiefs of the said Tribe have hereunto affixed our Seals…and have signed the same.' This statement is corroborated on the deeds by the signed affirmations of three white witnesses that the documents had been 'Signed, Sealed and Delivered' on 6 June 1835. It is also consistent with Batman's journal entry for the same day: 'The parchment the eight chiefs signed this afternoon, delivering to me some of the soil of each of them, as giving me full possession of the tracts of land'.[18]

Batman's journal entry for the following day reveals, however, that the signing process was somewhat more complicated and drawn out than the deeds implied. In his journal entry for Sunday, 7 June, Batman recorded that on that day he spent some time 'drawing up triplicates of the deeds of the land I purchased'.[19] He also described the process by which he obtained the 'Native chiefs' marks:

> I had no trouble to find out their secret marks. One of my natives (Bungett) went to a tree, out of sight of the women, and made the Sydney natives' mark; after this was done I took, with two or three of my natives, the principal chief, and showed him the mark on the tree; this he knew immediately, and pointed to the knocking out of the teeth. The mark is always made when the ceremony of knocking out the tooth in the front is done. However, after this I desired, through my natives, for him to make his mark, which, after looking about for some time, and hesitating some few minutes, he took the tomahawk and cut out in the bark of the tree his mark — which is attached to the deed, and is the signature of their country and tribe.[20]

In the act of disclosing his coup, Batman risks attracting accusations of forgery. He deflects attention away from his crime by using the passive voice, and locating his admission in a subordinate clause. He implies that he simply moved the mark from the tree to the document, as though this relocation is as innocuous as shifting a vase to a different spot on a table. Yet the placement or location of signs is crucial to their meaning. The meaning of written words is shaped very much by their location, whether we are speaking of the placement of a signature on a legal document, or the location of modern-day Aboriginal graffiti which says implicitly, 'This is my place, my land. I mark it as mine, in defiance of white law.'

According to the Batman treaty deeds, the Aboriginal signatures had been written and witnessed on the deeds the previous day. Either the 'Dutigallar' signatures were obtained the day *after* they were witnessed and verified, or

Batman was recollecting the events of Saturday in his Sunday journal entry. More important though is the fact that the 'principal chief' carved a mark on a tree. At no point did he or any other of the signatories put pen to parchment. Aside from Batman's ambiguous account, there is no evidence that the Woiworung elders laid eyes on any written documents at all. The 'Dutigallar' signatures on the treaty deeds were in fact appropriated copies — forgeries they would be called in Western print cultures.

Questions such as this were glossed over by Batman's contemporaries, and by most subsequent accounts of the signing event. With uncharacteristic mildness, John Pascoe Fawkner noted that Batman 'prevailed upon them to take pen in hand and make sundry marks upon One of the deeds'.[21] In an otherwise satirical account of Batman's trip to Port Phillip, the *Cornwall Chronicle* stated naively that:

> Mr. Batman was provided with the deeds in triplicate, the nature of which he explained to the chief as is the fashion upon such an occasion in the white man's country, who readily signed them and received one to preserve.[22]

The most explicit translation of a dendroglyph, or tree carving, into a signature on parchment was made by James Dawson in his *Australian Aborigines* (1881), widely regarded as one of the most authoritative late-19th century ethnographies.[23] Dawson's caption to the facsimile of the Geelong deed states that:

> The marks made by the chiefs on the parchment were their genuine and usual signatures, which they were in the habit of carving on the bark of trees and on their message sticks. The reader will be interested in these traces of civilization among a people who have hitherto been considered the least civilized of all nations.[24]

Popular histories of Victoria's origins also pushed out of sight any questions about the nature and authenticity of the dendroglyph signatures. Commenting in 1984 on William Barak's memory of the treaty signing, Shirley Wiencke assumed that 'the tribal elders…made their mark on the parchment.'[25] A century earlier, the *Picturesque atlas of Australasia* (1886) included a commissioned engraving by GR Ashton entitled *Batman treating with the Blacks*, which captured and reinforced the popular view at that time. This image was reproduced uncritically in 1979 in CP Billot's *John Batman: the story of John Batman and the founding of Melbourne*, and in the 1974, 1978 and 1982 facsimile reprints of the *Picturesque atlas of Australasia*.[26]

Batman treating with the Blacks shows Batman and an Aboriginal elder (designated as such by his grey beard) leaning forward over a large fallen log on which is spread the treaty document. Surrounding them is a cluster of Aboriginal men, some positioned as though lining up to add their signatures to the document. The right hands of Batman and the grey-bearded elder appear to meet at the point where they are both signing the deed, and it is difficult to tell which of them is holding the long feather pen. The stance of the Aboriginal elder and the merging of his right hand with Batman's may be interpreted in two ways: either the Aboriginal elder can 'sign' because penmanship is an innate human ability, or the signing process is difficult but Batman's guiding hand is solving the problem. The engraving thus opens and closes the practical question of exactly how someone who had never before seen a feather used as a writing implement might manipulate it. It also creates the impression that the Batman treaty consisted of a single document only, when in fact there were multiple copies of both the 'Melbourne' and the 'Geelong' deeds.

Harcourt has divided these copies into three categories.[27] First, there is the prototype or pro forma deed drawn up by Joseph Pettingell in Joseph Tice Gellibrand's legal office before Batman set out for Port Phillip. This manuscript initially had blank spaces into which John Batman and William

Ashton's engraving **Batman treating with the Blacks**, Andrew Garran, ed. Picturesque Atlas of Australia, *Vol. 1 (1886).* Courtesy Rare Books, Fisher Library, University of Sydney.

Todd later inserted details about the boundaries of the 'Melbourne' and 'Geelong' tracts of land, as well as the initial tribute and annual rental payments, and the names of the eight Aboriginal signatories. As well as stating that the 'Chiefs of the said tribe' had duly signed and sealed the document, the prototype deed records the names of the eight 'Dutigallar' signatories: Jagajaga, Jagajaga, Jagajaga, Cooloolock, Bungarie, Yanyan, Moowhip and Mommamalar. Only the first name has the dendroglyph signature beside it. This signature consists of three parallel wavy diagonal lines followed closely by a smaller elongated oval. Beside it is a small rectangular wax seal imprinted with a fine-grained, regular, cross-hatch pattern.[28]

Second, there are the main 'Melbourne' and 'Geelong' treaty deeds, which consist of one pair of so-called originals drawn up on 6 June, and duplicate and triplicate copies drawn up on 7 June.[29] These large parchment documents were copied by Batman and William Todd from the prototype deed, during and after negotiations with the 'Dutigallar chiefs'. On these six documents, the 'Dutigallar signature' appears beside each of the eight names, on both the front and back of each document. The third group of deeds, which does not concern us here, consists of approximately fifty small facsimile copies drawn up later for use in written submissions to Government officials.

Batman treating with the Blacks and other representations of the signing event entirely leave out of account the fact that the eight 'Dutigallar' men were alleged to have signed six documents, not just one. These representations foreclose the question of how eight members of a society without alphabetic writing could each have signed three copies of two deeds in two places — making twelve signatures for each signatory, and ninety-six signatures in all — using the unfamiliar technologies of pen, ink and parchment.

Two inferences may be drawn from the fact that there is only one 'Dutigallar signature' on the prototype deed. First, Batman intended the mark to be read as a communal signature — an ideograph for 'Dutigallar chief' — rather than as one of eight different individual signatures. Second, it seems likely that Batman copied the dendroglyph onto the prototype deed with a view to using it as a model for each of the two groups of eight identical signatures he subsequently copied onto each of the six parchment deeds. Batman's wording in his journal entry for Sunday, 7 June neatly sidesteps the issue of forgery. By writing in the passive voice that the Dutigallar chief's 'mark...is attached to the deed', Batman evaded the question of precisely who did the attaching. Looking at the regularity of the 'signatures', it is clear that they were made by a hand that had fully mastered the skill of writing on parchment with pen and ink. As Alistair Campbell has pointed out, 'It is inconceivable that Batman could have persuaded eight unrehearsed Aborigines in a few hours to have drawn the marks with the neatness and penmanship shown on the documents, not once but twelve times.'[30] Batman's first biographer, James Bonwick, surmised as much in 1883, reasoning that 'Batman copied the hieroglyphics cut on the tree, and placed that mark on the deed at the end of each of the supposed signatures of the chiefs.'[31]

Interestingly, Bonwick refers to the names of the chiefs as 'supposed signatures', and calls the 'hieroglyphics' copied from the tree a supplementary 'mark'. Bonwick's wording raises two questions about the treaty: How, given the foreignness of pen, ink and parchment, could the 'Dutigallar Chiefs' possibly have signed the deeds? And which marks constituted their 'signatures': The elders' individual names? The single mark copied from the tree onto the prototype deed? Or the ninety-six identical marks on the six 'original' Melbourne and Geelong deeds?

As well as constituting what Western print cultures would call a forgery, Batman's copying of the dendroglyph was also an act of cross-cultural media substitution — the transformation of a dendroglyph into a mark on a piece of parchment, which performed the functions of an original written signature as soon as it was copied onto a surface that was portable and could hence serve as a legal document. It was not the mark alone, not the naked mark itself, that was legally binding; the legal legitimacy of the mark was contingent on its placement and relocation onto a portable medium — or so Batman hoped. The place or surface on which a sign is written is part of the sign itself.

Batman's forgery involved copying the mark on the tree onto the appropriate places on the multiple copies of the documents. This action did not involve converting an ideograph into a phonograph. Dendroglyphs had the potential to work as legally valid signatures because, in modern Western cultures, signatures occupy a borderline space between ideograph and phonograph. The more illegible they are, the more ideographic. On the one hand, signatures are handwritten alphabetic renditions of the phonemic units of the signatory's name; on the other, they are marks that must be evaluated without any reference to sound, purely as an abstract visual configuration of lines. Accordingly, signatures are simultaneously writing and not-writing. They encode people's names, yet each signature

Forged signatures on the Batman treaty. Image from James Dawson, Australian Aborigines *(1881). Courtesy Rare Books, Fisher Library, University of Sydney.*

is so individually stylised that it becomes a performance or mark of the writer's body, like a thumbprint or fingerprint, and can therefore only be made authentically by its owner.

This dual aspect of signatures, without which the Woiworung dendroglyph would have been useless to Batman, is rooted in medieval European manuscript culture, in the notaries' practice of manually appending both his name and *signum* to documents, and in the English use of seals which combined both a *signum* and the signatory's name.[32] This dual ideographic–phonographic nature of the signature was consolidated after the advent of print. The printing press standardised writing, making the impersonal, standard hands of scribes and copyists obsolete. Literate people cultivated their own distinct, personal handwriting styles and signatures which, combining the functions of name and *signum*, became widely accepted as warrants of authenticity.[33] Paradoxically, the mechanisation of phonographic writing in Europe created the ideographic function of hand-written signatures, the function which Batman exploited in his appropriation of the Woiworung dendroglyph for his treaty documents.

Whether read ideographically or phonographically, signatures also work as memory aids. In that sense, they are not unlike dendroglyphs in traditional indigenous ritual contexts, or the broken knives and other symbolic objects that were sometimes attached to medieval European manuscripts to cue the relevant parties' memories of the documented agreement.[34] In south-eastern Australia (although not south of the Murray River according to Etheridge), dendroglyphs were used, along with ground-drawings, paintings, and ritual objects, to help explain the sacred stories imparted to young men during initiation ceremonies.[35] In so-called oral societies, dendroglyphs and other visual signs served as a means of storing information for later retrieval, just as alphabetic writing does in societies customarily designated 'literate'.[36] Yet according to Eurocentric definitions of writing as a phonographic code for words, these dendroglyphs were not a form of writing but ideographs working as memory aids. Signatures, too, may function as memory aids. They are *appended to* a document to commemorate the *making of* the documented agreement by the relevant parties. The signature not only consummates an agreement, it is also a trace of the moment of its making. As an object, the signature exists 'in witness to' the occasion of the making of the document on which the agreement is recorded.

If Batman's journal account of how he 'obtained' the 'Dutigallar' mark is true, it is a tale of trickery, deception and imposture. The Woiworung man's pointing to his front teeth, and checking for unauthorised onlookers, suggests that what he was making was an *initiatory* dendroglyph, a visual representation of secret sacred men's knowledge. Before Batman could view the mark he intended to use as the 'Dutigallar' signature, he had to convey to the Woiworung leader that he was lawfully authorised to see that mark. This he accomplished by having the Sydney Aboriginal man, Bungett, carve marks on a tree, thereby indicating his own initiated status, and Batman's status too, since Bungett had permitted Batman to view his mark. Only when convinced that Batman and Bungett were initiated men (albeit of another nation), and were thus lawfully authorised to view the mark, would the Woiworung leader carve his mark on the tree. By pretending to be initiated, and by assimilating the dendroglyph into the institution of the legal document, Batman was simultaneously breaking Woiworung law and endeavoring to subject the Woiworung to English law, which he was at that moment breaking himself.

Batman's trickery is completely erased from the third account of the treaty signing, his report to Governor Arthur, dated 25 June 1835, two and a half weeks after the signing took place. Composed by Batman's lawyer, Joseph Tice Gellibrand, using Batman's journal as the source, the report implies that all eight 'Dutigallar' leaders actively desired to show their special tribal mark to Batman. All mention of Batman's prompting of the 'signing' of trees, and copying of the dendroglyph, is omitted. The 'giving' of the special mark is described as a piece of secret men's business signifying the Aboriginal leaders' enthusiastic acceptance or initiation of Batman into the tribe:

> The chiefs appeared most fully to comprehend my proposals, and much delighted with the prospect of having me to live amongst them… On the next day the chiefs proceeded with me to the boundaries,[37] and they marked, with their own native marks, the trees at the corners of the boundaries, and they also gave me their own private mark, which is kept sacred by them, even so much that the women are not allowed to see it.[38]

Given these conflicting accounts of the signing of the treaty, it is difficult to separate fact from fiction. Even if Batman's accounts were complete fabrications, the theoretical possibility remains that an ideograph carved on a tree could be transformed into a signature on a legal document. In the case of the Batman treaty, parchment was substituted for country as both an inscribed surface and a *location* of the mark; a pen was substituted for an axe as a tool of inscription. It was through these substitutions that the glyph passed into the jurisdiction of British law — or so Batman hoped. New South Wales Governor Richard Bourke is unlikely to have been aware of Woiworung law, but he brought British law to bear on Batman's treaty on 26 August 1835, by declaring void 'every such treaty, bargain and contract with the Aboriginal Natives…for the possession, title or claim to any Lands'.[39] In London, Lord Glenelg, British Secretary of State for Colonies, upheld Bourke's decision. Yet Bourke and Glenelg declared the treaty invalid for reasons that had nothing to do with any suspicion that Batman had forged the signatures. Nor were they concerned that the Woiworung signatures were ideographic rather than alphabetic. Non-alphabetic signatures had long been accepted as valid in British law, and were common on treaties in New Zealand and North America.[40] Batman's treaty was illegal for one reason only: under British law, the Crown, not the Aborigines, had sole authority to sell off the land.

　　　○ ○ ○

John Batman stole or invented a Woiworung ideograph to do the work of a signature on a written legal document. His action serves as a reminder that in certain contexts within European culture, writing can function simultaneously as a phonographic code for a name, an ideographic configuration of lines produced through bodily performance, and a symbolic aid to memory of a document's making. While Batman used 'non-writing' improperly, the Wiradjuri carver and Charlie Flannigan both transformed alphabetic script into a non-phonographic medium. Unschooled in the principles of European literacy, the Wiradjuri carver used alphabetic characters to signify tradability perhaps, and used Europe's ideographic scripts such as Roman and Arabic numerals. His mimicry pointed to the fact that literate European cultures had not left the ideographic stage behind at all. Similarly, Charlie Flannigan used alphabetic characters not for their sound-values and their ability to encode spoken words, but for their decorative potential as visual art. Like those of the Wiradjuri carver, his inscriptions disarticulate alphabetic writing from its phonographic functions, thereby confounding Eurocentric narratives of cultural progress in which high civilisations leave 'primitive' visual signifying systems behind.

Borderland inscriptions such as the Batman treaty, the Wiradjuri clubs and Charlie Flannigan's drawings destabilise the Western conventions of reading that normally hold the distinction between 'writing' and 'non-writing' in place. They show how scripts are not *inherently* phonographic, ideographic or pictographic, but can change from one mode to another, or function simultaneously in more than one mode. Following recent inquiries into the ways trade recontextualises and transforms the identity of objects,[41] the Batman treaty offers access to the question of how these transformative processes apply to the communication technologies and signifying systems through which the trading parties reach, or legally ratify, their agreement. The Wiradjuri clubs and Charlie Flannigan's lettering also call for a historically grounded, non-Eurocentric, materialist approach to scripts. Such an approach calls implicitly into question the essentialist assumptions underlying much of what has been written on both sides of the current debate about what counts as 'writing'.

5

Textual battlegrounds in Van Diemen's Land

In 1546, when the Council of Trent reaffirmed the Vulgate as the only authoritative version of the Bible, it was endeavouring to protect the longstanding monopoly of the Roman Church over spheres of knowledge and belief that were politically crucial. Exclusive use of the 4th century Latin Bible meant that, even as literacy levels rose and printed copies of the Bible proliferated, the laity still needed their parish priests to translate and carry God's word to their ears. Protestant churches were founded on different readings of the Bible, but in turn protected the Scriptures from semantic disintegration by establishing their own authority structures and conventions to regulate biblical interpretation. Nonetheless, the Reformation involved a fundamental split between the Roman Church, which continued to mediate between the Latin Bible and the non–Latin speaking laity, and the Protestant churches which encouraged people to read the Bible themselves in their own languages.

In colonial contexts, however, this aspect of the Reformation was undone. Latin and vernacular European Bibles were equally unintelligible to the Indigenous peoples whose homelands were annexed into Europe's modern empires. In Africa, the Americas, Asia, Oceania and Australia, Catholic and Protestant missionaries alike had no *initial* option but to mediate between the Bible and the peoples they sought to Christianise. In each new colonial mission field, the Word of God was at first — and often for many decades — carried to the ears of colonised peoples by European mediators, regardless of whether these mediators were Catholic or Protestant. Only exceptional men such as Lancelot Threlkeld remembered that their own homelands in Europe had once been part of the Roman Empire, and that their own Vulgate or vernacular Bibles had been translated from Greek, Hebrew, and

Aramaic manuscripts. Although mass production and distribution of biblical texts facilitated the global dissemination of Christian doctrines, colonised populations were obviously prevented from reading the Bible for themselves until it was translated into their own languages and scripts, or until they acquired literacy in the language of the Bibles available to them. Like the pre-Reformation laity, colonised populations engaged with the Bible only as translated and selectively transmitted to them by church and government authorities who believed in their God-given right to exercise control. The Holy Word arrived in their country embodied in European languages and wrapped around with imperial and evangelical aspirations.

The politics of biblical interpretation in colonial contexts can be analysed within the theoretical framework jointly developed by Mikhail Bakhtin and VN Volosinov.[1] Working at the time of Stalin's 'Russianisation' of the Soviet Union, Bakhtin and Volosinov came to believe that all texts — and entire national languages — are subject to two competing sets of forces. On one side are centripetal influences exercised by dominant social groups who try to centralise hermeneutic authority, suppressing ambiguity and ambivalence by imposing reading practices that hold in place their preferred meaning. On the other side are dissenters who highlight language's ambiguity, and celebrate interpretative diversity.

Both sets of reading practices — the monologic and the dialogic — were clearly in evidence not only during the Reformation, but also in colonial contexts. The more widely the Bible was disseminated across cultural borders, and the greater people's ability to read it for themselves, the stronger was the pressure towards semantic fragmentation of the Bible through translation, dialogue and cultural recontextualisation. Stronger too, however, was the reactionary desire to hold that fragmentation in check.

According to Bakhtin and Volosinov, texts stay 'alive' in human history only as long as they remain subject to semantic reappraisal through dialogue and debate. If a single authority monopolises the power to determine and enforce scriptural meaning, the Bible becomes single-tongued and monologic. When a text is permitted only to 'say' the same thing to everyone under all circumstances, it becomes semantically ossified, stale, irrelevant and oppressive. To remain urgently meaningful, texts must remain multi-tongued, multi-voiced and semantically contested. While the Bible is often referred to as *the* (singular) living Word of God, European and colonial history both suggest that the Word degenerates into dogma unless it is continually 're-incarnated', as Walter J Ong puts it — continually re-voiced, re-heard, re-written, re-read, and re-enlivened in human thought and debate.[2] Semantically speaking, the Word 'lives' only by remaining in a state of perpetual becoming. Its meaning continually unfolds through translation, debate and recontextualisation in different cultural and historical settings. Yet this democratisation of the meaning-making process, when taken to the extreme, can lead to semantic chaos, cacophony and social conflict. In colonial contexts, uncontrolled reading of the Bible by local peoples would have meant that colonial government and church officials lost their monopoly over its immense power and moral authority.

Obviously, the struggle between centripetal and centrifugal forces unfolds differently in each region and each historical era. In some post-colonial contexts, language and literacy barriers have been overcome, and non-Western readers have developed their own locally relevant interpretations of the Bible. The Scriptures are being decolonised, and a 'second Reformation', global in scope, is unfolding as the Bible is reread in different locations and political contexts. Here, however, I look at a time, prior to this second Reformation, when the Indigenous peoples of Van Diemen's Land first engaged with the Bible, both as material object and as verbal text, largely, but not exclusively, under the watchful eyes of colonial officials who saw the Bible as a tool for cultural assimilation, and refracted their will to power through the voices of a tiny literate Aboriginal elite.

The text as object — red but unread

Aboriginal societies have lived in Tasmania for over 20 000 years, since before sea levels rose and cut off the island from mainland Australia.[3] Dutch, French and English explorers visited the island from 1682 onwards, and British and American sealers worked the Bass Strait islands from the late 18th century. The British first colonised Van Diemen's Land in 1803. The Indigenous peoples of Van Diemen's Land experienced this influx of convicts and settlers as an invasion:

> They consider every injury they can inflict upon white men as an act of duty and patriotic, and however they may dread the punishment which our laws inflict upon them, they consider the sufferers under these punishments as martyrs of their country...having ideas of their natural rights which would astonish most of our European statesmen.[4]

By the 1820s, Aboriginal resistance to the expansion of pastoral settlement was so effective that Governor Arthur imposed a state of martial law in 1828.

This move amounted to a declaration of war. Arthur established six roving parties to hunt Aboriginal people out of the so-called settled districts. The military had powers to arrest Aboriginal people without warrant or shoot them on sight if they returned. In early 1830, a bounty was placed on captured Aboriginal males and children, making 'black-catching' a lucrative commercial enterprise. Later the same year, 2000 men from the military, the police and pastoral communities joined together to form the 'black line', a heavily armed human chain that moved across south-eastern and central Tasmania in an attempt to make the land safe for colonists.[5]

Meanwhile, outside the 'settled' districts of the Tasmanian mainland and on Bruny Island in the south-east, a policy of conciliation was instigated. In early 1829, George Augustus Robinson, son of an East End London brickmaker, was appointed to minister to the remaining members of what he called the South-East tribe on Bruny Island. Over the next several years, Robinson also led a series of expeditions into the rugged Van Diemen's Land bush. With the help of a small party of Indigenous guides and mediators, his 'friendly mission' persuaded most of the Aboriginal bands remaining in the west, the north and the north-east to come with him to a place of refuge where they would be looked after and protected from the incursions of the white man.

On 22 August 1831, George Augustus Robinson recorded an extraordinary moment in the history of his 'friendly mission'. Trekking through the bush in north-eastern Van Diemen's Land, his party came upon a wooden dwelling, 'the largest of the kind that I have yet met with in the whole of my travels'.[6] This structure and its surroundings 'presented a remarkable scene'. More surprisingly, however, Robinson discovered in this wild, remote setting an artefact he saw as part of his own culture:

> All the ground in front of this habitation was thickly strewed with the feathers of the emu, and bones of this stately bird as also other animals such as the kangaroo covered the ground, which the natives had broken to pieces to obtain the marrow to anoint their head and body… On searching about, found the claw of an emu and some red ochre, but what appeared to me the most extraordinary was finding some pieces of the leaves of the Common Prayer Book, covered with red ochre. On examining these I found them to contain parts of psalms 30, 31, 32, 33 and 96, and on reading the first five verses of the 31st psalm, I found it so peculiarly adapted to me that I could not help exclaiming, 'Marvellous are thy ways, O Lord, and thy paths

are past finding out'; and on reading the 33rd psalm at the 13th and 14th verses, 'The Lord looked down from heaven and beheld all the children of men' &c, I thought them peculiarly applicable to this forlorn and hapless race of human beings... Ere I left this celebrated spot I collected some feathers of the emu and the claws, which together with the fragments of leaves of the Common Prayer Book I brought away with me as mementoes of the circumstance.[7]

Robinson's find repeats a motif that appears again and again in the literature of empire, a scene that Homi Bhabha has called 'the sudden, fortuitous discovery of the English book' in the world's 'dark, unruly places'.[8] Bhabha suggests that this moment of discovery exposes the potential ambivalence of the book, its dual aspect of being original, familiar and authoritative but also aberrant, foreign and vulnerable.

Unlike the Indian villagers who, in Bhabha's example, were alphabetically literate and had access to Bibles in their own language, the Aboriginal people of Van Diemen's Land had no way of deciphering the psalms as a verbal text. Nonetheless, they appropriated and transformed the text as a material object, and used it in accordance with their conceptions of what this foreign thing was, and what it might mean. Robinson discovered a book that was no longer a book but a scattering of 'leaves', coloured red — but unread. To Robinson, the *Book of common prayer* epitomised English civilisation, Christianity and colonial authority. Customarily the prayer book provided a script for Christian ritual. Rituals and ceremonies are (in principle if not always in practice) the antithesis of carnivals.[9] According to Bakhtin, carnivals temporarily do away with the distance ordinarily separating different voices and disparate varieties of discourse. All voices and discourses can potentially contextualise one another, and can thus mutually dialogise or determine each other's meaning and authority.[10] In English Protestant culture, the *Book of Common Prayer* would ordinarily have cocooned the psalmic text (and certain other parts of the Scriptures) within liturgical settings that secured their meaning and function by keeping potentially disruptive contextual influences at bay. In the Van Diemen's Land bush, however, the book had been displaced, dismembered, and torn away from its usual anchor points in English culture. The psalmic text was exposed to the transformative influences of one of the world's 'dark, unruly places'.

Robinson believed that the pages had been taken during a recent Aboriginal attack on a white settlement: 'No doubt exists in my mind,' he wrote, 'but these are the people who have committed the recent outrages in the vicinity of Launceston and on the east bank of the Tamar, these leaves having been taken in their predatory attack upon the white inhabitants, together with other plunder.'[11] Red ochre played an important part in Aboriginal ritual life, so it is probable that the pages from the prayer book — part of the script for Christian worship — were used for different ritual purposes by the people of north-east Van Diemen's Land. Although these people would not have been able to decipher the words of the text, they covered the pages with red ochre, perhaps ritually appropriating the power of what they correctly saw as one of the white man's sacred instruments.

Upon finding the stolen psalms, Robinson immediately repatriated the leaves into the category of written text, subjecting them again to the rules of both iconic and phonographic recognition upon which their usage, authority and meaning conventionally depended in his culture. On the one hand, he found the ochre-covered pages 'most extraordinary' and quite alien; on the other, the words of the psalms remained intimately familiar to him. Indeed, he read them as 'peculiarly adapted to me'. The first five verses of Psalm 31 ask God for protection from moral and physical danger ('come quickly to my rescue…save me…free me from the trap that is set for me'); the 13th and 14th verses of Psalm 33 describe God's gaze encompassing all mankind, including those whom Robinson called 'this forlorn and hapless race of human beings'.[12] Robinson therefore interpreted the found text as a promise of protection, and a vindication of his dangerous conciliatory quest. His discovery of the psalms of David in the Van Diemen's Land wilderness assured him of God's omniscience and omnipresence. Although — or perhaps because — the text-as-object had been expropriated, Robinson effectively undid its otherness and restored its conventional message by reactivating the phonographic function of the script, and reassigning familiar meanings to the words of the psalms.

The following day, Robinson reasserted his power to act as an authoritative transmitter of the psalms to the Aboriginal people who served him as guides and mediators. In his journal he wrote:

> I could observe that I informed the natives attached to the service that the paper I had found in the wild natives' hut was pieces of the word of God, and some of them who spoke English requested me to read it to them and which I accordingly did, when they paid strict attention. On this subject I had often spoken to them.[13]

Robinson validated his own ministry to the Aboriginal people of Van Diemen's Land by pointing to those from the mission as living proof that

that 'natives' were capable of engaging 'properly' with 'pieces of the word of God', provided of course that such words were conducted into their hearing in appropriate ways.

Robinson's repatriation of the psalms is evidence of his desire to make the Bible speak with a single voice in a single language. Throughout the colonial period, Aboriginal people in Van Diemen's Land, and in all other Australian colonies except South Australia, were rarely given access to the Bible in their own languages. Like priests of the Roman Church prior to the Reformation in Europe, colonial officials in Van Diemen's Land, sometimes aided by Indigenous agents, carried the Bible — or a particular reading of it — to the ears of the Pallawah people. Every effort was made to monologise the Bible, or render it as a single-voiced text, and to preserve the colonists' monopoly over the power of biblical knowledge. Every effort was made to prevent Aboriginal peoples from exploring what the Bible might say in the light of their own knowledge, culture and social values. These efforts, however, did not prevent non-literate Aboriginal people from appropriating and transforming the Bible as a ritual object, nor from challenging biblically-based colonial viewpoints.

Before Aboriginal people were schooled in alphabetic writing, their perspectives challenged orthodox readings of the Bible. Four weeks after discovering the ochre-covered pages in the bush, Robinson was resting at George Town in north-eastern Van Diemen's Land. While there, he received a letter from John Batman, passing on a story told by a Captain Kneale, who had taken a six-year-old Aboriginal boy christened George Van Diemen to England a decade before, in 1821. Robinson retold Captain Kneale's story in his journal:

> One night the boy was in conversation with him [Captain Kneale] and asked him who made the moon. He replied, God; God made everything. Then, looking steadily up at the Heavens for a few moments as if in deep reflection, he [the boy] said, do you see that star near the moon? He answered, yes. He replied, he supposed God made that star also? He replied, yes. Ah, said he, the moon's after that star and he will catch him too, and that he supposed the star was some poor black fellow and the moon would soon catch him.[14]

When Captain Kneale told George Van Diemen that God made the moon, and 'God made everything,' he was interpreting the beautiful night sky in terms of the first chapter of Genesis. In the wild beauty of Van Diemen's Land, Kneale perhaps glimpsed some remnant of an Edenic, unfallen world, a world confirming that God's creation was indeed 'good' as is stated in Genesis 1:18. The boy, by contrast, read the night sky in the context of his own people's recent historical experience. To him, moon and star were respectively predator and prey; they presented a picture of the way he and his people were being hunted down and killed or captured by white men. George Van Diemen read the sky as an allegorical tableau of the bloody war that was under way in Van Diemen's Land. He could not read the Bible for himself at the time, and may not have known about the story of the fall. Yet by reading the night sky differently, he disturbed Captain Kneale's reading of Genesis, implicitly shifting the emphasis away from the goodness of God's creation, and raising the possibility that colonialism as practised in Van Diemen's Land was a symptom of humanity's fallen state.

Genesis on Flinders Island

To house those Aboriginal people who accepted Robinson's offer of asylum, the colonial government in February 1833 set up the Wybalenna settlement on Flinders Island off the north-east coast of Van Diemen's Land, after several false starts on various unsuitable sites.[15] At the Flinders Island settlement, the Bible was foisted upon the people as an instrument of assimilation, part of a whole new way of life, complete with rituals designed to prevent aberrant interpretations of the holy book. The first translation of any portion of the Bible into an Indigenous Tasmanian language is ascribed to Thomas Wilkinson, who was appointed catechist at Wybalenna in June 1833. By mid-September of the same year, Wilkinson reported to Governor Arthur that he had translated 'the principal parts of the first four chapters of Genesis' into the language of the Ben Lomond people.[16]

Without acknowledging any assistance he may have received, nor considering the language differences that divided the Wybalenna Aborigines, Catechist Wilkinson proudly informed Governor Arthur that the people 'seemed to understand his [Wilkinson's] translation…and showed an interest in what they heard.'[17] Governor Arthur, however, judged the Ben Lomond translation 'imprudent'.[18] While insisting that 'scriptural religion should be the grand object of attention in the education of the aborigines,'[19] Governor Arthur thought it counterproductive to translate the Bible into the language of an 'uncivilised' society. Plomley has observed that the Governor 'could not understand that the only way to enter the hearts and minds of the Aborigines was through their own language'.[20] Governor Arthur believed that 'the Bible is the most effectual mode of introducing civilization,'[21] but he refused to countenance biblical translations into Aboriginal languages. For the Governor, Christianisation involved converting colonised peoples into 'proper' interpreters of the Bible, not converting the Bible into a foreign text whose familiar meanings could be lost through 'improper' assimilation into alien cultures. To allow Catechist Wilkinson to facilitate such an alienation on Flinders Island was to throw away the colonising society's monopoly over the power of biblical knowledge.

Catechist Wilkinson was popular with the Aboriginal people but was considered an irascible bigot by his fellow officers. After becoming embroiled in conflict with Wybalenna Superintendent Lieutenant William Darling and others, he was suspended from office in October 1833, and left the island permanently in April 1834.[22] No one else on Flinders Island attempted a *written* translation of any portion of the Bible into any of the Indigenous Van Diemen's Land languages. George Augustus Robinson, who took over as superintendent of Wybalenna in October 1835, had once preached a sermon in the Bruny Island language in 1829.[23] He did not repeat this experiment on Flinders Island, however, and strongly disapproved of attempts by the new catechist, Robert Clark, to preach in a pidgin English peppered with Indigenous words.[24] Until 1838, when some Aboriginal men spoke in their own languages on their (mediated) understandings of the Scriptures, the Aboriginal people on Flinders Island engaged with the Bible only as interpreted by white officials and two young Aboriginal teaching assistants, Walter George Arthur and Thomas Brune, both of whom had been educated at the Hobart Orphan School.[25]

The Bible became an instrument whereby the Aboriginal people on Flinders Island were inculcated into the English language and into a grotesquely degraded version of an English way of life. Walter George Arthur and Thomas Brune, together with Robinson and his officers, mediated the Bible in ways that implemented Governor Arthur's assimilationist agenda. The Governor was especially concerned, for instance, that the Aboriginal people should observe the Sabbath. In September 1833, having admonished Catechist Wilkinson for his 'imprudent' act of translation, Governor Arthur described the catechist's proper duties thus:

> Keep a school — have divine service twice on Sunday and…have the effect of leading the Aborigines to see at least at an early period one striking particular of the Christian Dispensation — I mean the strict observance of the Sabbath — during which day they may

readily be instructed that hunting and many other worldly pursuits give place to worship of an Almighty Creator.[26]

Governor Arthur's intentions were carried into effect by Superintendent George Augustus Robinson and those who served under him, especially Robert Clark. Having engaged with the Word of God primarily as mediated by their religious instructors and schoolteachers, the young Aboriginal men in turn passed on the Bible's messages to the rest of the Aboriginal people on the island. In October 1835, for example, Governor Arthur's preoccupation with the Sabbath was rearticulated in a short biblically based lesson written by his namesake, Walter George Arthur:[27]

Lesson the first

> In six days the Lord made the Heavens and the Earth, the sea and all that there in is. And on the seventh day God ended his work, and he rested on that day. For this Reason we keep the Sabbath holy, because the Lord rested on that day. Six Days are for working, in which our Labouring is to be done; but the seventh day is a day of Rest.[28]

This lesson paraphrases Genesis 2:2–3, which Walter had in all likelihood translated with Catechist Wilkinson two years previously. In the process of reinforcing the doctrine that God created the world, the passage functions as an instrument of cultural assimilation by teaching that the Sabbath should be observed as a day of rest. Walter was capable both of reading the Bible in English for himself, and of copying out the verses verbatim from the Book. This 'Lesson', however, is a paraphrase, not a verbatim copy of the Bible. Since its language differs from that of Walter's own biblical paraphrases and written compositions, it is probable that the paraphrase was not composed by Walter but copied by him. Copying was the prevailing mode of developing the Aboriginal students' handwriting skills on Flinders Island. The model text was usually written out by the catechist. Walter's 'Lesson' is evidently a copy of a paraphrase generated by Robert Clark, whose mediation of Genesis prescribes the manner in which the Aboriginal residents should conduct themselves at the Wybalenna settlement — precisely as Governor Arthur would have wished. The Governor's reading of the Bible was transmitted from the top down, throughout the colonial hierarchy. Governor Arthur's views shaped the way the catechist mediated the Bible to Walter, who in turn passed on the prescribed biblical messages to his countrymen.

Two years later, in the Wybalenna newspaper the *Flinders Island Chronicle*, Walter again admonished the people to observe the Sabbath. This time he composed the text himself, yet invoked the authority not of the Bible but of his teacher, Catechist Clark. Governor Arthur had by this time been replaced by Governor John Franklin, but the biblically authorised assimilationist agenda continued. Taking it upon himself to extend the catechist's biblically grounded pronouncement about the Sabbath, Walter admonished the people to wash with soap and stop painting-up with ochre (an ironic reproach given that Catechist Clark's own standards of personal hygiene were notoriously lax[29]):

> And now my Dear friends I want to tell you and I saw some women carrying woods upon Sunday so I walk to ask Mr Clark if it is right to carry wood on Sunday no I don't think it is right to carry woods on God's day so that I am sure it is not right for any one to do such things in his day You should not play or work on that day you should not do anything on God day... And also another thing you should not throw about the soap They have too much Mr Clark because when I am about the place I always see plenty of soap lying about I only want to put it down that you may all know that the soap is a fine thing to wash yourselves with and yet they don't care for it no they would sooner put on that there clay stuff what they have been always used and they like it better then they would have soap to wash they faces...[30]

Despite the biblical injunctions mediated through Robert Clark and Walter George Arthur, the non-assimilated Wybalenna residents had their own contextually determined views of the Sabbath. Everything relating to the Sabbath they termed 'Sunday'. Good cloth was referred to as 'Sunday'; Bibles and prayer books were 'Sunday books'.[31] Sunday or not, they were sent out to hunt for their food when the settlement's rations ran out, or when hostilities periodically erupted between the three main tribal groups.[32] For the Aboriginal people, Sunday also meant the tedium of long, unintelligible church services. Seeing his congregation's boredom and drowsiness, Robinson considered adapting the liturgy, believing it was 'absurd to persist in reading a set form of worship'.[33] Whether he could set aside the *Book of Common Prayer* was another question, however. He wanted to instigate 'true worship' by making liturgical language more intelligible, yet he could not condone Robert Clark's attempts to mediate Genesis in pidgin as 'God-a-mighty made us all, black and white fellows.'[34]

Literacy, power and traditional Aboriginal authority structures

The Flinders Island Aboriginal community was by no means homogenous. A small group of adults who had lived on the Bruny Island Mission and guided Robinson on his treks through the bush lived in a separate area from the Western, Big River and Ben Lomond peoples, between whom conflicts periodically arose. Fourteen women who had lived with sealers defied both Robinson and the Aboriginal men. Fourteen children lived apart from the adults in dormitories attached to the houses of the catechist and the storekeeper. These children were the main focus of Robinson's efforts to assimilate and Christianise. Ranging in age from six to fifteen in 1835, they lived a regimented life, rising at half past six to wash and say prayers before assembling at seven o'clock to read the Bible with the catechist and his family. They breakfasted at half past seven, attended school until noon, and after an hour's lunch break returned to school until half past three. Between six and eight, they helped the adults at the evening school, then returned to the catechist's house for family worship before retiring to bed at nine o'clock.[35]

Of these children, Walter George Arthur was the eldest, and Thomas Brune was between one and three years younger. These two teenage boys wrote virtually all the Aboriginal manuscripts now lodged in the Robinson papers at the Mitchell Library. Their writings consist of thirty-one issues of the *Flinders Island Chronicle* produced between September 1837 and January 1838, thirty-one sermons written between September 1837 and July 1838, and an assortment of miscellaneous lessons and fragments.[36] In these documents, many of which they read aloud to the assembled congregation, Walter and Brune carried selected parts of the Bible (in English) to the ears of the Aboriginal community at Wybalenna. George Augustus Robinson orchestrated these mediations. Whether trekking through the bush making contact with 'wild natives' or imparting religious instruction to the inmates of the Wybalenna settlement, Robinson's recurrent modus operandi was to create and/or exploit divisions within Aboriginal society, and use a small group of known and trusted individuals to mediate between himself and the larger, less familiar, less predictable group. Walter George Arthur and Thomas Brune played an important mediatory role between Robinson and the wider Flinders Island Aboriginal community. Walter's and Brune's sermons and reports in the *Flinders Island Chronicle* also carried biblical doctrines to the ears of the larger Aboriginal community at Wybalenna.

While these two young men were conduits for the power of the colonial administration, they did not derive their authority from precisely the same source, and they each had their own personal political agenda. Walter George Arthur was the son of Ben Lomond elder Drule.er.par, whom Robinson renamed 'King George'.[37] On Flinders Island, all the tribal groups were in alien country. In contrast to Coranderrk Reserve established in Victoria in 1863, for example, where Woiworung leader William Barak was senior traditional owner of the country on which the reserve was situated, no one was on their home territory on Flinders Island. None of the groups residing on the island was invested with the power that flowed from ancient spiritual ties to the Wybalenna site. Killings and displacements from homelands had disrupted the kinship networks and broken the physical bonds to specific sections of country that traditionally structured intra- and intertribal social relations. Nonetheless, memory-ties, spiritual ties, and knowledge-ties would naturally have lived on, and there is evidence to suggest that traditional ceremonial practices and power structures remained in place to some degree on Flinders Island.[38] Each of the main tribal groups retained an order of seniority which accorded authority to their elders. Robinson called these elders 'kings' and was partially successful in securing their cooperation with his plans. Thus, in traditional Aboriginal cultural terms, Walter was the son of a man of high degree, and had a certain social status, even though he had been taken from his country and family at a young age and had no recollection of his Aboriginal name.

Thomas Brune was in a rather different position. Born between 1820 and 1823 into the Nuenonne band on Bruny Island, he was taken to the Orphan School in Hobart.[39] Although he refers to being welcomed by 'brethren and friends' upon arrival at Wybalenna, Brune appears to have had no close family on Flinders Island, and his social status is difficult to determine.[40] Within the kinship structures through which Aboriginal social identities and relationships are traditionally defined, he appears to have had no authoritative position from which to speak. However, political relationships at Wybalenna were relatively unstable, and were complicated by Robinson's introduction of new forms of sacred and secular knowledge, new technologies of communication, and a pedagogical system where the young instructed the old, in direct contravention of customary practice in Aboriginal societies. In this context, a youth like Thomas Brune could create a niche for himself by using his language and literacy skills to mediate the power both of the Bible and of the secular colonial authorities. Although

Brune was slightly younger than Walter, and lacked the latter's kinship connections, both boys accrued power, social status and authority through their closeness to the Flinders Island Commandant, their knowledge of the English language, their ability to read and write, and their familiarity with the religious doctrines encoded in the white man's sacred book.

Walter and Brune both signed their writings with their names followed by the words 'Aboriginal Youth Editor and Writer'. Brune worked as a copy clerk for Robinson, and added 'Clerk of the Commandant Office' to this title.[41] Walter was referred to in the school reports as 'Prince Walter', and later signed himself as 'Chief of the Ben Lomond tribe'.[42] There are signs that the two young men were rivals at times. In the *Flinders Island Chronicle* of 2 October 1837, for example, Walter noted: 'When I am in school I always see Mis Thomas Brune. Laughing and playing away in the middle of school.'[43] Being 'put in the paper' like this was a mode of shaming, a dreaded form of punishment that Brune and Walter, young as they were, were deputised to mete out. When, for example, they threatened to put the sealers' women 'in the paper' for failing to clean their houses, Robinson recorded that the women 'begged they would not be put in the paper, [and] said they might KARNY speak but not write. They seemed to have a great abhorrence of being put in the paper.'[44]

The earliest document bearing Thomas Brune's signature is a biblically based writing exercise dated 24 July 1836:

> Protection
> Protection Protec [sic]
> 23rd Psalm
>
> The Lord is my shepherd: therefore can I lack nothing. He shall feed me in a green pasture: and lead me forth beside the water of comfort. He shall convert my soul: and bring me forth in the paths of righteousness for his Name's sake.[45]

In Thomas Brune's transcription of this section of Psalm 23, the archaic language of the King James Authorised Version has been simplified. In addition, in verse 3, 'He *restoreth* my soul' has been changed to 'He shall *convert* my soul,' perhaps in an effort to adapt the biblical text to the mission context. These changes suggest that Brune was not transcribing directly from the Bible but rather, in accordance with common teaching methods of the time, reproducing a copytext probably written by the catechist Robert Clark. Like Walter's, Brune's engagement with the Bible appears at this time to have been mediated rather than direct. Instead of having access to the entire text, and copying out whichever parts he found most meaningful, Brune reproduced a passage chosen and edited by his teacher, and may not have been aware of possible differences between the biblical text and Clark's copytext. In 1835–36, the catechist's mediations determined which parts of the Bible were accessible, opening up some parts but closing off others. The Bible was thus effectively rendered single-voiced and unambiguous. Until the people were able to read the entire text for themselves in an intelligible language, they had no way of knowing what they were missing, nor of deciding whether or how it might be meaningful or empowering.

For Thomas Brune, religious instruction and political instruction were delivered simultaneously by Psalm 23. At the top of the page, above the transcribed psalmic verse, the word 'protection' was written neatly in a copperplate hand, to be copied by Thomas Brune. Psalm 23 characterises God as a protector. While disease and high mortality rates made life for the Aboriginal people of Wybalenna a fearful 'walk through the valley of the shadow of death' (as in verse 4, before which Brune's transcription terminates), the official line was that the settlement was a safe, protected refuge where the Aboriginal people's needs were generously met by the grace of God and Commandant Robinson. The Commandant certainly saw himself as fulfilling the role of a protector, and was eventually to leave Wybalenna to take up the lucrative position of Chief Protector of Aborigines in the Port Phillip District. Discursively, Robinson inserted himself into the same position as God. In a sermon written in July 1838, Walter urged his Aboriginal audience to 'obey the king and all that are put in authority under him to submit myself [corrected to 'yourself'] to all my governors teachers spiritual partners and master and should order myself truly and reverently to all betters.'[46] The Bible was also used to explain why men such as Robinson and Clark had come from distant lands to Christianise the Aborigines. Thomas Brune noted in three of his sermons that 'Jesus Christ said a long time ago to his Disciples go ye and teach all nation baptising them in the Name of the Father and of the Son and of the Holy Ghost teaching them to observe all things whatsoever I have Commanded you and Lo I am with you always & even unto the end of the world.'[47]

Formulaic mediations

Walter's and Brune's sermons were a mixture of reportage, prayer and moral exhortation. It is likely that they were imitating the preaching style of

Robert Clark, whom Robinson described, with some irritation, as offering up 'a mixed prayer and exhortation'.[48] Walter and Brune quoted from and wrote about the Bible in their sermons. Walter's sermon of 6 October 1837 situates the Wybalenna people at the centre of a moral and cultural tug-of-war between the Bible and the bush, the latter being the place where they hunted and continued their traditional ceremonies out of sight of the Commandant:

> The people of Flinders Island…are learning to read now as fast as they can but they all run away into the bush and get sick and they say they will never come home again no they say there is too much work for them to do…
>
> [I]f you lose what God hast told you in the Bible God wont like you Nay God would like you no more he will cast you out of his presence…
>
> Now my dear friends learn…how to read this book and understanding it because there is no other [way] to get to God but by learning out of this book because there is no other book better than this Bible.
>
> Because the bible came from God and if it came from God it must be a Good book and those who learn of that book and understand it is a far better thing than into the bush and hunt for those things which is not of much Good.[49]

Formulaic repetition is a common feature of Christian liturgy in general, and of the sermon in particular as a written genre designed for oral delivery. Walter's and Brune's sermons are unusually repetitive, however. Although each sermon contains some new material, certain messages are reiterated again and again, using set verbal formulae. Formulaic statements are shuffled around from sermon to sermon, like pieces of a mosaic that have been assembled in a variety of ways to form different configurations of the same basic picture. Some of the most frequent are invocations of the authority of the Bible. Over a ten-month period, for example, Walter and Brune told the Aboriginal community eight times, using an identical form of words, that 'Jesus…came into our world *to die for our sins according to the scripture*.'[50] It is important to acknowledge that what comes across as formulaic repetition in a set of archival documents that can be read at a single sitting may not have been perceived that way in their original context, where each sermon was separated from the next by an interval of days or weeks. The exactness of these repetitions, however, is strikingly precisely because an identical form of words echoes again and again across large intervals of time.

Walter J Ong has noted that repetitive use of formulaic expressions is a distinctive characteristic of orally grounded discourse: where knowledge cannot be stored in written documents, it must be preserved through constant oral re-enunciation in memorable, formulaic verbal units. Parts of the Bible were mediated to Walter and Brune, whose writings were designed for oral delivery to, and memorisation by, an audience who could not read alphabetic script.

A more likely explanation for Walter's and Brune's repetitions, however, lies in the catechetical question-and-answer mode of instruction whereby Aboriginal people learned Christian doctrines. Throughout the time Walter and Brune were writing their sermons, they were engaged both as teachers and learners in a repetitive interrogational teaching process that gauged 'progress' on the basis of how accurately pupils could repeat prescribed forms of words in answer to set questions. Scriptural education at Wybalenna centred on repetitive, ritualised, ostensibly dialogic exchanges that in effect imposed a monologic reading of the Bible.

In Indigenous Australian societies, asking questions is considered offensive, especially if a younger person questions an older person. Traditionally, it is up to older members of the community to decide when the young are ready to be given new information. To ask a question is therefore a breech of social propriety. What must the residents of Wybalenna have made of the teaching system that Robinson introduced, where the literate young systematically questioned young and old?

The double positioning of speakers and audience

By early 1838, Thomas Brune was reading the Bible for himself, and reporting some of his findings in his sermons:

> And now my friends there is a passage in John's Gospel the third Chapter 'for can a man be born again when he is old can he enter the second time into is mother's womb and be born'
>
> Jesus said except a man be born of water and of the spirit he cannot enter into the kingdom of God...
>
> And now my friends I was reading in my house and I saw a verse in the chapter
>
> And now my friends if we are good in Christ well he would give us his word

> And now my brethren who is it that gave us the word Jesus Christ gives us his word and none [other] Do you know that Jesus Christ pardon all your sins The people of Van Diemen's land they are learning about God and his son Jesus Christ
>
> Do you think my friends that God is very good yes my friends and don't you think that Jesus is very good Yes and my friends don't you know that there is three persons in the Godhead perhaps you might say who are they why I should say the Father Son and Holy Ghost there are all one the Father his equal to the Son and the Son is equal to the Holy Ghost and these three all agree in one
>
> And my friends there is in the scriptures it says 'Thus saith the Lord of hosts consider your ways' do we consider our ways No my friends don't consider our ways No my friends we do not…and do let us pray to God for he will pardon our sins and if we do not well we have that place which burns for ever and ever
>
> And now my friends let us love the Lord thy God with all thy heart with all thy soul and with all thy strength love thy Neighbour as thy self
>
> Thomas Brune Aboriginal Youth
> Editor and Writer[51]

This sermon illustrates several features typical of both Brune's and Walter's writings. First, Brune's authority derives in part from the fact that he has read the Bible for himself. As well as delivering God's word to the Aboriginal congregation, Brune's direct biblical quotation functions to authorise him as a speaker. Quotations verify his claim that 'It tells me in the Bible.'[52] The question is: did the Bible tell Brune anything different from the readings imposed by the colonial authorities? And if aberrant readings did, on occasion, take shape in Brune's mind, would he have been punished for transmitting them to his countrymen?

A second notable feature of Brune's sermon (and Walter's sermons too) is that he speaks *for*, as well as *to*, the congregation. He asks rhetorical questions, a monologic form of pseudo-exchange in which the speaker answers the questions for his audience. The rhetorical questions in Brune's sermons pretend to activate a dialogue, but the dialogic form serves only to mask the monologic way in which the Scriptures are read and interpreted in the Flinders Island context. In this respect, Brune's rhetorical questions are entirely congruent with the catechetical method of teaching that situates teacher and pupil in a pseudo-dialogue that does not allow the pupil a separate, autonomous voice.

A third conspicuous feature of both Brune's and Walter's writings is the oscillation between first-, second- and third-person plural pronouns: the Aboriginal audience is referred to as 'we', 'you', and 'they'. Use of third-person pronouns was particularly prevalent in the *Chronicle*, although the practice also occurred in the sermons. Why did Brune and Walter need to tell the people of Flinders Island what they themselves had been doing? Given that the sermons and *Chronicle* issues were read out loud by their authors to the people assembled at the evening school, why did Brune and Walter adopt the apparently absurd practice of referring to their audience as 'they' rather than 'you', even to the extent of referring to themselves in the third person?[53]

These pronoun shifts may be accounted for in two non–mutually exclusive ways. First, they show that Brune and Walter sensed the uncertainty and ambiguity of their own social positioning. In his sermon of 7 February 1838 (quoted above), Brune begins in the first person ('And now my friends if *we* are good in Christ well he would give *us* his word'), but shifts between the second and third person in 'Do *you* know that Jesus Christ pardon all *your* sins. The people of Van Diemen's land *they* are learning about God and his son Jesus Christ.' In oscillations such as these, Brune and Walter shift between different speaking positions, crossing verbally back and forth between being at one with all Indigenous people of Van Diemen's Land, being part of some groups but not others, and being on the side of Robinson and his officers. Brune and Walter seem uncertain as to where they stand.

A second explanation for Walter's and Brune's pronoun shifts is that they are conscious of writing for more than one audience. Brune and Walter were often required to make fair copies of the texts they composed. Some of the neatest copies have the words 'Copy to Report' written in the margins in Commandant Robinson's handwriting. Although ostensibly written for an Aboriginal audience, Brune's and Walter's writings were produced under orders from Robinson, and were appropriated by him for enclosure in his official reports. One of Brune's sermons ends with a glimpse at its own circumstances of production: 'I cannot write no more on this paper Commandant hast directed me to do it and I will do it and obey him what he says to me.'[54] In terms of their content, form, and language, Brune's and Walter's writings served as proof of the success of Robinson's program of civilisation and Christianisation. Ostensibly they were reports *on* Aborigines *by* Aborigines, yet in effect they were ventriloquised by Robinson, and were aimed at a distant, non-Aboriginal group of addressees: the Governor of Van Diemen's Land and his superiors in London who, as Robinson well knew, would eventually read, and hopefully be impressed by, his reports and enclosures.

Learning by imitation

Thomas Brune urged his countrymen to 'learn the words of God'.[55] The question is: what exactly did 'learning' mean in the Flinders Island context? To implement Governor Arthur's wish that scriptural religion be the 'grand object of attention' in Aboriginal education, Robinson introduced three types of school on Flinders Island: a day school for the children and women, an evening school for adults of both sexes, and a Sabbath school. Catechetical dialogues — teaching the pupils by having them give rote answers to set questions — was the main form of instruction used in the schools. Teaching occurred through ritualised verbal exchanges or pseudo-dialogues wherein the correct answers were prescribed by the questioner. Robinson was a long-time advocate of Dr Andrew Bell's teaching method, which he had briefly outlined in a 1829 letter to Governor Arthur describing his amelioration program.[56] Bell had developed his system of teaching in Madras in southern India, his aim being to produce 'good subjects, good men, good Christians'. The more advanced pupils taught the less advanced, and the main method of leaning was by 'repetition which took hold of the mind'.[57]

No mode of education produces entirely predictable outcomes, especially in cross-cultural contexts. Repetition, copying and mimicry may serve as valid learning methods, as in traditional Aboriginal societies where people have learned how to do things from generation to generation by imitating their elders. Copying may also, however, consist of empty, mechanical repetition, as several non-Aboriginal historians have noted when suggesting that the Aboriginal pupils neither internalised nor utilised nor retained what they had learned at the Flinders Island school.[58] Post-colonial theorists have highlighted the subversive potential of verbal copying that almost *but not quite* conceals its parodic intent.[59] Others have noted the difficulty of distinguishing between acts of deliberate parody committed by colonised subjects, and parodic qualities assigned retrospectively at the moment of reading by post-colonial critics.[60] Finally, one might ask whether, strictly speaking, exact copying is possible at all, since every repetition is a recontextualisation, and every copy a re-creation because it is also implicitly a translation into what might be called the language of the new moment.

While there is evidence indicating that the Wybalenna Aboriginal people maintained some of their own traditional beliefs and cultural practices on Flinders Island, it is difficult to know today — as it was difficult for Robinson in his time to know — precisely what they 'learned' in the classroom. Robinson's records were highly selective and biased; his career depended on telling his superiors whatever they wanted to hear. Likewise, the people of Wybalenna were compelled to play out rituals of subordination before the colonial authorities. To avoid trouble, they told Robinson and his officers whatever they wanted to hear.

What seems clear, however, is that during 1837–38 Robinson lost faith in the catechetical schooling method that was effectively inverting the traditional Indigenous social order. He had to exercise all his ingenuity to keep up the charade of success before his superiors. Testing the pupils in January 1837, he received some very unpleasant surprises. Some Aboriginal pupils were deviating radically from the script. When he asked the pupils who is God, one woman replied, 'Eve' and 'heaven'. Davey Bruny corrected her, saying, 'God is a spirit, is not a woman; God is a white man.'[61] The previous day he had asked 'Who made me?' and one of the pupils had answered 'the Devil'. Robinson then offered five shillings to anyone who would get up and pray.[62] The following year, after testing the pupils orally, Robinson recorded that some of the people, 'when asked whether they liked the examination… replied that they did not like it, did not like the "damnation"'. Robinson explained that 'This of course was a mispronunciation.'[63]

In the latter half of 1837 the shortcomings of schooling-by-imitation were becoming increasingly obvious. In July, Robinson demoted the literate Aboriginal boys, other than Brune and Walter, from teachers to class monitors. He also formed the adults of both sexes into a separate class where they would be 'instructed in religious information, reading being considered by me superfluous.'[64] In October 1837, Robinson reported that the surgeon, James Allen, had begun to 'depreciate and underrate the intellectual acquirements of the aborigines. He condemns the mode of tuition and does not attend the evening school.'[65] Allen soon left the island, but his replacement, Matthew Walsh, together with Robinson's son, George, also 'found fault with the subject and manner of instruction'.[66] In early December, Robinson discovered that the west coast people misunderstood the concept of heaven, believing that 'when they die they go to PONE. DIM, i.e. a country a long way off to England and that they then appear as white people.'[67]

Around the same time, Walter George Arthur was discovered to have suffered a moral lapse: he was found in bed with Mary Ann Cochrane, a young woman of mixed descent who taught at the school.[68] Robinson married the couple in March the following year, but at the celebrations after the marriage ceremony the Aboriginal people 'mispronounced' the toast to the couple's 'good health' as 'go to hell,' and drank 'to the health of all' with words that sounded to Robinson suspiciously like 'go to hell all of you.' Thinking perhaps that such miscopying might reflect badly on him, Robinson explained the difference away by noting that 'the natives find it difficult to pronounce the "s".'[69] Whether such mispronunciations were accidental, or deliberate and tactical, is difficult to tell. What is clear, however, is that Robinson saw the political danger of the latter possibility. In order to maintain an appearance of proper order and control he explained away the difference — the recalcitrant otherness of the voicing — as an inadvertent error.

In January 1838, the new Governor, Sir John Franklin, made a short visit to Flinders Island accompanied by his wife and their retinue. Now Robinson's achievements would be put to the test. Robinson orchestrated the visit very carefully so as to hide anything that was not consistent with his glowing reports of success in Christianising and educating 'the natives'. When the Governor and his party inspected the school, 'the natives were well assembled in new garments accompanied by their teachers.' After roll call and an opening prayer by Thomas Brune, teaching commenced. Immediately, Robinson sensed danger and 'speedily stopped this part and ordered singing' so that the visitors would not perceive how little educational progress had been made.[70]

Vivienne Rae-Ellis has argued that, like the classroom display, Robinson's written records and official reports were instruments of deception. In the records of the school examinations carried out in mid-February 1838, each question and correct answer was recorded for each pupil in the same neat, clerical hand within ruled gridlines. The report is a chilling record of a dialogue scripted entirely from one side. After the Aboriginal pupils had learned the correct answers by rote, the examination ostensibly verified their understanding of Scriptural doctrines by recording their replies in writing. In effect, the teachers ventriloquised the pupils' answers. Robinson used the examination records as 'an additional voucher to my reports and other conclusive evidence of the superiority of the plan pursued at this settlement to every other that has been adopted towards the Australian savages'.[71] By enlisting the services of his family and officers to serve as teachers in the school, and recording the examination results for each class under the relevant teacher's name, Robinson implicated the teachers in his deception. Any who dared to contradict his glowing reports, or declined to endorse his records, would be calling their own competence into question.

In April 1838, however, in one of his last sermons at Wybalenna, Thomas Brune spoke openly of the inferiority of schooling on Flinders Island in comparison with the education he had received at the Orphan School in Hobart. In an uncharacteristically autobiographical vein, he wrote:

> I was took when I was young and I was brought to the [Orphan] school and I was taught to read the Bible and I understood it and I was taught to cipher and I was taught to learn the geography and the grammar and the catechism all them did I learn
>
> And then my friends I was come at Flinders Island and when I came on it and then two or three days afterwards I began to lose all the instruction what I have learn
>
> I am dunce that I cannot say anything at all[72]

The catechetical method imposed a Eurocentric colonialist reading of the Bible that was, as Bakhtin might have put it, a 'dead quotation'.[73] The correct verbal formula was supposed to wipe away the pupils' independent voice and traditional worldview.

Older men's rearticulations of the Bible

Brune and Walter were not the only Aboriginal males to convey biblical teachings to their countrymen. A handful of men, who could read not at all or only at an elementary level, also mediated biblical doctrines in their own languages to their people. Between February and April 1838, Robert Clark recorded English translations of these men's addresses at the weekly meetings for prayer and mutual instruction. Ranging in age from their mid-twenties to their mid-forties, some of them may already have attained a degree of seniority in traditional Aboriginal cultural terms, but it is difficult to know whether their authority as mediators was a cause or an effect of their existing social standing. In any case, the mediated nature of their received biblical knowledge did not prevent them from assuming authoritative roles themselves. They may not have been fluent in English, nor been able to read the ornate, archaic English of the printed biblical text. Nor were they schooled to a level where they could compose written sermons and reports for the *Flinders Island Chronicle*. What they did, however, was address the Wybalenna Aboriginal people on biblical themes in the Aboriginal lingua franca of Wybalenna, as well as in the traditional languages of the Big River, Northern, Western and Bruny Island peoples. The men's usual practice was first to address their own people in their first language, then address the community as a whole in the lingua franca. In line with both Aboriginal and European traditions, women and girls did not address the assembled community. Their role was to translate the men's speeches into English. The English translations of the Aboriginal men's addresses recorded in the archival records are in fact the words spoken by the female translators.

The youngest of the male orators were two Big River men, Dow.wring.gi ('Leonidas', also named 'David') and Drue.mer.ter.pun.ner ('Alexander'), and a north coast man, Drine.ne ('Neptune').[74] Estimated to be in their mid-twenties, these three were inclined to castigate the people from positions of moral superiority. On 10 March 1838, Leonidas urged the people to 'Love the Bible, it is a good book, it is God's book. Why do not you all learn to read God's book? It tells you plenty about God, about Jesus Christ. You are too lazy to learn.'[75] One week later, Neptune told the people, 'My brothers and sisters, why do you forget God?... You do not like God. I love God... [Y]ou are too fond of doing what is bad Learn to read the Bible. It is a good book. It is God's book...'[76]

Another man, Noemy (Mar.wer.reek), was from western Van Diemen's Land. Aged in his mid-thirties, he was appointed by Robinson to the role of constable in August 1836. One of his duties was to curb what Robinson saw as sexual promiscuity, a role that may have translated in his own cultural terms into the senior men's traditional responsibility of controlling younger men's access to women. In February 1838, Noemy was examined with two others by the chaplain, Thomas Dove, who remarked on 'the accuracy and extent of their scriptural knowledge'. Dove found that Noemy was capable of easily reading words of one syllable, and answered correctly a range of questions such as Who made you? Who is God? What is the soul? Does it survive the body? What kind of place is heaven? He also correctly answered questions 'relative to the creation of man, his original state and character, the cause of his expulsion from paradise, the story of Cain and Abel, the deluge and the great objects for which Jesus Christ came into our world'.[77]

Noemy was described by Chaplain Dove as 'not merely an eloquent but an elegant speaker'.[78] Robinson also remarked on his oratorical skills. Like Brune and Walter, Noemy was familiar with biblical doctrines. Unlike them, he probably did not read the Bible for himself, nor did he compose his addresses in writing, although he sometimes spoke with a small book in his hand, 'a primer, on which his eyes occasionally dwelt as a relief whilst he collected his thoughts'.[79] Noemy used a combination of English, the Western language, and the Aboriginal lingua franca of the settlement. On 24 February, he urged the Western people 'to live peaceably together, not steal from each other nor tell lies, nor scold each other'. He then shifted to the lingua franca to urge the Wybalenna women in general to 'not scold one another, clean your houses early in the mornings, do not be sulky, out your bad tempers away from you, love God, love Jesus Christ, do not remain too long in the bush when you go for firewood, doing what is bad.'[80] Like Neptune's addresses, Noemy's were translated into English by Pignaburg ('Bessy') and Ta.ne.e.ber.rick ('Clara').

The oldest orator, Wourraddy ('Doctor'/'Count Alpha'), was from Bruny Island and had accompanied Robinson on this treks through the bush in the early 1830s. His addresses to the Wybalenna Aboriginal people were translated into English by Pie.yen.kome.yen.ner ('Wild Mary'). In April 1838, he addressed the 'weekly meeting for prayer and mutual instruction', using the Bruny Island language to relate a narrative of what had happened to all the Van Diemen's Land tribal groups:

> The white men have killed us all; they shot a great many. We are now only a few people here and we ought to be fond of one another. We ought to love God. God made every thing, the salt water, the horse, the bullock, the opossum, the wallaby, the kangaroo and wombat. Love him and you go to him by and bye.[81]

Wourraddy's narrative of a shared Aboriginal historical experience announces the birth of a new, pan-Tasmanian Indigenous social consciousness, possibly based on Jesus' commandment to 'love one another' (John 15:12). Today, Aboriginal people from all parts of Tasmania refer to themselves as 'Pallawah', a word that means 'people' in Wourraddy's Bruny Island language.[82]

On the same day as Wourraddy delivered the above address, Clark's report of the weekly meeting recorded that a native youth read Matthew, Chapter 2, and 'translated some of the leading facts into the language of the settlement'.[83] By April 1838, Governor Arthur's earlier prohibition against translating the Bible into Aboriginal languages appears to have been forgotten. Biblical doctrines were being channelled to the Wybalenna

Aboriginal community through several Aboriginal voices speaking different Aboriginal languages, in addition to Walter's and Brune's English sermons. These new, non-English renditions of biblical doctrine represent the tentative beginnings of a second reformation, a reinterpreting of the Bible in Van Diemen's Land. In the context of the Wybalenna Aboriginal people's historical experience of being decimated, displaced and crushed violently up against groups from other parts of Van Diemen's Land, Wourraddy's injunction to 'be fond of one another' possibly appropriates one of Jesus' central teachings as a foundation for an incipient Aboriginal nationalism.

Crucial here is the possibility that if Wourraddy were using John 15:12 he may not have been de-authorising the Bible, but rather reclothing its words with meanings capable of advancing his agenda. At this moment, Wourraddy was not engaging with the Bible only as the white man's book, but rather as a political resource he could use to serve his people's interests. He actively chose particular biblical words to say something he already knew, instead of passively accepting foreign-imposed truths. If he was indeed rearticulating Jesus' message of love, it was as Bakhtin describes, 'interwoven with "one's own word"…half-ours and half-someone else's… [I]n each of the new contexts…this discourse is able to reveal ever newer ways *to mean*.'[84]

o o o

On a tiny island in Bass Strait, off the north-east corner of Tasmania, the beginnings of biblical translation and recontextualisation initiated a tentative appropriation of the Bible by Aboriginal Australians. Today, although it would be overly optimistic to say Australia has entered a post-colonial era, there are some Aboriginal communities where the Bible is no longer consumed entirely 'in a Western cup'.[85] In some localities today, Aboriginal Christianity replaces the notion of 'conversion' with metaphors of productive entanglement and transformation of both Indigenous and Western traditions. The gospel is no longer invariably viewed as a Western cultural artefact, a text woven solely from non-Indigenous stories, truths and values. Today, as Aboriginal theologian Djiniyini Gondarra maintains:

> We no longer see Him as the white man's God or a God that the missionaries brought to us, but He is our God who has lived with us in history. But not only in history, He is living with us now in the person of the Holy Spirit. He has given us the vision for the Aboriginal Church to think and theologize the gospel in the language and culture of the people.[86]

Unlike the Aboriginal residents of Flinders Island in the 1830s, who were relentlessly drilled and catechised on their hollow biblical knowledge, Djiniyini Gondarra is part of a second reformation. He insists that 'we cannot go on answering someone else's questions.'[87]

Postscript

In the second last edition of the *Flinders Island Chronicle*, Thomas Brune wrote to his countrymen, 'I got rite to you the same things over and over again. Commandant has directed me to work and if I dont attend to it I must be put in to gaol…'[88] In the previous edition, he had written, '…I am much afraid none of us will be live by and by as then as nothing but sickness among us. Why don't the black fellows pray to the king to get us away from this place.'[89] The final sentence is missing from other copied versions of this edition in Robinson's papers, suggesting that Brune smuggled the subversive suggestion in after Robinson had checked the original draft.[90]

On 17 February 1846, Walter George Arthur and seven other Pallawah men carried part of Brune's suggestion into effect by sending a petition to Queen Victoria protesting against the reinstatement of the unpopular former superintendent, Dr Henry Jeanneret, who had previously been dismissed from the position:

> The humble petition of the free Aborigines Inhabitants of V[an] D[ieman's] L[and] now living upon Flinders Island, in Bass's Straits &c & &c.
>
> Most humbly showeth,
>   That we Your Majesty's Petitioners are your free Children that we were not taken Prisoners but freely gave up our Country to Colonel Arthur then the Governor after defending ourselves.
>   Your Petitioners humbly state to Y[our] M[ajesty] that Mr. Robinson made for us & with Col. Arthur an agreement which we have not lost from our minds since & we have made our part of it good.
>   Your Petitioners humbly tell Y[our] M[ajesty] that when we left our own place we were plenty of People, we are now but a little one.
>   Your Petitioners state they are a long time at Flinders Island & had plenty of Superintendents & were always a quiet and free People & not put into Gaol.
>   Your Majesty's petitioners pray that you will not allow Dr. Jeanneret to come again among us as our Superintendent as we

hear he is to be sent another time for when Dr Jeanneret was with us many Moons he used to carry Pistols in is pockets & threaten'd very often to shoot us & make us run away in fright. Dr. Jeanneret kept plenty of Pigs in our Village which used to run into our houses & eat up our bread from the fires & take away our flour bags in their mouths also to break into our Gardens & destroy our Potatoes & Cabbages.

Our houses were let fall down & they were never cleaned but were covered with vermin & not white-washed. We were often without Clothes except a very little one & Dr. Jeanneret did not care to mind us when we were sick until we were very bad. Eleven of us died when he was here. He put many of us into Jail for talking to him because we would not be his slaves. He kept from us our Rations when he pleased & sometimes gave us Bad Rations of Tea & Tobacco. He shot some of our dogs before our eyes & sent all the other dogs of ours to an Island & when we told him that they would starve he told us they might eat each other. He put arms into our hands & made us to assist his prisoners to go to fight the Soldiers we did not want to fight the Soldiers but he made us go to fight. We never were taught to read or write or to sing to God by the Doctor. He taught us a little upon the Sundays & his Prisoner Servant also taught us & his Prisoner Servant also took us plenty of times to Jail by his orders.

The Lord Bishop seen us in this bad way & we told H[is] L[ordship] plenty how Dr. Jeanneret used us.

We humbly pray Your Majesty the Queen will hear our prayer & not let Dr Jeanneret any more to come to Flinders Island. And We Y[our] M[ajesty]'s servants & Children will ever pray as in duty bound &c &c &c

Sgd. Walter George Arthur, Chief of the Ben Lomond Tribes, King Alexander, John Allen, Augustus, Davey Bruny, King Tippoo, Neptune, Washington.[91]

Western commentators have often foregrounded the symbolically transgressive, openly indecorous aspects of the writings of subordinated groups. They highlight those moments when members of oppressed groups violate due process, commit unlicensed speech-acts, or break conventions of genre, grammar, tone, voice or narrative.[92] For many oppressed peoples, however, overt transgression is a luxury they cannot afford. Their vulnerability demands forms of risk-averse behaviour that may be misread (both by authorities of the day and by researchers who come after) as a sign that they have been ideologically manoeuvred into submission. James C Scott has argued that the outwardly deferential behaviour of powerless peoples is a mode of self-protection and camouflage, a 'ritual of homage' that keeps the subordinated group from harm.[93]

The etiquette of official communications is invariably imposed from above by the politically dominant group. It is an institutionalised product of, and means of perpetuating, a particular power structure. To violate such etiquette would have been entirely counter-productive for the Flinders Island petitioners. By adopting a submissive tone and observing all the correct formalities, the Pallawah petitioners created a rhetorically effective frame for their narrative of Jeanneret's previous reign of terror. Given the possibility of Jeanneret's return, the act of writing and sending the petition was risky enough in itself. Although the petition was supported by Superintendent Milligan, it so incensed Dr Jeanneret that, when he did eventually return to the island, he persecuted those involved in writing it. He imprisoned Walter George Arthur for seventeen days in an effort to make him renounce the petition, and 'says we will all be hung for high treason for writing against him'.[94]

Given that Jeanneret's return was always a possibility, and that the account of his misdeeds could trigger outbreaks of vengeful fury, it is perhaps not surprising that the Flinders Island petition conformed so strictly to norms of process, presentation, tone and language. In these regards the petition bears the stamp of the government, administrative and legal institutions within which it was produced and put to work. Although Walter George Arthur was capable of penning the petition himself, he chose not to do so, fearing perhaps that his handwriting, spelling or language might detract from the authority of the document. These were legitimate concerns for a colonised people writing to the British monarch from a tiny island on the other side of the world, in a climate of racial opinion that presumed alphabetic literacy was a primary criterion of biological and cultural advancement, rationality and full human status.

Walter George Arthur therefore wrote, on behalf of himself and his fellow signatories, to Dr Joseph Milligan (the Flinders Island superintendent whom Jeanneret was to replace), requesting him to ask Catechist Clark to draw up the petition to the Queen.[95] The terms of address employed by Clark — phrases such as 'we humbly pray', 'your petitioners humbly tell Your Majesty' and 'we Your Majesty's servants & children…as in duty bound…' — are part of a formula designed to reassure Queen Victoria, and all who governed in her name, that the petition was not a proclamation of rebellion. At no point did the petition question the legitimacy of colonial rule per se. Instead, it focused on Jeanneret's abuse of the powers invested in him. The petition's political leverage derived not from a demand for Aboriginal sovereignty or political autonomy, but from an invocation of moral values espoused by English abolitionists, philanthropists and other influential sections of British society.[96] As a tactical document, it played British colonial authorities at their own moral game. The petition worked by highlighting the discrepancy between officially espoused humanitarian ideals and Dr Jeanneret's abuse of his powers and neglect of his responsibilities as superintendent. The political force of this petition derived both from the content of the narrative of Jeanneret's previous actions, and from the tactically correct way in which that narrative was discursively framed.

The Flinders Island petitioners' account of Jeanneret's misdeeds is a communally generated story about the community's experience. Yet this communal voice is no more autonomous than the voices of the journalists who wrote for the *Flinders Island Chronicle* because, out of political necessity, the document was created with the help of, and for the eyes of, a series of white officials occupying positions of institutionalised power. The petition was clearly written with those others' sense of propriety in mind. Clark was the instrument through which Walter George Arthur and his fellow petitioners generated a document conforming to the norms of British bureaucratic supplication. Their story of Jeanneret's misdeeds, packaged in its proper discursive frame, was handed by Earl Grey, Secretary of State for the Colonies, to Queen Victoria in March 1847. This properly worded, properly produced document was a decisive factor in the removal of the Pallawah people from Flinders Island to the Oyster Cove settlement near Hobart later that year.[97] The Pallawah petitioners got what they wanted by writing the white right way.

6

Literacy, land and power: the Coranderrk petitions

Among the witnesses of the Tanderrum ceremony in 1835, whereby the Woiworung agreed to share their land with John Batman, were two adolescent Woiworung boys named Barak (c. 1824–1903) and Wonga (c. 1824–75). The two boys were cousins and both were closely related to Billibillary, one of the signatories of the Batman treaty.[1] By the time Simon Wonga and William Barak were in their mid-thirties, over half a million white settlers had flooded into Victoria, lured by gold and lucrative pastoral opportunities. The pastoralists quickly cleared and fenced all the habitable land. The Aboriginal economy was destroyed and the population was ravaged by violence, illness and starvation. Estimated at around 30 000 in the 1830s, Aboriginal numbers in Victoria had plummeted to just over 2000 by the early 1860s.[2] The Protectorate that operated between 1839 and 1849 had failed, despite the efforts of the Chief Protector, George Augustus Robinson, appointed on the basis of his 'success' in Van Diemen's Land.[3] After various Aboriginal schools and settlements had struggled to survive in the 1840s and 1850s, a system of large reserves and missions was established in the 1860s, with food, clothing, education and housing provided.[4] The purpose of these establishments was to give the 'dying race' a safe refuge to live out their remaining years, and to educate and train the young, especially those of mixed descent, so they could eventually obtain employment and 'make themselves useful', instead of being a 'nuisance' and a burden on taxpayers.

The first of the Aboriginal reserves established in Victoria in the 1860s was on the Acheron River in Taungurong country in central northern Victoria. The Taungurong people had secured the land with the help of Woiworung leader Simon Wonga and the former Protector of the

Melbourne region, William Thomas. In September 1860, however, after the Acheron community had cleared, fenced, ploughed, and sown seven hectares of crops, the newly formed Central Board to Watch over the Interests of the Aborigines ordered that the station be abandoned and moved to another locality, Mohican Station.[5]

A local white pastoralist, Peter Snodgrass, one of the Acheron Reserve trustees, had persuaded the government to purchase Mohican from one of his cronies at an inflated price, and to shift the Taungurong people to this cold and barren site, leaving the improved land at Acheron available for purchase by two of Snodgrass's other local squatter friends. Many of the Acheron residents refused to move, even after the squatters had broken their fences and brought cattle onto the reserve to destroy their crops.[6] A recurring pattern was begun wherein whites with a vested interest in the failure of Aboriginal initiatives became the main beneficiaries of government funding intended to assist Indigenous communities.

Not all whites saw Aboriginal people as an opportunity for exploitation, however. In August 1861, Reverend John Green, a 33-year-old Scottish Presbyterian minister, was appointed to the position of General Inspector of Aboriginal Missions and Reserves in Victoria. Green joined William Barak, Simon Wonga and William Thomas in lobbying the Protection Board for reserve land at Coranderrk Creek, a traditional Woiworung campsite. When the site was approved early in 1863, John and Mary Green and their four young children walked with the Taungurong families from Acheron and Mohican, to join with the Woiworung at the chosen site at Coranderrk. Mindful of the Acheron experience, everyone hoped that, this time, their tenure would be permanent and secure, but the reserve had not yet been officially gazetted. Although the land had belonged to Barak's and Wonga's clan since time immemorial, they had no legal right to consider it their home until the formal announcement of the land allocation had been published in the government gazette.

Batman's treaty, illegal as it was, had effectively dispossessed the Koori nations in the Port Phillip region. Now the remaining Taungurong and Woiworung clans were officially granted a place to live by the printing of a public notice in a government publication. Land was lost and regained not only by physical force, but by written documents produced and deployed in accordance with the white man's law. To the Koori peoples of Victoria in the latter half of the 19th century, it must have been clear that certain kinds of written document and particular practices of literacy were indispensable weapons in their struggles for land.

The gazettal of Coranderrk Aboriginal Reserve was unexpectedly prompt. In May 1863, two months after setting up camp at Coranderrk, Barak, Wonga, and eighteen other men and boys walked 67 kilometres to Melbourne to attend the Governor's public levee celebrating Queen Victoria's birthday and the recent marriage of the Prince of Wales. As well as bringing gifts for the Prince and the Queen, the men sent a written 'loyal address' to Her Majesty, Queen Victoria, and told her representative, Governor Henry Barkly, that they needed land. A month later, the first parcel of land at Coranderrk was gazetted and, after a time, the Coranderrk residents received copies of a letter from the Queen promising her protection. This course of events led many to believe that Coranderrk Reserve had been granted personally by the Queen.[7]

Barwick states that this belief was erroneous, and maintains that the promptness of Coranderrk's gazettal had nothing to do with the men's deputation and written address to the Queen.[8] Although other factors no doubt played a part, it remains difficult to dismiss as irrelevant the effect upon government officials of the knowledge that Aboriginal people were capable of communicating in writing to those in the highest seats of power. Whether or not the Queen intervened, the people of Coranderrk were correct in their perception that deputations and letters to people in high places were an effective way of asserting their needs and defending their interests. They used the medium of writing not to preserve words over time, but rather to carry their voices over the heads of local officials so they could be heard by higher authorities to whom the locals were accountable. In their future struggles to hold on to Coranderrk, the people used this bridging strategy on many occasions.

Despite the devastating impact of colonialism, Indigenous land-based and kin-based authority structures remained very much alive in colonial Victoria, as they do today in many parts of Australia. Coranderrk was the largest and most socially complex of Victoria's six major Aboriginal reserves and missions. It was located on the estate of the Wurundjeri-willam clan of the Woiworung people. As *ngurungaeta* (senior men recognised for their integrity and wisdom as a leaders), and as heads of the Wurundjeri clan on whose estate Coranderrk Reserve was established, William Barak and his cousin Simon Wonga were generally acknowledged to be the rightful leaders and primary spokesmen on matters concerning the Coranderrk community as a whole. Politically, this latter role was crucial. It was imperative that the Coranderrk residents spoke and wrote as a collective if they were to be heard and taken seriously by the government authorities responsible for their protection and welfare.

The Coranderrk community was not monolithic and its members were not always unanimous in their views, however.[9] As Diane Barwick has shown in her history of Coranderrk, the residents were divided by intersecting lines of social difference based on country of origin, language, age, moiety, gender, caste, clan and other kinship ties. Some social differences were traditional to Indigenous cultures; others, such as the distinction between 'half-castes' and 'full-bloods', were imposed by white legislators and popular white racist discourse.[10] One of Barak and Wonga's major achievements was to bring this community together as a political force: some of the large petitions are like snapshots of a political body in the process of constituting itself on paper. Even so, rifts and factional disputes periodically occurred, disrupting the social process of writing. In 1883, for example, Mrs Jeannie Rowan complained that 'as the half-castes and blacks are kept unfriendly with one another the blacks are unable to get their complaints put down in writing excepting by little children, whereas up till this time the half-castes always did the writing for all the people at the station…'[11]

From the early days, Barak and Wonga did all they could to uphold the authority of traditional Indigenous law. The Wurundjeri clan, on whose traditional estate Coranderrk was established, became hosts to the peoples of the Kulin nation, an already existing confederation of the Eastern Kulin-speaking societies (namely the Taungurong, Bunurong, and Ngurai-illam-wurrung peoples), and the Western Kulin-speaking societies (i.e., the Jajowrong and Wathaurung peoples).[12] The combined homelands of these peoples covered an area slightly smaller than Tasmania. As well as being neighbours, their languages were related, and their religious beliefs and social customs were similar. They believed the world was created by Bunjil (Eaglehawk), and they named their moieties Bunjil and Waa (Eaglehawk and Crow). As exogamous societies bound together through intermarriage and moiety affiliations, they shared a patrilineal moiety system wherein all individuals inherited membership of either the Bunjil or the Waa moiety. Strong intertribal alliances were built as Eaglehawk men married Crow women, and vice versa.[13] Upon marriage, women customarily moved to their husband's clan estate, but retained their ties to their country of origin. Children had rights to their birthplace, as well as to the clan estates of their parents.

At Coranderrk, people identified themselves not only by language, clan and moiety affiliations, but with reference to the places they were born and raised, even if they had long been driven away from those districts.[14] Family names such as Dunolly, Avoca, Terrick and Franklin allude to the (English names for) rivers, mountains and towns in people's homelands. Yet many who were born far away had traditional connections with Coranderrk through their Woiworung mothers, women who had left Woiworung country to live and bear their children on their husband's country. Two important figures in the history of Coranderrk, Thomas Bamfield (c. 1844–1893)[15] and Thomas Dunolly (1856–1923), were Taungurong and Djadjawurung respectively, but as descendants of Woirworung women of the land-owning clan at Coranderrk they had rights and responsibilities regarding the land on which the reserve was located.[16]

In the 1870s, a number of people from beyond the Kulin homelands were also sent to Coranderrk, particularly Burapper, Pangerang and Kurnai people whom the Kulin had traditionally considered foreign and hostile.[17] Over time, as they intermarried and had children at Coranderrk, they were bound together by their shared sense that Coranderrk was their home. Resentment against Board policies was also a strong bonding agent. These affiliations and divisions played a crucial role in shaping the internal dynamics of Coranderrk society, which in turn shaped the kinds of documents they wrote. By and large, however, the Coranderrk community differed from that of Flinders Island in Tasmania because its members were already bound together by intermarriage from the beginning. What's more, there was no power vacuum to elicit intertribal rivalry. At Coranderrk, everyone was living on the clan estate of two local men of high degree, William Barak and Simon Wonga.

The most detailed history of Coranderrk is Diane Barwick's meticulously researched *Rebellion at Coranderrk* (1998), which offers an almost day-by-day chronicle of the long battle to establish and retain the reserve. Barwick rightly presents the Coranderrk story as one of the great, but little known, epic struggles in Australian history. It was indeed a struggle, a paper war between the Aboriginal residents and the Board for the Protection of Aborigines (BPA) in which a vast number of documents were generated and deployed to serve political ends.[18] In this war of words over land and justice between members of two racial groups, both sides were internally divided in complex ways. Many of the Indigenous names alluded to places in their homelands. The names of some of the major white players match so well with their roles and personalities that the Coranderrk story reads at times like a moral allegory. Among the staunchest friends of the Coranderrk community were John Green, William Goodall and Ann Bon.[19] Among their foes were Messrs Strickland and Curr, and the arch-manipulator of documents and information, Captain Page, Secretary of the Board for the Protection of Aborigines for the twelve years between 1877 and 1889. Divided as it was, white Victorian society came closest to unanimity in its general ignorance and antipathy towards the Indigenous peoples it was dispossessing.

William Barak at work on a painting at Coranderrk, c. 1895. La Trobe Picture Collection, State Library of Victoria.

Power, knowledge and literacy

One of the main reasons why many Kulin were willing to leave their respective homelands and live at Coranderrk was that they wanted their children to go to school and master new survival skills in a place where the parents could live with, or very close to, them.[20] As on all reserves and missions, alphabetic literacy at Coranderrk developed far more rapidly among children and young adults than among their elders. The effect of this pattern of change on traditional Indigenous social hierarchies was varied and complex. Contrary to the views of Walter J Ong and other influential media theorists, literacy did not shift power automatically and invariably from the old to the young.[21] Young people's alphabetic literacy and knowledge of English could potentially either disrupt or consolidate traditional, orally based Aboriginal gerontocracies; hence, the diverse writing cultures and contrasting structures of intergenerational authority that developed on different Aboriginal missions and reserves in colonial Australia.

In Indigenous Australian societies, the most powerful spiritual and ceremonial knowledge has always been the responsibility of the older fully initiated men, although women have their own important spheres of sacred knowledge and political influence. This gendered gerontocratic social structure is preserved by customary laws that restrict the flow of some types of knowledge from the old to the young (and to unworthy or ineligible adults), and between men and women. The most potent songs and ceremonies for invoking the spirit-beings that shaped and controlled the universe were not disclosed to the uninitiated. Young people had to wait until their elders decided they were ready to receive these potentially dangerous tools for activating the powers of the spirit world.

Yet for those living on missions and reserves, literacy and the English language were powerful tools of another kind, tools that enabled Indigenous people to communicate with a new force that was shaping their world: colonial governments. As young people of both sexes became literate and fluent in English, their ability to negotiate with government authorities gave them a social status they would not otherwise have acquired at such an early age. The growth of alphabetic literacy among children and young adults thus created the *potential* for certain kinds of power to shift from older to younger generations.

In Van Diemen's Land, as we saw in the previous chapter, two teenage boys, Walter George Arthur and Thomas Brune, accrued a great deal of influence among the Pallawah peoples who had been taken to Flinders Island from their respective homelands on mainland Van Diemen's Land. Bearing in mind that the written record affords only a limited, partial view of Pallawah experience, and that the Flinders Island residents no doubt maintained a political and spiritual life unbeknown to the white authorities, it seems clear that these young men were able to use their literacy and language skills to form a close association with Commandant George Augustus Robinson, thereby gaining forms of power and influence they would not otherwise have had at such a young age.

At Coranderrk, however, literacy did not bring about a redistribution of power from the old to the young. The Coranderrk experience suggests that if a mission or reserve was located on the clan estate of one or more of the senior residents, the traditional gerontocracy remained largely in place. In such cases, the male head of the host clan was considered under traditional law to be the leader and spokesperson for the reserve or mission community. Although residents from other regions periodically gained favour with mission and reserve superintendents, a person's authority to serve as leader and spokesperson for the community as a whole depended primarily on their seniority in the kinship network and their associated rights and responsibilities in relation to the country on which the reserve was located. William Barak's and Simon Wonga's authority was based on their seniority in the land-holding clan upon whose traditional land Coranderrk had been established.

Numerous petitions were written at Coranderrk. In all but a few of these documents, William Barak's name heads the list of signatories. Barak could not write, but he remained the principal signatory because, in external affairs, he was considered the group's rightful representative.[22] Writing, like Kulin self-government, was based on traditional kinship and land-based authority structures. After Simon Wonga's death in 1875, William Barak was Coranderrk's *ngurungaeta* or speaker. Barak described a *ngurungaeta* as a man who was granted special authority by the people because he 'spoke straight and did no wrong'.[23] Barak also noted that 'beside each of the *ngurungaeta* there was the man to whom he gave "his words".'[24] Each *ngurungaeta* had a spokesman who could be trusted to understand and carry his words where they needed to go.

When the people of Coranderrk communicated in writing with white government officials, the social practice of written textual production was assimilated into traditional Kulin structures of authority and protocols of communication. The roles of author and scribe were respectively practised in accordance with the roles of *ngurungaeta* and speaker. As a *ngurungaeta* and head of the Wurundjeri clan on whose land Coranderrk was established, Barak was authorised by customary law to speak on behalf of those who lived there, and was responsible for deciding how the Coranderrk land was to be used and who should live in the Coranderrk community.[25]

The Coranderrk petitions occupy an important place in the history of Indigenous Australian writing because they attest to the resilience and adaptability of Indigenous cultures. The following petition was produced in late 1881, after almost half a century of serious disruption to traditional ways:[26]

'Coranderrk Station, November 16th 1881.

'Sir,
'We want the Board and the Inspector, Captain Page, to be no longer over us. We want only one man here, and that is Mr. John Green, and the station to be under the Chief Secretary; then we will show the country that the station could self-support itself.
'These are the names of those that wish this to be done.

'Wm. Barak, X	Alick Campbell, X	Ellen Richard, X	Edith Brangy
Thos. Mickie, X	Thos. Dunolly,	Harriett, X	Mary Ann McClennan,
Dick Richard, X	Alfred Davis,	Annie Hamilton, X	Bella Lee,
Thos. Avoca, X	Willie Parker,	Mary, X	Alice Grant,
Thos. Gilman, X	Willie Hamilton, X	Jessie Dunolly,	Thomas Dick,
Johnny Terrick, X	Johnny Charles,	Louisa Hunter, X	William Edmond
Lankey, X	Jemima Wandon,	Dinah Hunter,	Alexander Briggs,
Spider, X	Emma Campbell, X	Caroline Morgan, X	Abel Terrick,
M. Simpson,	Jenny Campbell,	Maggie Harmoney	Finnemore Jackson,
H. Harmoney	Lizzy Charles, X	Lizzie Davis	Joseph Hunter
Alfred Morgan,	Eliza Mickie, X	Metild Simpson, X	Johon Patterson.'
Robert Wandon,	Roy, X		

This petition is typical of many produced at Coranderrk. As a whole, such lists can be read as snapshots of a new, mixed regional community constituting itself as such. Yet the order of names also reflects the traditional gender, age and land-based social order. The local clan-head William

Barak is at the top, followed by the other senior men (who all sign with crosses), then the younger men (who wrote their own names), then the older (usually non-literate) women, then the younger (literate) women, and finally the children, who wrote their own names if they were old enough to attend school. The spatial ordering of people's names can be taken as evidence that when the senior clan-heads were on their own traditional country, the social process of producing written texts — and the layout of the pages themselves — could in fact consolidate the authority of the older generations, contrary to the expectations of theorists such as Goody and Ong, who see writing itself as the cause of a shift of power from the old to the young.

The Green years

To understand why this petition was written, we need to go back to the time when Coranderrk was established. During its first twelve years, from 1863 to 1874, the Coranderrk residents felt relatively secure in their tenure over the reserve land, and generally happy in their relationship with John and Mary Green who managed the reserve and taught in the school. Within a few months of arriving, they had built huts for themselves, and bought clothing and footwear using money obtained through the sale of possum skin rugs, baskets and other artefacts.[27] Against the grain of contemporary opinion, Green treated the Kulin as 'free and independent men and women', who would cooperate when led, but not when driven.[28] John Green worked beside the men as they cultivated the land. He recognised that they were every bit as intelligent as Europeans, and found them to be more truthful and honest. As manager, Green asserted his Christian morality over the people's customary laws; nonetheless, his method was, as he put it, 'to allow them to rule themselves as much as possible. When there is any strife among them this is always settled in a kind of court.'[29] All men and, after 1865, women participated in the court, which formulated a written code of conduct and handed out punishments to those who broke the rules, the ultimate punishment being banishment from the reserve. Green found that 'compulsion would make them kick against it, but if they get a voice in it themselves, and they once pass it as a law of their own, they would stick to it.'[30] Chairing the court, Green relied not on his externally instituted authority as manager but rather on his moral influence as a trusted friend and respected leader. He addressed the adult males 'as men and brothers'.[31]

6 ~ Literacy, land and power: the Coranderrk petitions

By the early 1870s, local pastoralists were lobbying the Board for the Protection of Aborigines to sell the land at Coranderrk into private hands, so it could be used 'more productively'.[32] Robert Brough Smyth, Board Secretary from 1860 to 1876 and Chairman from 1874 to 1876, had himself purchased land near Coranderrk, and stood to gain handsomely from economic development of the district. He was approached on the quiet by neighbours and local acquaintances who wanted Coranderrk broken up and made available to whites for leasing or purchase.[33] By 1874, the Board was seriously considering breaking up Coranderrk, selling off the land, and shifting the residents to distant reserves on foreign country near the flood-prone Murray River, ostensibly for the good of their health. John Green protested so vehemently against this proposal that the Board came to regard him as an impediment to their plans and a threat to their authority.

In August 1874, Green was goaded by the Board into resigning his post at Coranderrk.[34] He soon wished to withdraw his resignation but the Board refused to allow it. For many years, the Coranderrk residents lobbied for Green's return and for security of tenure on the reserve, mainly by writing letters and petitions. The Board called the Coranderrk residents' protests and requests a 'rebellion', as though writing and speaking were violent acts of armed resistance against a legitimately established government.

The double jeopardy of mediation

Colonial policy-makers around the world believed schooling to be the best way to 'advance' so-called primitive races. By the time John and Mary Green left Coranderrk in 1874, thirty-seven children and thirty young adults could read and write.[35] As time went by, they became regular readers of the newspapers. Some had books in their homes, and a number of the photographic portraits reproduced in Barwick show them holding a book (probably the Bible) in their hands. Barak was an accomplished painter[36] but, like most Indigenous Australians of his generation, had not been taught to read and write alphabetic script.[37] Nor was he able to express himself fluently in English, despite being a compelling speaker in his own Woiworung language.[38] To fulfil his responsibilities as head of the clan on which Coranderrk was located, Barak therefore enlisted others to write for him and those who resided on his clan estate. His first scribes were white men. In September 1874, Barak asked Reverend JH Stahle, Green's temporary replacement, to write a petition to the Board asking that Green be reinstated as manager.³⁹ Although this petition was unsuccessful, the people of Coranderrk had found a written genre that accorded with their need to speak as a collective. Stahle, however, was dismissed for supporting Green and for writing 'improper' letters to the Board on behalf of the Coranderrk residents.⁴⁰ Through the intervention of Anglican Board members, Stahle was appointed as superintendent at Lake Condah Mission, where we'll revisit him in the following chapter.

Barak had gone through the first stages of initiation in his youth but is reputed to have been converted to Christianity under John Green's influence, and to have memorised sections of the Bible he sometimes carried.⁴¹ In October 1875, Barak enlisted the services of an unidentified scribe to write another petition defending their land and requesting John Green's reinstatement. It is a men's petition, and the language reflects the influence of Green's Christian teachings (see p. 135, 136).

It is likely, judging by the handwriting, the spelling and the style of English used, that Barak dictated this petition to one of the youths who had been taught to write by Mary Green at the Coranderrk school. These young scribes were making themselves useful in a manner not anticipated by colonial policy-makers. Only Barak the clan-head was authorised by traditional law to speak for the community; only the young knew how to write, to put Barak's message before the eyes of white officials in high places. By this time, Barak and the other senior petitioners expected little joy from face-to-face appeals to the Board. Their deputation to a Board meeting three months previously had proved futile. This time, therefore, they sent their written message over the Board's head to the Chief Secretary, JA Macpherson.

They did not send this petition *directly* to the Chief Secretary, however. Given that the petition had been penned by one of their own young men, Barak and his co-signatories may have judged that white mediation and authentication of the document were required. They therefore sent the petition to local judge and parliamentarian George Harker, who forwarded it to Chief Secretary Macpherson with a covering letter supporting the men's wish to remain at Coranderrk. Harker served as a credible witness to verify to the Board that the petition genuinely expressed the residents' wishes, and to confirm to the Coranderrk leaders that their written message had been sent to the appropriate destination.

Coranderrk
Oct 20th 1875
(the day the Month we had a Meeting here)

I William Barrak
    Remember of Coranderrk

    I would if you be so kind to help us for we are in trouble and I will Name the Names of those who are willing to live and die here these are them that agree to stop

Harry	Willie Barker
Bobby Wandon	Willie Buskumbe
Johnny Webster	Martin Simpson
Jemmy Webster	Johnny Phillip
Dick	Tommy Avoca
Peter Hunter	Tommy Were
Tommy Banfield	Jemmy Barker
Samson Barber	Willie Tulgium
Tommy Dunolly	Tommy Hanet
George	Jemmy Race
Edward	
Johnny Terrick	all present
Tommy Farmer	
Johnny Charles	

    We want a man whom God chosen to lay the foundation of Coranderrk Station for he it is appointed us to the living God and that's Mr Green for if it wasnt for him we what a been all dead and that's all we require Just now & many the Lord bless you Sir and give you good knowledge

I remain you
Kind Friend
William Barrak[42]

Unlike personal deputations, written protests could not be ignored by the Board: writing put the Coranderrk residents' requests on the record. In this case, the Board responded by denying the petitioners' political agency, deliberately misconstruing Harker's involvement as evidence that the protest had merely been incited by white troublemakers. Another Board tactic was to 'misplace' or simply ignore documents that revealed their high-handed negligence and incompetence. Much of the Board's correspondence for

> I William Barak Remember of Coranderrk Coranderrk Oct 20th 1875
>
> (the day the Month we had Meeting here)
>
> I would if you be so kind to help us for we are in trouble and I will name the Names of those who are willing to live and die here these are them that agree to stop)
>
> Harry
> Bobby Wandon
> Johnny Webster
> Jemmy Webster
> Dick
> Peter Hunter
> Tommy Banfield
> Jackson Barber
> Tommy Donally
> George
> Edward
> Johnny Terrick
> Tommy Farmer
> Johnny Charles
>
> Willie Barker
> Willie Bushumbe
> Martin Simpson
> Johnny Phillip
> Tommy Arooa
> Tommy Wise
> Jemmy Barker
> Willie Ferguson
> Tommy Hunet
> Jemmy Race
>
> all present
>
> We want a man whom God chosen to lay the foundation of Coranderrk Station for he it is appointed us to the living God and thats Mr Green for if it wasn't for him we what a been all dead and thats all we require Just now & may the Lord bless you Sir and Give You good knowledge
>
> I Remain you Kind Friend William Barak

Petition from William Barak et al. dated 20 October 1875, asking that John Green be reinstated as manager. Collection of Public Records Office Victoria.

the troubled years of 1875 and 1877 was mysteriously 'lost', and the Kulin petition of 20 October 1875 was not mentioned at all in the minutes of the relevant Board meeting.[43] The Board defended its own credibility and authority by tampering with the records and controlling the flow of information to parliament, to government departments, to the press and the general public, as well as to those whose welfare they were ostensibly protecting. The Coranderrk residents learned quickly that to defend their home, they themselves had to become adept in using written documents and the English language as political weapons. The challenge they faced was how to do this in a manner consistent with their own protocols of lawful communication.

Messengers and mediators played a recognised role both in European cultures, and in intra- and intertribal communications within Indigenous cultures. On the question of whether to enlist white mediators for their letters and petitions, however, the Coranderrk residents found themselves in a double bind: they were damned if they did but equally dammed if they didn't. If they asked their non-Indigenous friends to intercede on their behalf, the Board treated their requests and complaints as inauthentic, merely the work of meddlesome white do-gooders. If the Coranderrk community penned their own letters and petitions, however, their wishes were dismissed as baseless whims of an irrational, childlike race. Either way, their words were rendered impotent.

On 1 April 1876, former police sergeant Hugh Halliday took over from Stahle as manager of Coranderrk.[44] The Board, dominated at the time by Anglicans, ordered Halliday to forbid John Green's monthly visits to Coranderrk to conduct Presbyterian church services for the residents. The residents responded by drafting a petition objecting to Green's exclusion. They sent their draft by post to a Melbourne friend for presentation to the Chief Secretary. Before the petition had left the reserve, however, it was officiously intercepted by Halliday, who sent it to Christian Ogilvie, the recently appointed BPA Chairman, after the suspension of 'the half-mad bureaucrat' Robert Brough Smyth.[45]

The BPA took the petition not to be a sign of Indigenous initiative and political agency but as evidence that 'some well and some ill intentioned white people' were bent on undermining the Board's authority.[46] Ogilvie viewed Aboriginal complaints as a product of white indulgence: 'As long as there are people who listen to blacks' complaints I think it is very natural, with such a race of people, that they will complain.'[47] The possibility that Indigenous Australians were autonomous agents and writers was inconceivable to most Board members. Edward Curr, for instance, whose error-ridden four-volume ethnographic study *The Australian race* (1886–87) later made his reputation as an expert on Aboriginal affairs, asserted that:

> ...natives are children, and in anything I have recommended I have inferred that they would be treated as children... [T]he blacks should, when necessary, be coerced just as we coerce children and lunatics who cannot take care of themselves...[48] Their will is nothing.[49]

Curr and the majority of his fellow Board members persisted in such beliefs despite the fact that, on several occasions, they had been outwitted by members of this 'childlike' race. In September 1876, for instance, the people of Coranderrk had generated a petition that foreclosed all possible doubts regarding its authenticity. Having read in the newspapers that the Board was seeking to prescribe their places of residence and control their movements, they held a meeting to formulate a response to the proposed regulations. The reserve manager, Mr Halliday, stated in his covering letter to the Board Chairman, Christian Ogilvie, that 'the Natives of this Station' had asked him to ring the station bell as they wished to hold a general meeting of the kind first held in the era of John Green. When all were assembled, the men asked Halliday for another witness, so Mr Deans, the schoolteacher, was called in to record the proceedings. To make sure the document reached its target, Mr Halliday expressly asked Ogilvie to put the document before the Board at his earliest convenience.[50] The petition read as follows:

> Memorandum of Resolution Passed at the Coranderrk Aboriginal Station at a meeting of the Native's on the 11th Septr 1876.
>
> 1st Resolution
>
> Resolution proposed by James Barker and seconded by John Charles that the Natives of Coranderrk are well satisfied with the treatment they have received from the Central Board and also the present local management and request that they may not be removed from the present station, and that the Board will forward the said resolution to the present Government for consideration—
>
> 17, <u>For</u>   6, against,   resolution carried
>
> <u>2nd Resolution</u>
>
> Proposed by John Briggs and seconded by Martin Simpson that if the Station at Coranderrk is broken-up they will <u>not</u> proceed to any other mission station in the Colony

Carried unanimously

3rd Resolution

Proposed by Robert Bains and seconded by James Edgar, that this Meeting approves of Mr Halliday's management of the station since his arrival on it

Carried unanimously

Signatures

Edward Hunter	Willie Morris
Thomas X Bamfield	Freddy
Willie Parker	Peter X Hunter
James X Reece	Alfred X Davis
James X Rowan	John X Briggs
William X Hamilton	Bobby Wandon
A, X Campbell	Thomas X Hodnath [?]
Leonard X Kerr	Thomas X Avoca
Danhall	John X Phillips
Bobby Bain	Thomas X Farmer
James X Edgar	William X Berrick
Martin X Simpson	Lankey X
Johnny Charles (his mark)	James X Barker
Samson	

Witness to resolutions and signatures
James S Deans

Much as they wished to discredit such mediated expressions of Indigenous views, the Board could not deny that this petition had validly documented the signatories' wishes. Such a denial would have cast aspersions on the manager and the schoolteacher, staff members that they themselves had appointed.

The petition is unusual in several respects. First, it is not a Woiworung initiative; second, it is one of the only documents to register non-unanimity overtly on paper; and third, it records something of the oral context of its own making within a European protocol for conducting formal meetings. It indicates that after some discussion,[51] individuals made resolutions which were then put to a vote, whereby they were formally accepted or rejected by those in attendance. The resolutions and votes were recorded in a written text that represented the decisions of the collective. The first resolution was made by Taungurong leader James [Jemmy] Barker, and Djajaworung John Charles. The six men who voted against this resolution were non-Kulin Burapper men who had come to Coranderrk just four years previously, and wished to avoid foreclosing the possibility of returning to their traditional country.

The second resolution was put by Djadjawurung Martin Simpson, and Pallawah Tasmanian John Briggs (husband of Woiworung woman Louisa Briggs). Robert Bains and James Edgar, who put the third resolution, were Pangerang and Burapper respectively.

The dominance of voices from outside the Kulin confederacy makes this petition highly unusual; however, it provides an idea of configurations of authority that cut across the traditional Kulin clan- and land-based social order. The relative positioning of the twenty-seven names on the petition was probably determined by the order in which the men lined up to sign. Of the six men who made and seconded the resolutions, all but Briggs stood in a group in the second quarter of the queue. Barak stood at a distance, near the very end, in second last place. The order of signatures on the page reflects the position of the signatories' bodies in space, which in turn reflects the political grouping of the men on the day of the meeting.

The entanglement of orality and literacy

In the eyes of the Protection Board officials, the authority of the September 1876 petition derived not only from its endorsement by Halliday and Deans, but from certain features of the document itself. In its recording of the resolutions, votes and names of persons present, the document conformed to well-established Western bureaucratic conventions. It thus bore the marks of its own authenticity as a true record of a particular set of oral statements and exchanges. The written record was not inherently authoritative; its authority was based on the formal record-keeping conventions whereby it signified its fidelity as a transcript of spoken words, which in turn were authorised by having been written down in the 'proper' way. Writing thus deferred to oral utterance which had no authority but that bestowed by writing.

Such paradoxes call into question the simple binary opposition between 'primitive' oral cultures and 'advanced' literate ones, and the Eurocentric colonialist idea that, over time, 'progress' from orality to literacy was necessary and inevitable. By adopting alphabetic script, Indigenous Australians did not step over a threshold between orality and literacy. Instead, they wove back and forth between oral and literate institutions *within* European culture, as well as *between* European and Indigenous cultures. Far from putting an end to talk, their writings served often to empower their spoken words.

6 ~ Literacy, land and power: the Coranderrk petitions

Many of the documents produced at Coranderrk were designed specifically to be read aloud in face-to-face contexts of communication. For the 1881 parliamentary inquiry into conditions at Coranderrk, a number of Aboriginal witnesses composed written statements to be read aloud at the hearings. By submitting their testimonies in writing, the Aboriginal witnesses gained a measure of control over the inquiry's agenda, raising issues deliberately avoided by some of the commissioners in their ordinary lines of oral questioning. In the written statements prepared beforehand, the Aboriginal witnesses were able to express themselves more fully and freely than would have been possible when standing up to be questioned in the intimidating atmosphere of the inquiry. For example, the following men's petition, submitted by William Barak, correctly diagnosed managerial incompetence and proliferating bureaucracy to be the major reasons why the station remained unproductive and the residents lacked the basic necessities of life:

> Coranderrk,
> Sept. 5th 1881
>
> Sir — The only complaint we have is this, we all wish Mr. Green back here in Mr. Strickland's [the manager's] position. Mr. Strickland is not a fit man here in regard to work and also to the sick people; he has no idea of tilling the ground or making any improvements on the station, or doing any good for the welfare of the black here; no potatoes or hay here on the station, and the station ought [to] keep itself in meat, but it does not: we all have to buy meat. When Mr. Green was here he used to be doing what Mr. Strickland is doing now, that is, he used to preach the gospel and also do the farming work, and also do what Mr. Capt. Page is doing now as inspector, and made a good improvement; and now it takes three men and there is no improvement. If Mr. Green had the use of the money what is laid now since he left, there would (be) something what the station would be able to pay back. We are all sure if we had Mr. Green back the station would self-support itself. No wonder the visitors that come here and go away and say the station ought to be sold, when we won't be allowed to clear the ground; the Central Board, and the manager too, are only leaving this open for to give room to the white people to have something to say about it. The only thing we wish is Mr. Green removed back here, and then they will see that (the) station will (be) improved better, and will also see that those who speak against us will see we have a head manager of us. So that (is) all we all have to say. These are the names of our men what are

agreeable and hope to be carried out – Wm. Barak, Thos. Banfield, Dick Richard, Thos. Avoca, Terrick Johnny, Thos. Gillman, Lankey, Willie Hamilton, Alick Campbell, Thos. Dunolly, Martin Simpson, Alfred Morgan, H. Harmony, R. Wandon, J. Briggs.[52]

By submitting evidence in written form, the witnesses ensured that their views would be accurately recorded in the official minutes of evidence.

The witnesses' testimonies were also reported in the newspapers. Reading the testimonies of Manager Strickland, Captain Page and other members of the Board, the Coranderrk residents were incensed at the lies they told. The Coranderrk residents used the inquiry to criticise the white officials who governed their lives. Writing proved to be a great means of talking back to the white men who were abusing their power. In writing, one could marshal one's thoughts and arguments, and plan how best to approach the dangerous issues that were likely to cause a stir at the hearings. Thomas Dunolly challenged the testimony and criticised the ethics of those whose decisions governed their lives. His astute rebuttal of evidence given by Captain Page and Manager Strickland revealed the hidden agendas behind government policies and managerial passivity that diminished the productivity of the reserve lands:

> Coranderrk, November 17th, 1881.
>
> Sir,
>
> I have seen in the newspapers that Mr. Captain Page said that we get two suits of clothes per year. That is false. We only get one suit of clothes per year; and it is true that the women have to make flannel shirts for the men out of their flannel which they get for their petticoats. And he said that it never reached his ear about meat. He was told on three occasions about want of meat… And I have seen Mr. Strikland; I and Boby Wandon saw him on the 5th of February 1881 with liquor in him; and when we tell Mr. Captain Page anything, he don't care about listening to anything said. We could see what Mr. Captain Page wanted to do. He did not want to make any improvement on the station. He wanted to leave it open for every visitor to see it laying waste, so the visitors go to Melbourne and report it. It is not our fault, because we were not allowed to go further than the orders left by Mr. Captin Page…
>
> I remain your most obedient servant,
>
> 'Thos. Dunolly.'[53]

While writing was often needed to prepare for and authorise oral testimony, the Coranderrk residents knew that writing did not obviate the need for face-to-face dialogue. Although a postal service operated between Coranderrk and Melbourne, the Coranderrk men on several occasions walked the 67 kilometres through the night to present their petitions personally to the Chief Secretary in Melbourne, before walking another 67 kilometres home. These long, tiring walks placed a great strain on their health. Barak walked with a painful limp from a broken leg that had never healed properly. Bamfield had severe rheumatism. Other men had debilitating chronic illnesses such as tuberculosis or hydatid tumours. On a number of occasions the men went without food for more than twenty-four hours. Clearly, they believed strongly that it was necessary to speak face-to-face with those to whom they wrote, rather than trusting the written document to do its work alone.

Having witnessed the devastating results of the Batman 'treaty', Barak could be forgiven for not entirely trusting the medium of writing. Another reason for presenting written documents in person may have been that he wished to head off anticipated accusations of forgery and outside interference by whites hostile to the Board. In the hand-delivered petitions, spoken and written words worked to authorise each other. The Coranderrk men were not only communicating in two verbal media, they were consciously working within two quite different discursive regimes, one vesting final authority in the written word, the other in the spoken word. As far as the white government authorities were concerned, the physical presence of the signatories verified the authenticity of their petition, and the Coranderrk men knew they had to satisfy the white man's criteria of authenticity. From their own traditional, orally grounded point of view, however, an obverse relation between writing and speech may have pertained: the petitions were perhaps viewed as symbolic objects that functioned in the manner of message-sticks to identify the delegated speakers and authorise their spoken words. In the petitioners' minds the primary locus of their message may have been in their oral utterances. Crucial as they knew documentation was in white political institutions, from their own cultural perspective they may have seen the written versions of their messages as a way of preserving and carrying their words between one context or oral communication and another. To work effectively, the written petition had to be delivered *as though it were an oral message.* Power and meaning did not reside inherently in the alphabetically written document itself, but were activated through the ceremonial process of its face-to-face delivery and re-voicing.

Authors, scribes and owners

So determined was the Board to de-authorise the Coranderrk residents' letters and petitions that on more than one occasion they hired detectives to investigate whether they were forged. There had indeed been a case of forgery at Coranderrk in 1878–79. Following Frederick Strickland taking over as manager from Hugh Halliday in September 1878, Halliday's adult children had lodged accusations against Strickland by forging autograph letters from non-literate and non-existent Aboriginal people.[54] Four years later, in 1882, the Board used these earlier forgeries as a convenient excuse for questioning the authenticity of all letters and petitions lodged by the Coranderrk residents. Aboriginal people who penned written complaints were dismissed as puppets of white agitators. A police detective was again sent onto the reserve to gather handwriting samples from suspected forgers. In the archives, these documents are labelled as exhibit 'A', 'B', and so on. After comparing these samples with the handwriting used in the body of the Coranderrk residents' petitions, they found to their embarrassment that the petitions had in fact been penned by Thomas Dunolly, and that they genuinely expressed the views of all the signatories.

In particular, the Board cast doubts on the authenticity of any signature that took the form of a cross, alleging that these non-literate cross-makers had no notion of what they were signing. In a letter published in the *Argus* in 1882, ten Coranderrk men expressed their concern about the Board's plans to impose strict rules on the station. As can be seen from the following transcription, four of the signatories' names, including William Barak's, were signed with an 'X'.

> To the Editor of *Argus*,—Sir,—We beg of you to put our little Column in you valuable paper please. We have seen and heard that the managers of all the stations and the Central Board to have had a meeting about what to be done, so we have heard that there is going to be very strict rules on the station and those rules will be to much for us, it seems we are all going to be treated like slaves, far as we heard of it,-- We wish to ask those Managor of the station Did we steal anything out of the colony or murdered any one or are we prisoners or convict. We should think we are all free as any white men of the colony. When we all heard of it, it made us very vex it enough to make us all go mad the way they are going to treat us, it

6 ~ Literacy, land and power: the Coranderrk petitions

seem very hard. We all working in peace and quietness and happy pleasing Mr. Goodall, and also showing Mr. Goodall that we could work if we had a good manager expecting our wishes to be carried out, what we have ask for, but it seem it was the opposite way. So we don't know what to do since we heard those strict rules planned out. It made us downhearted. We must all try again and go to the head of the Colony,— We are all your Most Obedient Servants, Wm. Barak (X). Thos. Avoca, Dick Richard (X), Thos. Mickey (X), Lankey (X), Lankey Manto[n], Thos. Dunolly, Robert Wandon, Alfred Morgan, Wm. Parker. Coranderrk, August 29th, 1882.

On the day this letter was published, the BPA Chairman, Captain Page, wrote to the Coranderrk manager, William Goodall, asking him to:

> ...please find out if all these men knew what they were signing. I hope they did not. It is monstrous that the Board can do nothing without that clique remonstrating. It has frequently happened that many of the signers do not know what they have signed. Please enquire into it and let me know.[55]

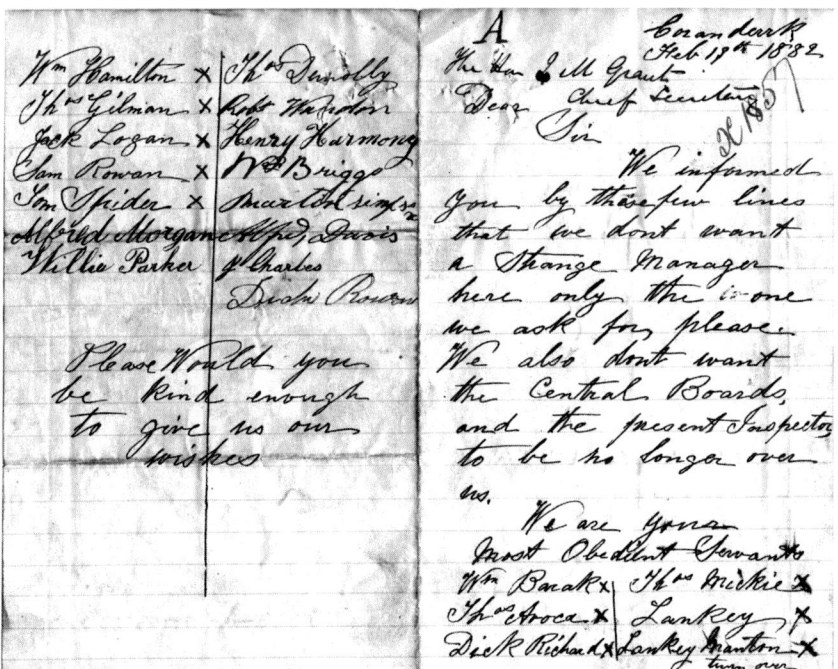

'Exhibit A': a petition from William Barak and others to the Hon. JM Grant, which the Board wrongly suspected of being forged. From the collection of Public Records Office Victoria.

145

Goodall had some difficulty establishing the extent to which the cross-makers knew what they were signing. There was no neat fit between European and Aboriginal views on what it meant to sign a document. The European norm was that the author, the scribe and the owner of a document were one and the same person. In the petitions produced by the Coranderrk community, however, these roles were divided between different individuals. William Barak could not write and had signed with a cross, yet as the local clan-head he was the principal author. His name heads the list of signatories on the vast majority of the Coranderrk petitions because he was head of the clan lawfully responsible for looking after the land where Coranderrk was situated. Thomas Dunolly, one of the lower ranking signatories, served as Barak's scribe. In that role, he penned most of the petitions, including the letter to the *Argus*. Nonetheless, all the signatories, including the cross-makers (all senior men), 'owned' the letter because Barak had presided over its making and was considered the Coranderrk residents' rightful representative in external affairs.[56] Irrespective of whether they knew precisely what was 'in' the letter, as co-signatories they owned it nonetheless. These cross-makers could neither read nor write, yet they endorsed and accepted responsibility for the letter by virtue of their allegiance to Barak, the senior traditional owner of the country in which, and about which, the letter was written.

Thomas Dunolly

Dunolly was a young Djadjawurung man from the Loddon River area, over 100 kilometres north-west of Coranderrk. He had been educated at Edward Stone Parker's school at Mount Franklin. In 1882, Barak explained to ethnologist AW Howitt the traditional basis of Dunolly's role as amanuensis:

> Beside each of the *ngurungaeta* [leader or clan-head] there was a man to whom he gave 'his words'... Beside me are Robert Wandin, Tom Mansfield [Bamfield] who gets 'the word' from me, and Tom Dunolly.[57]

For Barak, the question of who could speak for whom was resolved by referring to traditional law. Robert Wandin was a 'speaker' by virtue of being Barak's nephew. Thomas Bamfield was a 'speaker' because he was head of a Taungurong clan, the Taungurong having been closely allied with the Woiworung since the pioneering days when the people walked from

Acheron and Mohican to Coranderrk with John and Mary Green. Why did Barak 'give his words' to Thomas Dunolly, a young man of mixed descent born outside the Corranderrk area, who had no inherited rights in that part of the country? It appears Barak chose Dunolly because of his proficiency as a writer in English. Barak even told Howitt he intended to name Dunolly as a *ngurungaeta*.[58]

Yet writing skills alone made neither a 'speaker' nor a *ngurungaeta*. Dunolly's abilities as a scribe would certainly have elevated his importance in the community, yet writing also consolidated Barak's traditional authority. Barak's name headed the list of signatories on most of the Coranderrk petitions. His standing in the community was signalled in spatial terms on the page. As principal signatory and author, Barak's authority was reinforced, and the continuing strength of this traditional social hierarchy was demonstrated in 1884 by Dunolly's failed attempt to marshal wide support among Coranderrk residents for the one and only petition he wrote that lacked William Barak's imprimatur.[59]

Judging by the formality of the language, Dunolly's petition, dated 21 January 1884, appears to have been dictated by the Coranderrk manager, William Goodall. It states:

> Ever since Mr Goodall has managed this station our condition has been considerably improved we are better cared for in every respect and were never happier or better looked after in our lives. We do not wish any alterations made and when we have any complaints to make we feel that we are quite capable of doing them our selves and do not wish Mrs Bon or Dr Embling or any one else to make them for us or in any way interfere with our manager or his management[60]

The purpose of the petition was to reject Annie Manton's and Jeannie Rowan's complaints against Goodall's favouring of young men of mixed descent, especially those on Coranderrk's cricket team.[61] Of the twenty-nine signatories on Dunolly's petition, twenty-one were members or relatives of the team; the remaining eight were children from the station dormitory.[62] Needless to say, this petition did not represent the views of Barak and the other senior men.[63] In this instance, the manager and the Board appear to have made a puppet of Dunolly, using his rebuttal of Annie Manton's and Jeannie Rowan's complaints as a means of reprimanding 'interfering whites' such as Mrs Ann Bon and Dr Thomas Embling, long-time friends and supporters of William Barak, Thomas Bamfield and other senior Coranderrk residents.

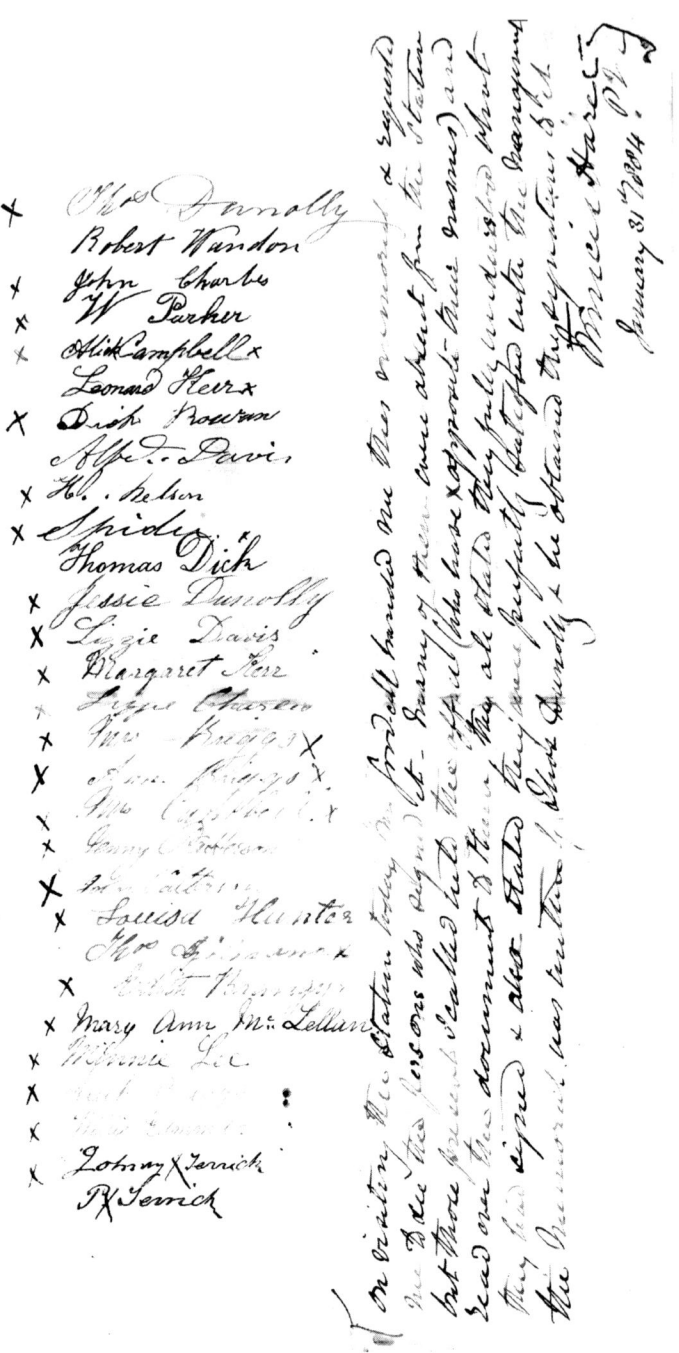

Signatories to Thomas Dunolly's 1884 petition. The note alongside details William Goodall's efforts to legitimise it. From the collection of the National Archives of Australia.

Mrs Bon was an especially aggravating thorn in the side of the Board. She was a philanthropic termagant, and a longstanding friend, advocate and employer of William Bamfield and other Taungurong shearers. She corresponded regularly with Aboriginal people throughout Victoria for many years (but unfortunately, the whereabouts of her papers, if they still exist, remain unknown). For twenty-five years, Mrs Bon criticised the prejudice, ignorance, corruption and negligence of the Board before becoming a Board member herself in 1904, in which role she endeavoured to defend Aboriginal interests for a further thirty-two years, until shortly before her death in 1936 at the age of ninety-eight.

Apart from this one occasion, Thomas Dunolly used his language and literacy skills in a manner that preserved traditional protocols of communication and perpetuated traditional power relations between the generations. In terms of how writing worked in relation to intergenerational politics, the Coranderrk and Flinders Island reserves were diametrically opposite. On Coranderrk, the ink that flowed onto the paper from Dunolly's pen became a medium through which Barak's authority was perpetuated, and the rows of words on the page were lifelines that helped Kulin political traditions remain alive. Although young people had the *technical ability* to write, only Barak, the senior clan-head, had the traditional *authority* to negotiate with outsiders on behalf of the community. The history of Coranderrk shows that when young people acted as scribes for their elders, they made themselves important only in so far as they reasserted the elders' traditional authority in the community. At Coranderrk, writing worked, paradoxically, to consolidate the traditional, orally based gerontocracy. On Flinders Island, however, where no one was on his or her own country, Thomas Brune's and Walter George Arthur's literacy worked to turn the traditional power structure upside-down. In making this comparison, it is crucial to bear in mind, however, that what we know today about the Flinders Island settlement is only that portion of the community's life set down in writing in the Commandant's records.

Tearing the generations apart

In 1886, the *Aboriginal Protection Act 1869* (Vic.) was amended. These amendments effected a dramatic reversal of the 1869 legislation, which had classified people of mixed descent as 'blacks', and had aimed 'to keep the blacks together, and bring them as seldom as possible in contact with other races'.[64] Explaining the rationale for the 1886 amendments, Moravian missionary Reverend FA Hagenauer highlighted the need to separate 'our half-caste friends' from the 'full-bloods' and to raise the former to 'self-reliance' and absorption into the European population.[65] To facilitate this process, new rules were introduced regarding who could be deemed Aboriginal.[66] People of mixed descent born after 1852 were no longer to be counted as Aboriginal. Unless granted special permission, people of mixed racial descent between the ages of thirteen and thirty-four had to leave the reserves and missions and go out to work. This Act caused tremendous suffering and hardship. It tore families apart, and threw people of mixed descent into a hostile white world on the eve of the depression of the 1890s. The 1886 amendments also threatened the intergenerational collaborations on which Aboriginal writing depended.

When different age groups within a society are separated from each other, 'the teaching generation' cannot pass on its knowledge and cultural practices to 'the learning generation'.[67] For mission and reserve communities in late–19th century Victoria, the 1886 Act threatened traditional lines of cultural transmission. But it did something else: it separated the *speaking* generation from the *writing* generation, thus jeopardising a crucial line of communication between Aboriginal communities and white government authorities. As a result of the 1886 Act, the old people, who had authority to speak for the community, were kept apart from the young people who had the technical ability to transform their elders' speech into writing. Those who could lawfully speak for the community had not been taught to write; those who could write were not authorised by traditional law to speak on their own initiative for the community. The power of literacy could, in theory, only be used by breaking with traditional Kulin law. In practice, however, there was some play in the system, and people found ways of sidestepping the rules.

o o o

In 1886, Thomas Dunolly was probably around thirty years of age, but was given permission to stay with his wife at Coranderrk temporarily, although their children were sent out into service. The Board expected him, however, to 'behave properly and particularly not to act as "letter-writer" any more'.[68] When Dunolly continued as Barak's scribe, the Board lured him away from Coranderrk by offering him the opportunity to farm a piece of land on the Victorian side of the Murray River near Cumeroogunga.[69] He returned to Coranderrk in 1905, after the death of his wife, and eventually married Jemima Burns Wandin (1855–1944), the widow of

Robert Wandin. Barak had passed away in 1903, and Thomas Bamfield had died ten years previously.[70] After 1917, when the BPA had voted to close Coranderrk, Dunolly embarked on another writing campaign, which he continued until his death in 1923. The reserve was officially closed in 1924, although Dunolly's widow and a handful of other families were permitted to remain in their cottages on 20 hectares of 'poor land not required by the government'. A number of descendants of the old people were camped outside the reserve fence, but were 'moved on' by the local police constable who acted as Local Guardian.[71]

Mrs Jemima Burns Wandin Dunolly was the last permitted resident of Coranderrk. She passed away in 1944, but members of her family continue to live in the district today. At a conference at La Trobe University's Melbourne campus in July 2002, Joy Murphy Wandin welcomed the international body of conference delegates by handing out sprigs of Eucalypt, an action that forms part of the traditional Tanderrum ceremony through which the Woiworung agreed to share their country with John Batman. Joy Murphy Wandin continues the tradition of assimilating foreign elements into her people's traditional cultural practice.

7

Hidden transcripts at Lake Condah Mission Station

In the winter of 1876 Robert Sutton, a young Kerrupjmara resident of Lake Condah Mission Station in south-western Victoria, took the unprecedented step of issuing a summons against the station superintendent, Reverend John Heinrich Stahle. He charged Reverend Stahle with assault. Shocked and angry, Stahle duly appeared before the local magistrate. The magistrate dismissed the charge, and severely reprimanded Sutton and his two Aboriginal witnesses. He warned them that if they ever told a similar story again they would be put in the lock-up.[1] The magistrate's message was clear: although Stahle had no legal right to use physical violence against the Aboriginal people in his care, should he happen to do so, the victims were not to bring the matter to public attention. By threatening to lock Sutton up for calling violence by its name, the magistrate was not only pushing colonialism's coerciveness out of sight, he was issuing a clear message to Robert Sutton and his people: you must behave as though you are satisfied with your lot, or you will be punished.

What we see in the magistrate's orders is the drawing of a line between what Yale political scientist James C Scott has called 'hidden and public transcripts': that which can safely be said publicly and that which must remain concealed.[2] In *Weapons of the weak* (1985) and *Domination and the arts of resistance* (1990), Scott examines what he describes as 'the fugitive political conduct of subordinate groups': those covert, indirect modes of physical and ideological dissidence that dare not speak their own name.[3] These hidden forms of resistance pose a challenge to some of the key principles developed within Marxist theory. Scott argues that followers of Gramsci, in particular, have tended to overestimate the effectiveness of hegemonic control; that is, domination that is exercised with the consent of the people who are being dominated, the people who have been made to believe that their own subordination is natural, right and inevitable. Scott argues that hegemonic control appears to be effective because researchers have looked only at public transcripts, leaving out of account the hidden transcripts, the concealed records and disguised expressions of anger, resentment and resistance of very powerless peoples.

Traditional understandings of hegemony, Scott argues, have failed to consider two possibilities. The first is that powerless groups, far from being unable to imagine political change:

> ...have learned to clothe their resistance in ritualisms of subordination that serve both to disguise their purposes and to provide them with a ready route of retreat that may soften the consequences of possible failure.[4]

The day-to-day survival of powerless peoples may depend upon their ability to *feign* willing consent to their own subordination. This pretence involves observing the boundary between public and hidden realms of expression. To violate that boundary would be to commit an open act of insubordination, a risk-laden luxury that very vulnerable groups are seldom able to afford, especially if they are living within total institutions such as slave plantations or Aboriginal reserves.

The second possibility overlooked in the Gramscian model of hegemony is that dominant groups have their own reasons for concealing resistance to their ideological leadership. As subaltern peoples tactically hide their contempt for the powerful, the powerful may in turn conceal their knowledge of being defied and despised, and may concomitantly hide the degree to which they must use brute force to preserve their position of dominance.

Powerful and powerless alike are thus bound up in a conspiracy of silence about physical oppression and resistance. Both act out a public performance of control and subordination. This principle is neatly encapsulated in an old Ethiopian proverb: 'When the great lord passes, the wise peasant bows deeply, and silently farts.'[5] Here, not only does the peasant's expression of contempt remain anonymous, inaudible and unprovable, the great lord also preserves his dignity by pretending everything is sweet. The peasant's deep bow and the lord's serene bearing are both part of a performance of hegemonic order. The foul smell is a protest expunged, a protest without trace, as though it never happened.

Scott's approach is not without problems of its own, but it does broach an important question: if hegemonic control is invariably accompanied by at least a threat of physical force, how is it possible to gauge the degree to which a group may have been ideologically manoeuvred into genuine, spontaneous submission, as distinct from being physically coerced or threatened into *a pretence* of submission?

Strategic performances

These questions are especially pertinent in post-colonial contexts, where the Eurocentric biases of Gramsci's 'hegemony', Althusser's 'ideology', and the Frankfurt school's 'false consciousness' are now becoming apparent. As Simon During has pointed out, these theorists assume both dominant and subordinate groups are 'citizens of a single state and work within a shared cultural horizon', which is clearly not the case in colonial contexts.[6] Ranajit Guha also argues that the colonial state is fundamentally different from the metropolitan bourgeois state that established it:

> The difference consisted in the fact that the metropolitan state was hegemonic in character with its claim to dominance based on a power relation in which the moment of persuasion outweighed that of coercion, whereas the colonial state was non-hegemonic with persuasion outweighed by coercion in its structure of dominance... We have defined the character of the colonial state therefore as a *dominance without hegemony*... For there can be no colonialism without coercion, no subjection of an entire people in their own homeland by foreigners without the explicit use of force.[7]

Guha grounds his argument in the history of the Indian subcontinent, which differs in several respects from the history of Australia. In Australia, there were two contrasting orders of persuasion and dominance. In areas where free settlers were numerically and economically dominant, and where colonists did not rely on Indigenous knowledge or modes of production, the Australian colonies resembled the British bourgeois state where hegemony outweighed coercion. Yet Aboriginal people (and convicts in the early years) lived under direct rule and physical coercion on reserves and missions, in prisons and children's homes, and on pastoral properties outside the metropolitan regions. In these institutions, coercion clearly outweighed ideological controls.

On Aboriginal reserves and missions, civil and state spheres were rolled up into a single institution where ideological apparatuses such as school and church were combined with physically coercive state apparatuses such as the gaol, the children's dormitory and the forced labour camp. Many factors militated against overt Aboriginal protests. Oppressive as they were, the reserves were viewed by many Aboriginal people as their only place of asylum and/or their only option for staying on or near their traditional country. Individuals who complained could be exiled to distant reserves far from kin and homeland. A sustained chorus of Aboriginal complaints could lead to closure of the reserve altogether, and thus the loss of the whole group's traditional or adopted home.

Reserve superintendents, too, had their reasons for pretending Aboriginal residents were happy. The reserves were funded by government and church money on the understanding that they provided protection, schooling, religious teaching and other forms of 'improvement' for Aborigines. At Lake Condah, Reverend Stahle's salary was paid by the Board for the Protection of Aborigines, which was in turn accountable to the government and to taxpayers. Lake Condah Mission Station also received some funding from the Church of England Mission Society. To protect his own position, Stahle had to pretend his charges were enjoying his protection. Aborigines and mission superintendents thus entered into a strange collusion: each had their own very different reasons for engaging in a public performance of hegemonic order.

In Victoria during the second half of the 19th century, reserve and mission managers and other government officials generated public transcripts typical of those produced by powerful groups. They were discursive performances that affirmed, naturalised and justified their power over Aboriginal people. For public view, these administrators painted flattering portraits of themselves and the reserve system, portraits that concealed or euphemised 'the dirty linen' of the white man's rule.[8]

These pretences of benevolence made it possible for Aboriginal people, in their own public transcripts, to make certain kinds of modest claims on their self-proclaimed benefactors. Without raising fears of sedition, or fundamentally challenging protectionist policy, Aboriginal people could request additional food rations, better housing and other incremental improvements to their living conditions. Much of their correspondence with government officials, and their testimony in official inquiries, was of this non-threatening kind. As such it typifies the public transcripts of powerless peoples. For the most part, the public transcripts of Aboriginal reserve and mission residents were discursive performances of subordination, not manifestations of ideological or cultural assimilation. Complaints and requests were usually made politely and deferentially, and were signed with the conventional formula 'your most obedient and humble servant' — a poignant form of words given that they were forced to live, quite literally, in servitude.

This formulaic, deferential language worked to camouflage bitter feelings that could not be expressed openly. The camouflage had its cost, however: the Aborigines' deference appeared to hail white officials as superiors, and to ratify white domination. Yet knowing they were likely to be punished for anything resembling open rebellion, the majority of Aboriginal residents on the Victorian reserves stifled overt expressions of anger and resentment. Sometimes for years at a time they refrained from all but the most covert and oblique modes of resistance. To do otherwise was to risk being beaten, deprived of food and clothing, exiled to distant stations, and separated from their families.

From time to time, however, these performances of paternalistic care and submissive acquiescence would suddenly collapse into open expressions of mutual contempt and hostility. While anger and racial hatred periodically disrupted colonialist public discourses of protection and improvement, Aboriginal people likewise periodically dropped all pretence of gratitude, obedience and equanimity, and protested against actions of individual reserve managers and/or oppressive policies formulated by the Protection Board.

Doublespeak

If dissent is kept *entirely* hidden within a tightly-knit group, it is obviously not registered in the written archive, nor is it guaranteed to be preserved in oral memory. One can therefore only guess at the extent of Aboriginal people's hidden expressions of dissatisfaction. Given the elusiveness of this evidence of concealed unrest, we might question how anyone knows that these expressions of anger and resentment against whites circulated on a continuous basis at Lake Condah. Why, for instance, are public protestations such as Robert Sutton's legal action against Stahle viewed as signs of *chronic* resentment and resistance, rather than as mere flashes of anger in an otherwise peaceful existence?

The answer is twofold. First, open dissent does not spring out of nowhere. Robert Sutton's legal action against Stahle could not have been mounted without some degree of preliminary discussion, advice and preparation.

Charging Stahle with assault was thus the culmination of a series of actions that remained hidden until the moment Stahle received the official summons to appear in court.

Second, between times of open protest, the public transcripts of subaltern groups often contain coded, sanitised, oblique expressions of resistance.[9] These veiled protests may remain entirely hidden from the dominant group, yet as a form of doublespeak, they express subaltern people's chronic dissatisfaction.

In September 1877 on Lake Condah Mission, for example, Stahle thrashed two fifteen-year-old boys for alleged sexual misconduct with two teenage girls. One of the boys was John Sutton Jr, younger brother of Robert Sutton, who had taken Stahle to court for assault the previous year. The other boy was Henry Albert, a member of the Green family who were closely connected to the Suttons. As part of their punishment, Stahle made the boys write letters of confession and apology to Captain Page, Secretary of the Board for the Protection of Aborigines. Stahle's aim was to shame the boys by forcing them to expose their actions to official scrutiny, just as Robert Sutton had exposed Stahle's actions in court fifteen months previously. Yet the boys' letters are also readable, against the grain imposed by Stahle, as another allegation of assault. John Sutton Jr in particular says almost as much about Stahle's punishment of the boys as about the boys' actions with the girls. His letter to Page may be read as a complaint disguised as an apology. He describes how Stahle:

> …called us up to his house and gave each one of us a good whipping and after that sent us to work in the rain, and after we were done working he gave us another good beating. This is all what done to us.[10]

The final words of this letter — 'this is all what done to us' — suggest that Stahle's 'good beatings' were felt as a violation by John Sutton Jr. Given his brother's earlier protest against Stahle's use of violence, could John Sutton Jr possibly have believed Stahle's whippings were unequivocally just and good? It is reasonable to assume that, like most families dealing with a recurrent problem, the Suttons would have discussed Stahle's behaviour among themselves and their friends. The boys' accounts of being beaten by Stahle may therefore be read as oblique offshoots of a hidden transcript that had existed at least since the lead-up to Robert Sutton's court case. These letters of confession put Stahle's violent propensities once again on the public record, yet unlike Robert Sutton's charge, the boys' accusations were made at Stahle's command, and were so camouflaged and ambiguous that no one (including myself) could see them unequivocally as a mode of protest.

The 'grateful Aborigines' petition

Subordinate groups may signify acceptance of their position not only by remaining silent, but by actively proclaiming themselves to be satisfied with their lot. Why can't subaltern peoples' expressions of contentment be taken at face value and read as evidence that potential unrest has been hegemonically controlled? One gauge of a people's power is their ability to speak for themselves, *and be seen to do so*. When Aboriginal people protested against the degrading conditions in which they were forced to live, the authorities often attributed their protests to the influence of 'interfering whites'. When they expressed their gratitude and contentment, however, the authorities insisted they were speaking freely and spontaneously for themselves. Overt expressions of contentment cannot be taken at face value, not only because powerless people risk punishment if they show dissent, but because their voices may either be drowned out, mediated or ventriloquised in radically distorting ways.

In September 1877, the same month John Sutton Jr and Henry Albert wrote their letters of confession, Stahle recommended to Page that the boys' fathers, John Sutton Sr and Thomas Green, along with Billy Gorrie and Jackie Fraser, be refused work certificates. He alleged that while away shearing the previous year they had spent their money on alcohol and 'came back to the Mission Station in rags'.[11] In protest against Stahle's unwillingness to let them go, the men refused to work on the station. Stahle stopped their food and tobacco rations but found the situation so trying that he earnestly requested the Board 'to take steps in the matter'.[12]

Stahle took steps of his own to show the Board how disruptive Sutton's group was. He wrote a petition to Captain Page on behalf of nineteen Aboriginal men who, he asserted:

> ...requested me on their own account to write for them to the Board for the Protection of the Aborigines informing them that they are dissatisfied with the conduct of the men
> Tommy Green
> John Sutton
> Billy Gorrie

and their boys
Henry Albert &
John Sutton Jr.

I asked the men why they wished me to forward their names and they said that they are desirous to express their thankfulness for that which is done for them by the Board and also to tell them that it is their desire to go on quietly & steadily to labour on their own home. [A]s the Aborigines have requested me to forward their names along with the expression of the thankfulness to the Board — I considered it my duty to comply with their wish. I have the honor to be

Sir
Your obedient Servant
J. H. Stahle[13]

After Stahle's signature, the petition lists the names of nineteen men, five of whom sign for themselves. The remaining fourteen names, all with identical crosses beside them, are added in Stahle's writing.

Taking this petition at face value, we might read it as proof of the power of hegemony, a confirmation that the majority of Aboriginal residents at Condah consented willingly to their lot. A second possibility is that the document may have originated in the signatories' wish to maintain *a pretence* of contentment. Stahle had cut off the food and tobacco rations of the 'troublemakers', and was refusing their requests for certificates to obtain employment outside the station. The nineteen petitioners who declared themselves dissatisfied with the conduct of Sutton's group and satisfied with Stahle's management may well have being trying to shield themselves and their families from any blanket disciplinary measures the Board might have been considering. A third possibility is that since fourteen of the nineteen signatures and crosses were in Stahle's writing, they might have been made without the signatories' knowledge and informed consent. If such was the case, Stahle may be seen as literally writing the public transcript of the Aboriginal signatories, ventriloquising the Lake Condah majority's enunciation of consent to their own subordination.

The 'Aboriginals' Narrative' — a suppressed and hidden transcript

At Lake Condah there is evidence to suggest that John Sutton Sr and his group harboured resentments against Stahle and the Protection Board on an ongoing basis over many years. Their protests alternated between being suppressed from above and deliberately concealed from below. Such was the case with a document known as 'The Aboriginals' Narrative', which contains the story of its own difficult emergence from the hidden to the public realm.

In March 1878, something happened at Lake Condah that angered John Sutton Sr and other senior men on the reserve. Stahle failed to look into the men's allegations that two of the younger men had engaged in sexual misconduct with two young women. His inaction appeared both to defy Christian morality and to slight one of the senior men's traditional responsibilities as uncle to the young women involved. Remembering perhaps how their own sons had been physically beaten for sexual misconduct, John Sutton Sr and Thomas Green were surprised and angered that Stahle made no move even to reprimand the alleged culprits. When the men were gathered for ration distribution — a humiliating weekly display of their impotence and Stahle's power — tensions escalated to such a degree that Stahle abruptly shut the ration store and sent for the police. Sutton and his group tried on several occasions to notify Board and church officials of their grievances against Stahle. Their complaints were either blocked or explained away by Stahle. Yet these grievances continued to circulate in the Condah community, where they were a powerful focus of resentment against Stahle.

John Sutton Sr and the other men did not forget what had happened; in fact, Stahle's attempts to suppress the men's story helped keep it alive. In May 1880, twenty-six months after the incident occurred, the men tried to make their complaints known to a visiting church official, but he was hurried away by Stahle. Two months later, John Sutton and his group enlisted the aid of a local white man, Mr F Elmore, who wrote down their complaints in detail. The document is headed 'Aboriginals' Narrative' and consists of four closely written foolscap pages. It is signed with crosses by John Sutton, Thomas Green and Billy Gorrie. The men kept this document to themselves for a further four months until November 1880, when they sent it to Captain Page, to whom Stahle was accountable. In total, this set of Aboriginal complaints remained hidden for thirty-two months, before finally being exposed to official scrutiny.

Whenever John Sutton Sr and his group enlisted outside help to put their grievances on paper, Stahle ascribed their recalcitrance to 'white interference'. Stahle's position in the middle of a bureaucratic hierarchy was a difficult one. On the station, he could behave autocratically; in relation to his Aboriginal charges, he wielded almost absolute power. On the station he expressed hostile attitudes towards those he governed, attitudes which a more self-disciplined manager might have kept hidden. Officially, Stahle's role was to look after the Condah people's day-to-day welfare. Yet, since his abrasive managerial style could be construed as a sign of unfitness for the job, he would not have wanted everything that went on at Lake Condah to be known outside the station. Powerful as he was in the closed Condah setting, he occupied a relatively powerless position in the government and church hierarchies. In official communications with superiors, therefore, we often see him choosing his words carefully, and attempting (not always successfully) to respect professionally appropriate principles of discretion. Stahle, in effect, had two sets of public and hidden transcripts, the boundaries of which shifted depending on whether he was speaking up the power hierarchy to those who paid his salary, or speaking down to the Aboriginal people whose lives he controlled. What he could say openly to each audience had often to be hidden from the other.

The problem Stahle faced was keeping these two audiences from speaking to each other. He was safe from criticism from above as long as knowledge of his actions and attitudes remained confined to the station, or was conveyed to the Board solely by himself in carefully chosen words. Such was not the case, however. As the younger Condah residents learned to read and write, and as the older ones gained support from local whites willing to write on their behalf, Stahle found it increasingly difficult to control the flow of information into and out of Condah station. The technology of writing enabled the Condah Aborigines to communicate with the outside world without Stahle's help and without his knowledge. Protests or requests that they might have been too afraid to make to his face could now be made in writing, behind his back, to his superiors.

Supporters of John Sutton Sr and his group, such as Mr Elmore and local Justice of the Peace JN McLeod, undermined Stahle's power by breaking his monopoly over the channels of communication between the Aboriginal residents and the Board. Through such intermediaries, the Condah residents could bypass Stahle and convey their grivances directly to his superiors. When Captain Page received the 'Aboriginals' Narrative' in early November 1880, he forwarded it to Stahle with a request to 'please explain'. Stahle duly explained by labelling his accusers liars, profligates and rebels. In his letter to Page of 6 November 1880, he boldly asserted that 'All the statements made in the "Aboriginal Narrative" are false and unfounded,' but had to add lamely '(with the exception of those to which I have refered as being correct in my letter)'.[14]

Stahle was clearly rattled. Later the same day he wrote a second letter to Page refuting the latter's remark that Mr Elmore 'seems a nice old gentleman'. Furious at Elmore's involvement, Stahle asked 'whether proceedings could not be taken against a man like Elmore for forwarding such statements to those in authority without having made any enquiry into the truth of them'? Fearing his credibility was shaky, Stahle sent Page a collection of favourable remarks culled from the Lake Condah visitors' book, together with 'a few lines from Miss Gregory [the school teacher] testifying to the correctness of my statements'.[15] One wonders whether, under the circumstances, Miss Gregory could possibly have declined to corroborate Stahle's word.

Dangerous wanderers

The boundary between hidden and public transcripts is a zone of constant struggle. By limiting what can be *said* publicly (as distinct from what is publicly known or thought), dominant elites lock up much of the latent power of subordinate groups' knowledge. They can seldom entirely prevent counter-hegemonic discourses from coming into being, but by keeping expressions of dissent from being freely transmitted they can stop them spreading between subordinate groups and being translated into large-scale, coordinated political actions. The restrictions placed on Aboriginal people's movements under the reserve system meant that they had limited opportunities to transmit their hidden transcripts beyond their own reserve boundaries. The more cut off each reserve was both from non-Aboriginal society and from other Aboriginal reserves, the narrower the social reach of the Aboriginal residents' hidden transcripts.

Yet no reserve could be hermetically sealed. People wrote letters to relations and friends on other reserves, and sometimes to non-Aboriginal friends.[16] At Lake Condah, Stahle is known to have intercepted some of these letters. Occasionally people gained permission to visit relations on other reserves, and they maintained contact with Aboriginal people who lived in the districts around the reserve. Another channel of communication was the 'troublemakers' who were banished periodically to distant reserves by Orders in Council. Also influential were the 'dangerous wanderers' who slipped through the net of the reserve system altogether, and carried hidden expressions of dissatisfaction between reserves.

When hidden transcripts are transmitted for the first time between isolated cells of an oppressed group, members of that group can recognise themselves *as a group* for the first time. They learn the extent to which their political circumstances and living conditions are shared, and see the degree to which their feelings of anger, humiliation and frustration are held in common. Without adopting an essentialist approach to Aboriginal people or any other group, it is reasonable to suggest that those who live within the same structure or system of domination are likely to have a common body of shared experiences, patterns of behaviour, speech habits, ideas and feelings about their circumstances. In so far as their conditions of subordination have been similar, it is valid to assume there will be some family resemblance between their hidden transcripts (as well as between their public ones).[17] By carrying hidden transcripts between different reserve communities, itinerants could ignite a new, politically formidable sense of social cohesion among previously atomised groups. The hidden transcripts of different groups could thus coalesce and consolidate into more fully developed counter-hegemonic public transcripts, which in turn supported open expressions of insubordination. For these reasons, Stahle and other reserve officials regarded itinerant and unconfined Aboriginal people as a potentially serious political threat.

One such 'dangerous wanderer' was James Scott, who arrived at Lake Condah Mission Station in early November 1880.[18] At that time, the 'Aboriginals' Narrative' had sat dormant for four months in the hands of John Sutton and his group. It is surely not coincidental that just after James Scott's arrival at Lake Condah, the damning narrative was sent to Captain Page. Because Scott did not live on the reserve, he may have been more willing than the permanent residents to risk airing his inflammatory views within Stahle's sight and hearing. Scott could leave the reserve at will. Unlike the permanent residents, he did not have to bear the brunt of the superintendent's acrimony in the long term. His brazenness may well have stimulated others into showing their resentment more openly. As well as being an influential speaker, Scott may have exerted considerable political influence as an audience — an outspoken outsider in whose eyes the men wished to appear similarly forthright. The outspokenness of this 'dangerous wanderer' may have triggered the Condah men's decision to unhide their hidden transcript, take their document out of mothballs, and make their grievances known at last to Captain Page.

Stahle seems not to have connected Scott's arrival at Lake Condah with the men's decision to send their complaints to Captain Page. However, within days of having explained his side of the story to the Board, he wrote again to Page complaining about Scott's disruptive influence:

> I am quite alarmed about the half-caste James Scott. Whenever & wherever he sees a few men sitting together he joins them & commences his yarns [about] what ought what could & should be done with regard to this place & that they should not rest until the Government would give them their rights.
>
> It is a matter of the greatest regret to see men who have been for over two years contented happy & cheerful go about with the same sulky & discontented look as some of them have done some two years ago.[19]

Stahle believed — or wanted Page to believe — that prior to Scott's arrival, the Condah men had been 'contented happy & cheerful': hegemonically controlled, in other words. He believed — or wanted Page to believe — that Scott had caused the men's discontent, yet he half understood that there was some connection between their present 'sulky and discontented' look and the troubles of two years ago, recounted in the 'Aboriginals' Narrative'. Stahle seems oblivious to the possibility that the men had been carrying grudges from years ago, or that their cheerful countenances were masks worn to avoid aggravating him. He appears to have thought their anger and resentment had been quelled in 1878. In fact, the documentary evidence suggests the men's bitter feelings had merely gone underground, and that as well as introducing new information and ideas to Lake Condah, Scott's rebellious talk was acting as a catalyst to bring the Condah men's *existing* hidden transcript into public view.

On the same day as Stahle informed Page of Scott's activities, his wife, Mary Stahle, wrote to Page without her husband's knowledge, telling him how serious the unrest at Lake Condah was becoming:

> Scott [is] telling the blacks how badly they are treated — and how they should not rest until their wishes are fulfilled, until they become their own masters, not to be led like children any more.[20]

Mary Stahle's covert communication with her husband's superior reveals the presence of a new Aboriginal public discourse on the reserve. James Scott was not agitating merely for additional food or tobacco rations, nor was he urging the men to repudiate Stahle for failing to live up to the ideals that allegedly validated colonial domination. He was instead renouncing the hegemonic public discourse of protectionism altogether. Echoing the talk of abolitionists and freedom fighters, Scott was taking the far more radical step of repudiating the very principle through which Aboriginal peoples' lives were controlled by others.

Itinerants such as Scott could potentially electrify an entire region by carrying previously isolated hidden transcripts from place to place. The Protection Board, already contending with complaints from Aboriginal residents of Coranderrk, Ramahyuck and Ebenezer reserves, appear to have seen James Scott's activities at Lake Condah as a serious political threat. They acted swiftly to isolate him and curtail the effects of his visit. They ordered Scott to leave the reserve and called in the police to confiscate the Aboriginal men's firearms. They also transferred John Sutton to Ebenezer Mission Station, threatened to expel those who had written letters of complaint, and instigated regular fortnightly police visits to the station.[21] Again, state authorities were drawing a firm line between what could be said publicly and what must be hidden.

Women's voices

The early Lake Condah residents were a relatively homogenous cultural group; almost all were members of the Kerrupjmara people.[22] As time went by, however, Stahle exploited and intensified factional divisions in the community, to the point where John Sutton and his group accused the manager of treating 'the blacks like dogs while the half-castes are told to come in'.[23] Over time, the make-up of the Condah community was changing as a result of sexual unions between white men and Aboriginal women. How did Aboriginal women view their political position? What kinds of public and hidden transcripts did they generate as individuals, as members of families, and as constituents of the Condah community as a whole?

While Stahle clashed with Aboriginal men over rations, work certificates and the right to control sexual conduct on the station, he also endeavoured to direct the lives of Aboriginal women in matters to do with their sexual relations, the custody of their children and their place of abode. With one notable exception, the Condah women wrote to government authorities about themselves and their immediate families, rather than as representatives of larger groupings.[24] Some women's voices are elusive, refracted several times through the writings of other people, including Stahle, who usually insisted the women were happy and contented at Lake Condah.

While many women used highly mediated and meek modes of address, Maggie Mobourne was an outspoken female warrior. She detested Stahle, his family and the Condah schoolteacher, and when angry she expressed her contempt openly. From the late 1890s onwards, Maggie Mobourne, acting both alone and with her husband, Ernest Mobourne, challenged Stahle on a range of issues.[25] The records show, however, that the Mobournes alternated strategically between overt and covert resistance, sometimes protesting bluntly and directly but at other times pleading abjectly or refracting their complaints through the voices of high-ranking government officials. Clearly, the Mobournes played a crucial role in an *ongoing* subculture of resistance, yet they adjusted their tactics as circumstances changed from one moment to the next.

In early 1900, Maggie launched three trenchant public blasts against Stahle. After he reproved her for her husband's and children's absence from prayers, Maggie's anger boiled over and could not be hidden any more. In a letter to the *Hamilton Spectator*, she accused Stahle of being a treacherous hypocrite who:

> ...doesn't practice what he preaches. He's not a fit person for the position he holds but is dragging us down to hell rather than helping us to rise. What I say here is true and I can take a solemn oath before God and before any Christian people as I have proofs for his falsehoods. We who know his ways often wonder he is not punished by the Master he professes to serve.[26]

So incensed was Maggie that she also wrote two petitions, one to parliamentarian DN McLeod who was Vice-Chairman of the BPA, and the other to a local Justice of the Peace, Mr Duffit. The former petition is worth examining in detail:

> Mission Station
> Lake Condah
> February 27th, 1900
> D.N. McLeod, Esqre. M.L.A.
> and Vice Chairman
>
> Sir
> Having returned in September last to the Mission Station with the object of endeavouring to live in peace and in accordance with the

rules of the Station I am sorry to inform you that Mr Stahle seems to take every opportunity to find fault with us, and it seems as if our efforts to live peacefully are of no use here because Mr Stahle seems determined to annoy us and to take every opportunity of reporting us to the Board for insubordination.

On the 18th inst. Mr Stahle spoke in a threatening manner to me and stopped our rations, which he denies and I say that <u>he is a liar and has always been</u>. (See full particulars in another letter). <u>and he doesn't treat us justly</u>. I would ask you to get up an impartial Board of Inquiry to investigate and see fairness and justice.

I am prepared to substantiate my statements to be true and also can get the majority here as witnesses to prove that we have been living peacefully.

I am

Sir

Yours respectfully

Maggie Mobourne

(We the following corroborate the statements given above)
Signatures

Ernest Mobourne	Isaac McDuff his X mark	
Robert Turner	his X mark	Bella Mobourne
Thomas Willis	his X mark	
James Cortwine	his X mark	
Jenny Green	her X mark	
Albert White		
Fred Carmichael		
Louisa White	her X mark	
Edward P. Cortwine[27]		

This petition seems at first glance like a triumphant outburst of previously silenced voices, a loud and strident protest against Aboriginal oppression. However, the politics of this document are more complex than they might initially appear. First, only a small proportion of the Condah community signed Maggie's two petitions. Eleven people (at least three of them close relations)[28] added their names to the petition to DN McLeod; ten signed the petition to Mr Duffit. Against these small numbers we might compare Ernest Mobourne's politely worded petition of 2 July 1907, to which no less that forty-eight people appended their names. Although Maggie's petitions said what others may have wanted to say, it appears many of the

Mission Station
Lake Condah
February 27th 1900

D. N. McLeod, Esqre. M. L. A.
and Vice Chairman

Sir

Having returned in September last to the Mission Station with the object of endeavouring to live in peace and in accordance with the rules of the Station. I am sorry to inform you that Mr Stähle seems to take every opportunity to find fault with us, and it seems as if our efforts to live peaceably are of no use here because Mr Stähle seems determined to annoy us and to take every opportunity of reporting us to the Board for insubordination.

On the 19th inst Mr Stähle spoke in a threatening manner to me and stopped our rations, which he denies and I say that he is a liar and has always been (See full particulars in another letter) and he doesn't treat us justly. I would ask you to get up an impartial Board of Inquiry to investigate and see fairness and justice.
I am prepared to substantiate my statements to be true and also can get the majority here as witnesses to prove that we have been living peacefully.

I am
Sir
Yours respectfully
Maggie Mobourne

(We the following corroborate the statements given above)
Signatures

Ernest Mobourn   Isaac McDuff   his × mark
Robert Turner   his × mark   Bella Mobourn
Thomas Willes   his × mark
James Cortwine   his × mark
Jenny Green   her × mark
Albert White
Fred Carmichael
Louisa White   her × mark
Edward Cortwine

Maggie Mobourne's letter to DN McLeod, which later became a petition but with limited support. From the collection of the National Archives of Australia.

Condah residents were too afraid to join Maggie in saying the unsayable about Stahle.

The second issue complicating the politics of Maggie's petition to DN McLeod is that it did not begin as a petition at all, but rather as an individual letter. Powerless groups may not only hide their rebellious ideas and feelings, they may also conceal the extent to which they constitute themselves as a group. Maggie wrote the body of her petition to DN McLeod in the first person singular, beginning with '*I* am sorry to inform you that' and ending with '*I* am, Sir, Yours respectfully, Maggie Mobourne'.[29] When she described the wrongs committed against 'us', she meant against Ernest and herself. Initially, Maggie spoke for herself and her family, not as a spokesperson for her community. Nonetheless, as soon as she obtained wider corroboration of her charges against Stahle, her letter was effectively transformed into a petition. In contrast to other petitions,[30] the signatures on Maggie's document were appended as a postscript. After her signature, a note was added, saying: 'We the following corroborate the statements given above,' followed by eleven signatures. The most radical and daring aspect of Maggie's letter is perhaps not its content or vituperative tone, but the fact that it becomes a site upon which (a few) Aboriginal protesters constitute themselves momentarily as a visible political group.

A third significant element in Maggie's petition (and in her letter to the *Hamilton Spectator*) is that, for all her sharp criticisms of Stahle, Maggie's claims did not amount to an attack on protectionism or Christianity per se. She fired her shots at Stahle's character — his hypocrisy, his cruelty, his lies — but did not lash out against the *systematically* oppressive effects of colonialist ideology as institutionalised through the reserve system and the church. Strategically or otherwise, she did not denounce Christian principles but invoked them as a source of standards Stahle was failing to live up to. She did not denounce protectionism as such, but accused Stahle of failing in his duty of protective care. Maggie clearly did not pretend to consent to her own subordination, but nor did her letter and petition articulate the more radical emancipatory politics espoused by the 'dangerous wanderer' James Scott. Although Maggie's petition openly expressed anger and frustration, it neither advocated an anti-colonialist ideology, nor proposed an anti-colonial program of political action. Even so, Maggie and Ernest were banished to Lake Tyers.

The Mobournes were permitted to return to Condah in 1903, but were soon involved in conflicts with Stahle over Maggie's elopement with Dunmore widower Henry Albert, and over Ernest's refusal to work or to sit through Stahle's excruciatingly dull church services. In the midst of these conflicts, the Protection Board announced plans to close Lake Condah. In his best copperplate writing, Ernest penned a petition to the Cabinet on behalf of elder Peter Hewitt and forty-seven other Condah signatories, requesting that the mission station not be closed down. This petition is a public transcript, a humble supplication in which 'the Aborigines residing at Lake Condah would earnestly pray the Cabinet to reconsider their decision and allow us to remain at Lake Condah.'[31] Ernest supports his request by offering an idyllic narrative of the mission's history in which Stahle is characterised as a kind friend and benefactor:

> Our fathers…with their loved missionary Mr Stahle whose labours have blessed and who is still with us then put their minds and hands together fencing in the whole reserve…and have built stone and wooden cottages for our use, a fine church wherein to worship God, a Mission House for their much loved missionary…[32]

In contrast to Maggie's angry letter/petition of February 1900, Ernest's document is signed by forty-eight people: the whole Lake Condah community. It was safe to sign Ernest's petition because its humble, supplicatory tone reassured government and Board authorities that they were in control. There was one rupture, however, in this communal performance of subordination: the order of petitioners' names suggests that, despite Stahle's attempts over a period of three decades to eradicate the Condah residents' 'primitive ways', the community's traditional structure of authority had not been destroyed. Although Ernest Mobourne penned the petition, his name does not head the list of signatories. This honour is reserved for senior law-man and clever-man Peter Hewitt, whose name is immediately followed by the names of other senior men, below which in turn appear the names of the other residents. As was the case with the Coranderrk petitions, the order of names may be read as a coded assertion of cultural and political autonomy, a sign of defiance that probably remained invisible to the authorities. Ernest's petition managed both to honour the Condah elders and to conform to white epistolary decorum. The petition achieved its objective. Lake Condah was not closed down.

7 ~ Hidden transcripts at Lake Condah Mission Station

> A 5318
> Lake Condah
> Mission Station
> July 2nd 1907.
>
> To The Hon Members of the Cabinet
> Gentlemen
>
> We the undersigned Aboriginese of the Lake Condah Mission Station noticed in the columns of the Portland Guardian and Argus with very great sorrow that the Cabinet had decided to dissolve two of the Mission Stations in Victoria, one of these being Lake Condah on which we reside, and the other Lake Wellington. We the Aboriginese residing at Lake Condah would earnestly pray the Cabinet to reconsider their decision and allow us to remain at Lake Condah. Our fathers were brought here some forty years back to form a mission station here and were then informed that if they built houses, fenced in and cleared the reserve, that the Mission Station would remain theirs for them and their childrens children. They with their loved missionary Mr Stähle whose labours have blessed and who is still with us, then put their minds and hands together fencing in the whole reserve with a good substantial fence, clearing it and have built stone and wooden cottages for our use, a fine church wherein to worship God, a Mission House for their much loved missionary a schoolroom wherein our children are taught to read and write. It would be very heart breaking to us if after

Ernest Mobourne's petition to Cabinet on 2 July 1907 adopted a suppliant tone but preserved the Lake Condah residents' traditional structure of authority. From the collection of Public Records Office Victoria.

these promises by the then Government, the present Government would still retain their decision, and transfer us to another station. Our fathers have passed peacefully to rest and we would wish to live and work and be buried beside them. Praying that you will grant us our request.

We are.
Gentlemen
yours respectfully.
The Aboriginese of Lake Condah

Peter Hewitt his mark	Lizzie Carter
William Carter Senior his mark	Fanny McDougall
James Cortwine his mark	Joseph McDougall
Isaac McDuff his mark	Louie McDougall
Henry Rose his mark	Ethel Mobourne
Jocas Johnson his mark	Elizabeth Carmichael
John Dutton his mark	Leslie Johnson
Edward Cortwine	Fanny Carter
Albert White	Anthony Johnson
Daniel James Cortwine	Ernest Mobourne
Annie Turner	Annie Harrison
Donald Turner her mark	James Young
Maria McDuff her mark	Jennie Green
Agnes Carter	Lawrence Young
Louisa Carter	William Carter
Louisa White her mark	Sam Mobourn
Janet Turner her mark	Flora Stewart
Dinah White	Jackson Stewart his mark
Catherine Cortwine	Hughie Cortwine
Bessie Johnson	Henry Dawson his mark
Maggie Mobourne	Ellen McCallum
Jessie Carter	Eddie Mullett
Wallace Carter	Elsie Florence Evelyn White
John Mullett	

Articulating silences

In this account of Lake Condah Mission Station, which is based mainly on Protection Board documents in the National Archives of Australia, I have been able to examine hidden transcripts only to the extent that they have *not* remained entirely hidden. This kind of archival research tries to read a silence by looking at its shadow, or its moments of breaking, in the written archive. Leela Gandhi has noted the importance of 'attending more carefully to the silence of the archive' and interrogating the 'construction of history as certain knowledge'.[33] For me, it has sometimes been necessary to speculate on the basis of scant evidence, to acknowledge that archival silences can be inscrutable, and to remember that, like Stahle, I may be ventriloquising Aboriginal voices from a non-Indigenous position of power and privilege. Even with contextual knowledge, it is not always possible to determine whether absences and silences in the archive point to the presence of non-players, or tacitly express the equanimity of colonised subjects, or are the shadow cast by a hidden culture of resistance.

Elaborating on Ranajit Guha's statement that 'there can be no colonialism without coercion,' one might say that different (post?) colonial cultures, and indeed different regions and classes within nations, have been shaped by different varieties and blends of coercive and hegemonic control.[34] At Lake Condah Mission Station, where civil and state apparatuses operated together, there is less evidence of hegemonic control than of real or threatened coercion, and less evidence of spontaneous consent to oppression than of feigned consent to avoid punishment. Like many other missions and reserves, Lake Condah was a place where, as Guha might have predicted, physical coercion clearly outweighed hegemonic control.

What role, then, did hegemony play in the oppression of Aboriginal people at Lake Condah and across the mission and reserve system in Australia? Broadly speaking, I would suggest that while Aboriginal people were coerced into submission, most non-Aboriginal people were persuaded by hegemonic racist and colonialist discourses that such coercion was natural, just or a matter of necessary discipline. Until the late 1970s, Australian school children were taught that Aboriginal peoples offered no significant resistance to white settlers, and that those who lived on missions and reserves felt themselves fortunate to be protected and culturally uplifted.

This hegemonic fiction of Aboriginal consent to the 'civilising mission' was central to settler ideology. It blinded the majority of non-Aboriginal people to the devastating consequences of dispossession, cultural suppression, institutionalised violence, the breaking up of families, and other 'dirty linen' of the white man's rule. In Australia, hegemonic discourses worked primarily to elicit the consent of the silent urban settler majority to the systematic oppression of fellow human beings. Hegemony did its work less on Aboriginal minds than on the minds of those who wanted to reap the benefits of colonialism without ever having to admit they were morally culpable or personally implicated in Aboriginal peoples' suffering. Ideas about hegemony were thus themselves hegemonic. The myth that Aboriginal people were hegemonically controlled was itself a hegemonic force that helped — and is still helping — large sections of the non-Indigenous Australian population see themselves as innocent non-players in an ongoing process of racial oppression.

8

Early writings by Aboriginal women

Relations of domination and subordination exist within, as well as between, colonising and colonised societies. As each society's internal political structure shapes its external relations, so its dealings with outsiders affect its internal political dynamics. The prevailing assumption in colonial Australia was that governing Aboriginal people was men's business. Colonial officials were invariably male, and on the rare occasions when women intervened their efforts were seldom appreciated. When Scottish philanthropist Ann Bon sided with the Coranderrk residents against the Protection Board, for example, this august body of men dismissed her as an interfering woman who 'forgets her sex and enters the arena of public life and dons the unmentionables and the kilt'.[1] The Board's prevailing assumption that women had no legitimate role in public life meant that *anything* Ann Bon did could be dismissed as mere female meddling. The male Board members believed they alone should wear the political pants.

Men's monopoly of colonial government positions had a bearing on who did the writing in Aboriginal communities. By and large it reinforced the traditional Indigenous patriarchal practice whereby senior male clan-heads and other male leaders represented the community, and younger literate males were trained up as future leaders. Men were by no means the only ones to take up the pen in defence of their interests, however. The recent publication of *Letters from Aboriginal women of Victoria, 1867–1926* (2002) shows that Aboriginal women wrote hundreds of letters to BPA members and other government officials. Writing mainly for themselves and their families rather than for larger community groups, women addressed colonial officials on a wide range of issues, including children and family, land and housing, their right to personal freedom, the behaviour of mission and reserve managers, and their need of financial and material assistance.[2] These women's letters, like those of their menfolk, show how Aboriginal women viewed their own lives, and interpreted the broader political context within which they and their families were living. Questions remain, however, about women's circumstances as writers. Under what conditions did they pick up the pen themselves rather than refract their voices through documents written by men? When, why and what did Aboriginal women read? How was their literacy, or lack thereof, viewed by their own menfolk and by white colonial officials? How did they authorise themselves as writers between colonial and Indigenous patriarchies?

Writing, race and gender

Opinions vary widely as to how colonialism changed the lives of Aboriginal women. Some have argued that women were doubly subordinated by racism and sexism; others say that gender roles on missions and reserves benefited women rather than men, and that in certain respects women fared better under colonialism than their menfolk did. It is risky to generalise about the political position of Aboriginal women under colonialism. Possible vested interests lurk behind all the arguments. In addition, gender and race relations differed from place to place and from one period to another. Irrespective of these differences, women invariably experienced sexism in culturally specific ways, and all Aboriginal people felt the force of colonialism in gender-specific ways.

From the arrival of the First Fleet in 1788, the speech of women and girls, as well as men and boys, was transcribed by Governor Phillip and his officers as they attempted to document the Indigenous languages spoken around Port Jackson. As time went by, and young women such as Boorong and Truganini learned the language of their captors, their English utterances were also recorded by white officials.[3] Aboriginal women and girls did not normally serve as spokespeople for their communities; however, they did serve as intermediaries and translators for their menfolk. As was noted in Chapter 5, George Augustus Robinson's journals refer to Pallawah men's addresses in their traditional languages, but it is actually the women's English translations of those addresses that we read in the journals. The erroneous assumption that translation is a form of passive copying has rendered women's agency invisible, and obscured their authorial contribution to the making of the English records.

Distinct patterns of gendered literacy and language use developed in different colonies. In Van Diemen's Land and South Australia, young, literate, English-speaking Aboriginal men were groomed to be future missionaries and community leaders, and their written communication skills were further enhanced in such roles. Yet women's and girls' literacy and language skills were sometimes more developed than men's and boys', again for reasons related directly to their gender. Some of the women on Flinders Island had learned English from the seal hunters who had captured them for sexual usage and other forms of unpaid labour. On other missions and reserves, girls and young women often developed higher literacy and language skills than boys whose school time was frequently interrupted because their labour was required for outdoor rural labouring work on which the survival of the station depended. Because Aboriginal girls were seen by mission and reserve managers as sexually vulnerable, they generally spent more years than their male peers under white women's supervision in the dormitories. While boys trained as rural labourers, girls were trained as domestic servants in the homes of missionary families, where some became fluent in 'polite' forms of written and spoken English.

Also significant was the fact that the British monarch was a woman, and that Aboriginal communities' diplomatic communications with the Queen may have been viewed as women's business. For Queen Victoria's birthday in 1863, for example, a young woman known as Ellen penned two letters on behalf of the Djadjawurung community at Mount Franklin, and sent them, together with a collar she had crocheted, to the Queen.[4] The Queen's reply mentioned Ellen's crocheting specifically, and requested that she make known to her people the Queen's interest in their welfare.[5] Without further knowledge of the circumstances and content of Ellen's letter to the Queen, it is difficult to know whether she was acting as an intermediary for male Jajowrong leaders, or had taken it upon herself to write the letters on behalf of her community. In either case, her gender must have been a crucial consideration in this early written diplomatic communication with the Queen.

Ellen's letters were not the first written Aboriginal communications with Queen Victoria. In February 1846 in Van Diemen's Land, Ben Lomond leader Walter George Arthur and seven other Pallawah men sent a petition to the Queen requesting that the cruel, abusive former commandant, Dr Henry Jeanneret, not be reinstated to his post at the Wybalenna settlement on Flinders Island.[6] Walter's wife, Mary Anne Arthur (nee Cochrane), did not sign the petition. It was signed by men only, despite Mary Anne's involvement in its planning. James Bonwick, Batman's first biographer, described Mary Anne as a woman with 'vigour of intellect' whose 'strength and independence of will was stamped on her expansive features'.[7] Nonetheless, she often remained an invisible partner in her husband's protests and campaigns for land and other rights. When Bonwick visited the Arthurs' home at Oyster Cove he observed that 'books lay on a side table. The Bible occupied a conspicuous position. The daily newspaper was there, as Walter was a regular subscriber for the press.'[8] Like her husband, Mary Anne Arthur saw clearly the connection between writing and power, and played a central role in an emerging culture of Pallawah literacy.

Mary Anne Arthur's 'behind-the-scenes' involvement in early Indigenous political writing arose from her own complex political position as a Pallawah woman whose life was shaped by and within colonial institutions. She had taught at the Flinders Island school before being hastily married off to Walter George Arthur by Commandant George Augustus Robinson.[9] A few days after her wedding, she and her husband were sent to tiny Chalky Island, where Walter was employed as an assistant shepherd. Sally Dammery argues that Commandant Robinson saw Mary Anne as 'a good Christian woman' who would exercise a positive moral influence over her husband, especially with regard to his drinking. In line with the thinking of the temperance movement of the day, Robinson implicitly granted Mary Anne a degree of authority over her husband by making her responsible for his sobriety and morality.[10] In May 1838, Mary Anne reported to Commandant Robinson that her husband had been beating her. Robinson reprimanded Walter, who retaliated by inflicting further violence upon his wife.[11] Mary Anne was caught, in effect, between two patriarchies, a position occupied by many Indigenous women, then as now. Her challenge to Pallawah male dominance was a politically ambivalent act. She protected her interests as a wife by exercising the authority delegated to her by a white patriarchal colonial official, and was beaten by her Pallawah husband as a consequence.

Despite the beatings, Mary Anne remained with Walter, and played an important part in his political activities. As well as being closely involved in planning the 1846 petition to Queen Victoria, she wrote her own letters to government officials. In June 1846, she informed the Chief Secretary in writing that the newly reinstated Dr Jeanneret was persecuting the men who had petitioned against his return. This letter is one of the few cases where a woman speaks for people other than herself and her immediate family. Writing for her compatriots as well as for the petitioners and, of course, herself, she wrote that they did not:

...like to be his slaves nor wish our poor country people to be treated badly or made slaves of... I hope the Government will not let Dr. Jeanneret put us into Jail as he likes for nothing at all as he says he will do it and frighten us to much with his big talk about our writing to the Queen.[12]

Women's roles in communal writing

The early petitions written in Victoria and Van Diemen's Land fall into two broad categories: all-male petitions and community petitions where women are among the signatories. Some of the men's petitions deal with men's concerns only. Other all-male petitions raise matters relevant to the whole community. Community petitions address issues that concern everyone on the mission or reserve. I have not come across any petitions signed solely by women, nor any community petitions concerned primarily with women's issues. Women seldom wrote on behalf of their communities. Three that stand out in the present context are Ellen of the Mount Franklin Jajowrong, Mary Anne Arthur in Van Diemen's Land and Bessie Flower Cameron at Ramahyuck in Gippsland, eastern Victoria. Although these women wrote at least one letter in the first person plural — as 'we' rather than 'I' — these letters were not produced in the context of community meetings where everyone was present to sign their name or to mark the document with a cross. It is impossible to know whether these letters were written in solitude, but the fact that each is a monograph, signed solely by the woman who wrote it, makes it likely that the writer composed the letter while she was alone. With the possible exception of Ellen's letter to Queen Victoria, these women appear to have written on behalf of their communities on their own initiative, not at their menfolks' request. Their authority to write may have derived from Aboriginal women's customary role as go-between, and/or from their writing skills and their fluency in English. Yet the fact that so very few women took it upon themselves to write on behalf of their communities attests to the resilience of traditional Aboriginal male gerontocracies, and to the male monopoly over colonial government positions.

Scribes, too, were almost invariably men. A significant exception is the petition penned by Betsy Bamfield in October 1893, from William Barak and thirty other members of the Coranderrk community to Charles

Officer, Vice-Chairman of the BPA.[13] As in many other petitions, land was the issue:

> Coranderrk
> Oct 23/93
> To Mr Officer.
>
> Sir,
> Dear Friend,
> We have much pleasure in writing these few lines to you. We heard little about our land going to be taken from us. There is not many of us blacks here they ought to leave us alone and not take the land from us it is not much. We are dying away by degree. There is plenty more land round the country without troubling about Coranderrk. We Aboriginals from Coranderrk wish to know if it's true about the land. Please we wish to know. We got plenty of our own cattle and we want the run for them and if the White People take it from us there will be no place to put them. We mean cattle for the use of the station. We never forgot Mr Berry said to us in the Town Hall when we Passed the native weapons to him he told us we can go away and come to our home here again any time to our station.
>
> We don't forget Mr Berry's word and also when we go into any of the White People's paddock to hunt or fish they soon clear us out of their private premises very quick and yet they are craving for Coranderrk. We only go enough run for to have our sports and game's.
>
> | | |
> |---|---|
> | William Barrak X | Dick Richards X |
> | Thomas Avoca X | Thomas Smythe X |
> | Johnny Phillip X | William Major X |
> | Dick Puchell X | Tom McClennan X |
> | Edward McDougall | Harry Wheeler |
> | Woodford Robinson X | Robert Wandin |
> | Ellen Richards X | Jemima Wandin |
> | Harriet Smythe X | Margaret Harrison X |
> | Mary Phillip X | Betsy Banfield |
> | Kate Friday X | Maggie McClennan X |
> | Lizzy Davis X | Sarah Barrack X |
> | Alfred Davis | Maggie Purcell X |
> | Bill Russell X | Louisa Russell X |
> | Peter Hunter | Jane Donnelly |
> | Alice Login | Alexander Login |
> | Ellen Wandin | |

Not all scribes had identical responsibilities, and without corroborating evidence it is difficult to know how, if at all, the actual composition of the letter — the choice of words — was shared between William Barak and Betsy Bamfield. In any case, the signatories' claim to the land was based first on a ceremonial agreement performed some years earlier with then Chief Secretary Graham Berry. In 1893, when this petition was written, Berry's party was no longer in power, but his long-ago promise was nonetheless invoked as a basis for the people's right to own Coranderrk forever. The petitioners' second claim to land was based on a moral appeal to racial equality: Why must there be one law for whites and another for Aboriginal people? Why is white people's land held as private property, while even long-term Coranderrk residents, some with ancient ties to the country in question, have no land that is exclusively and permanently theirs?

Why was Betsy Bamfield the one to serve as scribe for Barak? At the time this petition was written, Thomas Dunolly's right to live at Coranderrk had been revoked by the 1886 amendments to the Aboriginal Protection Act, the 'half-caste' act that forced young Aboriginal adults of mixed descent off the Victorian reserves. He had been coaxed off the reserve like many other young literate men, and was trying to establish a farm near Cumeroogunga on the Murray River. In 1893, however, at the time Betsy Bamfield penned this petition, a number of young literate men, including Barak's nephew Robert Wandin, remained at Coranderrk and were therefore still available to act as scribes. Why, then, was Betsy Bamfield chosen? Was it because her English was good and her handwriting very neat? Or because she was the daughter of one of Barak's speakers, Taungurong leader Thomas Bamfield, who had died earlier that year? If that was indeed the reason for assigning Betsy to the role of scribe, the traditional Indigenous social hierarchy was being at once perpetuated and adapted. William Barak, the senior male Woiworung clan-head, had allocated to this young woman a role formerly reserved for young men because she was the closest literate relation to a recently deceased senior man. In terms of the connections it reveals between gender, writing and power, this letter is thus, paradoxically, both conservative and innovative.

What was at stake in the question of whether or not an Indigenous woman could read and write? The archival records offer few clues about Aboriginal men's attitudes to female literacy, but white men's views emerge somewhat more clearly. Comparing the stories of Annie McDonald (nee Rich) at Lake Condah and Bessie Cameron (nee Flower) at Ramahyuck,

> Coranderrk
> Oct 23/93
>
> To Mr Officer.
> Sir,
> Dear Friend.
> We have much pleasure in writing these few lines to you. We heard little about our land going to be taken from us. There is not many of us blacks here they ought to leave us alone and not take the land from us it is not much. We are dying away by degree. There is plenty more land round the country without troubling about Coranderrk. We Aboriginals from Coranderrk wish to know— if it's true about the land. Please we wish to know. We got plenty of our own cattle and we want the run for them and if the White People take it from us there will be no place to put them. We mean cattle for the use of the station. We never forgot Mr Berry said to us in the Town Hall when we passed the native weapons to him he told us we can go away and come to our home here again any time to our station.
> We don't forget Mr Berry's word and also when we go into any of the White People's paddock to hunt or fish they soon clear us out of their private premises very quick and yet they are craving for Coranderrk we only got enough run for to have our sports and games.

William Barrack x
Dick Richards x
Thomas Avoca x
Thomas Smythe x
Johnny Phillip x
William Major x
Dick Purcell x
Tom McLenan x
Edward McDougall
Harry Wheeler
Woodford Robinson x
Robert Wandin
Ellen Richards x
Jemima Wandin
Harriet Smythe x
Margaret Harrison x
Mary Phillip x
Betsy Banfield
Kate Friday x
Maggie McLenan x
Lizzy Davis x
Sarah Barrack x
Alfred Davis
Maggie Purcell x
Bill Russell x
Louisa Russell x
Peter Hunter
Jane Donnelly
Alice Login
Alexander Login
Ellen Wandin

William Barak's petition for which Betsy Bamfield acted as scribe, a role usually reserved for young men. From the collection of the National Archives of Australia.

it appears that white male authority figures could have quite different investments in Aboriginal women's literacy, or lack thereof.

Literacy and the construction of 'the helpless': Annie Rich

One of the most elusive voices refracted through the archival record is that of Annie McDonald (nee Rich), a young woman, who arrived at Lake Condah in 1880, eight months pregnant. Born in South Australia, Annie had been dispatched by her white pastoralist father into domestic service in Victoria at the age of ten.[14] While working in the home of a respectable family in Echuca, Annie had fallen pregnant to her white employer, a local businessman. Whatever affection he had for Annie was apparently outweighed by his wish to avoid a scandal. Annie was ejected from the household and, with no family nearby, she had little option but to seek refuge at Lake Condah Mission Station. After the birth of her baby boy, the Lake Condah Mission Superintendent, Reverend J Heinrich Stahle, requested that Annie be detained on the station by an Order in Council to prevent her returning to a situation where she might again be sexually exploited. Stahle's involvement was typical of a pattern wherein he clashed with the men over rations, work certificates and the right to control women's sexual conduct, and tried to control the women in matters to do with their sexual and marital relations, the custody of their children and their place of abode.

Annie had no family around her. Her kin and country were far away, making her a stranger to Kerrupjmara country where Lake Condah was located. Stahle's main rival in the struggle to control Annie's life was her former employer, the father of her baby. This man went by the names Alexander Jeffrey and Andrew Jackson, but Stahle eventually surmised that they were one and the same.[15] The deliberate confusion of names suggests that he wished to remain anonymous to protect his family's reputation. Stahle judged Jeffrey/Jackson to be a scoundrel, and disapproved when he began writing and visiting Annie and the baby in 1881. He viewed Annie as a helpless young woman, a naive victim of white male sexual desire, backing up this view with an erroneous claim that she was unable to read or write. His assertions regarding Annie's illiteracy were part of a white patriarchal discourse that denied Aboriginal women's agency, and legitimised government control over them as being for their own protection. Annie Rich McDonald was in fact able to read and write. Her granddaughter, Dawn Lee, has several of Annie's letters, as well as her

Bible with her personal inscription and the marriage certificate she signed upon marrying Alf McDonald in 1883.[16]

Back in 1881, however, when the father of Annie's baby had just re-entered her life, Stahle was so intent on protecting her that he grilled her confidante (and future sister-in-law), Euphemia McDonald. Having been coerced by Stahle into betraying Annie's trust and violating her privacy, Euphemia found the strain so great that she began to suffer violent fits and bouts of amnesia, eventually declining into a state of grave illness.[17] Given the detail of Stahle's knowledge of Annie's incoming letters, it is possible that Euphemia McDonald was not his sole source of information. Stahle was not above intercepting and reading the Lake Condah residents' mail. When a letter arrived from Jeffrey/Jackson in November 1882, Stahle wrote immediately to BPA Secretary, Captain Page, asking in effect (in convoluted syntax that betrayed his breathless anxiety) for permission to open and read it:

> Fearing that the letter might contain similar advice as in former ones, in which she was advised to run away & instructed how to proceed & at the same time not wishful to have a girl in my house who might be driven through bad influence to an act of desperation & having no place otherwise on the station where I could leave her in safety, I would ask you kindly to inform me what I shall do. Shall I hand over the letter into her hands or forward it unopened to the Board or shall I have the letter read in my presence?[18]

Annie asked Stahle to let her leave the station and return to the Jeffrey/Jackson household, but he told her he was powerless to grant such permission because of the Order in Council. He thus effectively imprisoned her at Lake Condah for her own protection.[19] However, he informed Jeffrey/Jackson that if he would marry Annie, or at least provide maintenance for the child, the Order in Council might be rescinded. Although unwilling to acknowledge publicly his relationship with Annie, Jeffrey/Jackson mounted a legal challenge to the Order in Council in 1882. He also asked Annie to write to Captain Page, confirming that she wished to leave Lake Condah. Annie accordingly produced the following letter:

> In reply to the letter that I received from Mr Jeffrey last month, requesting me to write to you myself, I beg you if you can apply to the Board for me to leave the Mission Station, that I do not wish to stay here.

> Two years ago I came to the Mission Station, not to settle down, but to visit some of my friends, and to return home again to Echuca after my visit.
>
> But there was an Order in Council telling me to stay on the Mission Station to settle down, But I do not wish to stay here.
>
> <u>Therefore will you please</u> to investigate into the matter to the Board if they can give me permission to leave.[20]

To strengthen the case that Annie should be allowed to leave the station, Jeffrey's/Jackson's solicitor argued that she was an educated woman, a responsible adult capable of making her own decisions about where, and with whom, she would reside.[21] Having her write to the Board herself strengthened this case, and contradicted Stahle's characterisation of Annie as a helpless, uneducated girl. Literacy was a sign of intelligence, personal agency and independence of mind — precisely the qualities that Annie had to prove she possessed in order to persuade the BPA that she did not need to be kept at Lake Condah for her own safety.

Despite Annie's letter, the legal challenge failed. Annie therefore voted with her feet, running away from Lake Condah with her child, only to be recaptured by the police the following day.[22] In the time leading up to her flight, Annie had openly expressed her resentment and anger towards the Stahles. She was 'disagreeable and unpleasant' and, according to Stahle, 'it was evident that she tried to weary us out so that she might have a chance to get away.'[23] Yet Stahle continued to see Annie as Jackson's/Jeffrey's puppet, a victim of seduction rather than an agent of her own actions. He believed that '…she would never have thought of leaving & especially in such a manner, if she had not been continually encouraged and urged to it by Jeffrey or Jackson.'[24]

Stahle's interests were served by characterising Annie as a victim of white male desire; Jackson's/Jeffrey's interests were served by characterising her as a responsible, literate adult, capable of making her own decisions as to where, and with whom, she should live. It is impossible to know fully, however, what Annie herself thought and felt. The Board records indicate that after 1881, once she was past the crisis of giving birth to a baby whose father wished to avoid scandal, she consistently wanted to escape from Lake Condah. That much seems clear. But the precise politics of Annie's relationship with her employer remain obscure. Did he genuinely care for her, or was he preying on her vulnerability as an Aboriginal woman who had no family of her own in the district? Did she love him, or did she judge living with him to be the lesser of two evils, a tolerable price to pay for escaping Lake Condah? Annie eventually married Euphemia's brother, Alf McDonald, with whom she had seven children.[25]

White vested interests in black women's literacy: Bessie Flower Cameron

While Annie Rich's literacy was denied by Stahle in an effort to characterise her as helpless and thus in need of protection at Lake Condah, Bessie Flower Cameron's reading and writing abilities were publicly displayed and applauded by whites who sought financial support for missions and reserves. Accomplished Aboriginal women such as Bessie were a public relations asset: they showed taxpayers and mission supporters that their money was indeed 'uplifting' the Aboriginal race. In February 1868, several of Bessie Flower's letters were published in the *Church of England Newspaper* in Western Australia, the editor's aim being to refute recent criticism of the Annesfield Anglican Mission in the local papers.[26]

Bessie Flower, a member of the Meananger (Benang) people, was the most prolific and highly educated Indigenous woman writer of her time. Born in 1851 near Albany on the south coast of Western Australia, she grew up at Annesfield, an Anglican residential school run by Anne Camfield.[27] Bessie was genuinely devoted to Mrs and Mr Camfield, whom she and the other children called 'Martie' and 'Missie'.[28] So loyal and loving was she towards Mrs Camfield that she called her 'dearest more than mother'.[29] She was also devoted to reading, as Mrs Camfield noted:

> Bessie…was never without a book in her pocket by day or under her pillow at night. Her love of reading often brought her into scrapes, from reading at inconvenient times but it was improving to her as (though she liked to read stories as well as any girl) she is much interested by History, Travels and more serious works.[30]

Mrs Camfield obviously viewed reading as a good thing in general, but she endorsed the prevailing view that romantic fiction was a frivolous, morally suspect feminine genre that compared unfavourably with serious masculine non-fictional material. After passing the government examination with credit, Bessie spent two years at a model school in Sydney, where she studied academic subjects such as English literature and language, arithmetic, history, geography and scripture, while also developing her ladylike accomplishments with lessons in piano and singing.[31] Returning to Albany in 1866, she became assistant teacher to Anne Camfield at Annesfield, and served as organist at the local Anglican church.[32] As a young Indigenous woman with a middle-class white education, her social standing was highly ambivalent and precarious.

In 1867, Bessie and her younger sister, Ada, were among five young Nyoongah women who travelled to Ramahyuck Mission Station in south-eastern Victoria, where Christian Aboriginal women were urgently needed to marry the young male Kurnai converts. Like other Aboriginal societies, the Kurnai were accustomed to gender divisions in ceremonial and religious life. They viewed Christianity primarily as men's business because white ordained missionaries were invariably male. If Kurnai Christianity was to stick, however, women had to be integrated into the congregation. Moravian missionary Reverend FA Hagenauer accordingly devised a plan to import female Aboriginal converts from other parts of Australia. Apparently unaware of traditional Kurnai marriage laws, Hagenauer assumed that these women from the other side of the continent would happily marry the young male converts and hold them firm in their faith, thereby establishing the foundations for a stable Aboriginal Christian community on Ramahyuck and Lake Tyers mission stations.[33] Bessie Flower did not travel to Victoria to be married, however. Having assisted Anne Camfield as a teacher, her plan was to teach temporarily in the Ramahyuck school before returning home to Annesfield in Western Australia. Shortly after her arrival in Victoria, she wrote to Mrs Camfield, 'I wish I were at home' but consoled herself by thinking, 'Never mind, I won't have long to stay.'[34]

Bessie's letters to Anne and Martie Camfield are polite and warmly affectionate. There are flashes of wit and humour and, although she was obviously homesick, Bessie seemed to be enjoying the adventure of new people, places and experiences; for example:

> On Thursday I wished I was going to the church instead of rocking about in the steamer. One day when we were on deck the second officer came to us & was talking about Albany, he said they considered it a great punishment to be sent there, that nothing grew but rocks & stones & I said that added to the beauty of the place, he laughed so, & said a good deal more, but when I could not say any more, I spoke about the climate being the best & he said — 'Oh, you are right there, it is the best.'[35]

Although Bessie had been thoroughly Europeanised by her education, her memory of, and attachment to, her beautiful unpicturesque country remained strong. Her love of even the rocks and stones suggests that despite her polite, chirpy, feminine tone, she is not a Jane Austen heroine admiring the pretty English countryside, but a young Nyoongah woman using writing to bridge the distance between her body and her homeland.

When Bessie arrived at Ramahyuck, she set to work teaching in the school. The mission Superintendent, Reverend Hagenauer, reported that she 'does well' as a teacher, but her education in his view was excessively academic, as she 'seems to have not had the practical turn one would wish'.[36] More physical work was expected of Bessie than of white women in her position. As well as conducting lessons in the school, she was required to help Mrs Hagenauer with her housework, teach the Hagenauer children for an hour each day, and help Mrs Hagenauer conduct sewing classes for the Aboriginal women. Bessie also played the harmonium for the daily services in the mission chapel.[37] In this busy new setting, however, Bessie soon found her feet, as Hagenauer noted:

> Bessie Flower is getting into the real work and harness, and we not only like her very much but she gets everyday more useful. She keeps her school very well together, which is of great importance... The children love her and all are obedient to her, and she does well.[38]

Hagenauer complained about Bessie's 'excessive' love of reading, but he showed Bessie off at the mission open days, and highlighted her accomplishments in press releases and annual reports. Her high level of literacy reflected well on her teachers, and proved that with adequate funding of missions and reserves, 'aboriginals [*sic*] can be educated and made useful.'[39]

Bessie was also a woman, however, and before long a white labourer working at Ramahyuck asked her to be his wife. Hagenauer, taking charge of the situation, promptly packed her off to Lake Tyers Mission Station, and arranged for her to wed Donald Cameron, a young Jupagilwournditch man from Ebenezer Mission Station. Bessie and Donald were married in November 1868, and early the following year, when Carl Kramer returned to take over the Ramahyuck school, Bessie was demoted from her position as schoolteacher and relegated to routine housekeeping duties. She and Donald were assigned to look after the new Ramahyuck boarding house, where Aboriginal children removed from their parents were to reside.

Bessie and Donald's first child was born in 1869, and others followed in close succession.

Ethnographer Alfred Howitt, visiting Ramahyuck in 1871, described the Cameron family's quarters:'Their little rooms are very neat and just as whites might occupy, a few books, some [needle]work and some nicknacks were lying about.'[40] Bessie and Donald spent their leisure time writing letters, reading newspapers and 'self-improving' books from the mission station library.[41] One of Bessie's letters was published in the *Gippsland Mercury* on 1 May 1874. It was addressed to the Secretary of the Board for the Protection of Aborigines, and was especially significant because it was written by an Indigenous woman from Western Australia, 'in the name of the Aborigines of Ramahyuck', defending Hagenauer against recent anonymous criticism published in the local newspapers:

> Mission Station Ramahyuck
>
> Sir
>
> We the aborigines residing at this station have heard and read in the Argus and the Gippsland Times, that our kind friend and protector, the Revd. F. A. Hagenauer has been accused of unkindness and cruelty to the blind man Bobby, & also that he prevented us from giving food and shelter to him, which we beg to assure you, is an intolerable lie. We cannot suffer such accusations to pass, without stating to the Board of Protection, that we feel sorry such unfounded complaint, should have gone abroad, especially by such a man who did already everything to injure us, and tried to burn our fences and grass in the paddocks.
>
> I have the honour to be
> Sir
> your most humble servant
>
> B. Cameron
> in the name of the Aborigines of Ramahuck[42]

This is one of the rare occasions when an Aboriginal woman served as author for a community. Whether Bessie wrote and published this document at Hagenauer's request is not known, but the fact that she regularly read the newspapers means that she may have exercised her own initiative in writing it. Three days after its publication in the *Gippsland Mercury*, Hagenauer had Bessie write a copy of the petition, to be sent to Robert Brough Smyth in Melbourne. Bessie's letter brought credit to Hagenauer not only on the basis of its content and style, but from the mere fact of its existence. Samples of good Aboriginal writing served as concrete evidence that Hagenauer and other missionaries were 'improving' and 'uplifting' the race whose land the colonists had expropriated. Betsy's authority to act as author of the petition depended neither on her ties to the Kurnai land on which Ramahyuck was located, nor on her position within the Kurnai kinship network. Her role as a female spokesperson for her Indigenous community was based exclusively on her command of English and her ability to express her community's views in writing.

While AW Howitt had been impressed with Bessie and Donald's immersion in a culture of books and writing, Reverend Murdoch MacDonald, visiting Ramahyuck three years later, in 1877, thought that Bessie's literacy was perhaps too much of a good thing. Reverend MacDonald observed that Bessie was 'literally a constant reader'.[43] She consumed everything she could lay her hands on, including Macaulay's essays. Bessie stood out from other Aboriginal readers because she consumed 'literary' texts, novels as well as newspapers, fiction as well as factual writing. At this time, Bessie's obsessive reading may have been driven by a need to distract herself after the deaths of her sister, Ada, and her baby son, Boyd. Hagenauer complained that although 'her superior education helps her wonderfully well', she was by no means as 'useful' as she could have been. MacDonald opined that 'it would be better on the whole if she looked to her house more and read less,'[44] a view voiced today by many men whose wives spend 'too much time' reading popular women's romances.[45]

Another reason why Bessie may have buried herself in books was that in 1878 her husband, Donald, became involved with another woman. Bessie wanted to leave him, but in doing so would have risked losing custody of her children. Hagenauer sided with Donald, who wanted the children to live in the Ramahyuck boarding house, believing that they 'will not improve under Mrs Camerons [sic] direction, but will certainly be a comfort to the deserted husband.'[46] Bessie moved to Lake Condah, refusing to relinquish the children. She returned to Ramahyuck, however, where she was reconciled with Donald, who soon resumed his extra-marital relationship.

By February 1883, Bessie had had enough, and asked permission to leave Ramahyuck and live at Lake Tyers with her friend Emily Brindle (nee Peters), one of the four young women who had come from Western Australian with Bessie sixteen years earlier. Hagenauer forbade Bessie's request to move, telling her that 'We could never be a party of recommending that you should separate from your husband.'[47] Instead, Donald and Bessie were sent unwillingly to Ebenezer in Donald's traditional country in north-west Victoria, the aim being to put as much distance as possible between him and his lover.

For Bessie, the move to Ebenezer represented a second exile. In August 1883, she wrote to Captain Page, asking permission for the family to return to Ramahyuck. Page referred the matter to Hagenauer, who refused to countenance their return, saying that the 'repeated immorality and drunkenness of [Donald] Cameron are the strongest reasons to keep him and his family away from here.'[48] Bessie was effectively being punished for her husband's wrongdoings. In reply to her repeated pleas to be allowed to return to Gippsland, Hagenauer fumed that 'if they return it would become a public scandal.'[49] Bessie, for all her attainments, was no longer a public relations asset. Tarred with the same immoral brush as Donald, she was now merely an embarrassment.

In late 1883, Bessie and Donald gained permission to return to Gippsland, but not to live on either Ramahyuck or Lake Tyers reserves. In April 1884, Bessie wrote to Captain Page, asking again for permission to live at Lake Tyers:

> I hope you will allow us to stay on this station, it comes hard on the children & myself wandering about without a home, & I feel it the more as I had a good home when I was young & then to be tossed about in old age, Please listen to my prayer for it is a prayer for a home. Hoping you are quite well Dear Sir, I remain your obedient servant, B. Cameron.[50]

Her request was initially refused but later that year the BPA finally agreed to let her and Donald live at Lake Tyers.

By April 1886, Bessie was again publicly defending the Ramahyuck and Lake Tyers mission stations. The mid-1880s were a time of debate about how best to 'manage' Aboriginal people. Major amendments to the Aboriginal Protection Act in 1886 resulted in the expulsion of most young adults of mixed descent from missions and reserves, the expectation being that they would cease being a burden on taxpayers and make a living for themselves by working in the wider community. Writing as 'The Vagabond' in the *Australasian*, John Stanley James's contribution to the debate on the wisdom of this law was to label mission Aboriginal people 'useless blackfellows'. In reply, Bessie published the following letter in the *Argus*:

Having read in the Australasian of the 27th of March an account of 'The Vagabond's' impression of the people of Lake Tyers, I was moved to write a letter in defence.

In the first place, I will not say much on his style of calling us niggers, as he told us in his address that he was an American. Now, all respect to Mr Vagabond, but I know the way the niggers have been treated in America.

Secondly, Mr Vagabond says it was related to him that the Rev. F. A. Hagenauer knocked down a loafing blackfellow three times. Now, I have lived on Ramahyuck many years, and never in my time did it happen, nor before as I was told. Mr Hagenauer is not [of] a fighting nature; he managed us by kindness.

Thirdly, Mr Vagabond said he 'did not find the houses particularly clean and well kept.' He forgot that he went around inspecting at 9 o'clock on Saturday morning, just in the middle of cleaning.

If Mr Vagabond was a Benedict he would know all about the business of house-cleaning on a Saturday; but, then, in his own house there would be a room set apart for visitors, and we have only two rooms, so he must excuse us at not finding that houses clean and tidy at 9 o'clock Saturday morning.

In conclusion, I must say the words, 'Very lazy and useless is my summary of the Lake Tyers blackfellow,' are very sad, as there is some truth in them, yet still there is some work done, or else the station could not go on as it has done. But, as Mr Vagabond asks himself, 'Would I, in this place' and goes onto say, 'As I am a truthful judge of my own character I am compelled to admit I would not,' so we will take courage from that, and go on our way, trying what is in our power to bring up our children to earn their own living, and be useful members of society, and ourselves to be grateful to the board and our missionaries for all their kindness and patience to us aboriginals.

Hoping, Sir, you will excuse my taking up a little of your valuable time, as I am writing this in the name of all my coloured brethren and sisters of Lake Tyers.[51]

Bessie is again writing in the first person plural, articulating her by now strong allegiance to the Aboriginal community in Victoria, despite the fact that she was not a member of the Kurnai people on whose land she lived, and that her high level of education set her apart from most mission and reserve residents in Victoria. Numbering her points like a lawyer, Bessie addresses The Vagabond's criticisms one by one, deploying incisive analysis, rhetorically effective allusions and polite, scathing irony. By noting The Vagabond's use of the derogatory word 'nigger' she implies that he is a racist. By mentioning that he is an American, she addresses her readers implicitly as Australian, interpellating them as humane people who find the racial oppression of American slavery abhorrent. Bessie's reply to The Vagabond's criticism of the untidy state of the residents' houses implies that he is not only unfamiliar with the Christian practice of cleaning on Saturday in preparation for the Sabbath, but is also oblivious to his own privilege as a free white man who has never raised a family in cramped, poor quality housing. Bessie's view is clear-eyed and balanced. She admits there is some truth in The Vagabond's accusation that the Ramahyuck residents do not work as hard as they could, but she goes on to say that they do what is needed to keep the station running. She also seizes on The Vagabond's confession that, were he in the residents' shoes, he would not be motivated to invest his labour in the station. This confession is important to Bessie's rhetorical purposes because it admits that black and white react similarly to oppressive circumstances, and implies, moreover, that the mission residents' lack of industry and initiative is not an inherent racial shortcoming but an attitude arising from the demoralising political and economic circumstances in which they are constrained to live. Bessie ends by claiming a right to speak in the public domain as a spokesperson for 'all my coloured brethren and sisters', an Aboriginal community that is also a Christian congregation structured like a (patriarchal) family.

Bain Attwood has argued that Bessie 'internalised what amounted to European domination, and did not perceive it as destructive' largely because she was taken from her family at a very young age.[52] As she grew older, however, she suffered as a result of the racially based paternalism of white men such as Reverend Hagenauer and Captain Page, who placed her needs second to those of her unfaithful Aboriginal husband. Bessie's reading doubtless played a major role in structuring her social and moral awareness, and in her writing we can see over time her transformation from a deferential, submissive girl to an assertive, self-authorising woman who wanted to live outside the judgemental gaze of white male authority figures. Her writing not only reflected this change, it facilitated it. Being able to express her views publicly, especially when she wrote on behalf of her 'coloured brethren and sisters', must have given her a tremendous sense of power and achievement (even though whites took credit for her accomplishments), and may also have consolidated her feelings of belonging and social worth even though her kin and country were far away.

Bessie Flower and Annie Rich were immigrants, not wives complying with the Aboriginal custom whereby women go to live in their husband's country. Bessie Flower Cameron's life was shaped not only by other people's attitudes to her race and her gender, but also by her being an immigrant. Like Annie Rich, she was a kinless stranger living in the country of a foreign Aboriginal nation. Both women lived out the paradox of Australia's Aboriginal diaspora, the experience of 'leaving country without leaving the country', as Noelene Brasche puts it.[53] Bessie Flower never returned to her Meananger country, 3000 kilometres to the west; nonetheless, it seems somehow fitting that Bessie Flower, the most 'literary' Indigenous reader and writer of the 19th century, is a member of the same people as Kim Scott, whose novel *Benang* (1999) won the Miles Franklin Award, Australia's most prestigious literary prize.

Writing to bring people close

At the 1881 parliamentary inquiry into Coranderrk Aboriginal Reserve, Mrs Caroline Morgan enlisted her Jajowrong kinsman, Thomas Dunolly, to write out the following narrative:

> This is my evidence. Coranderrk, November 16th 1881. I have asked Mrs. Strickland [wife of the reserve manager] for a pair of blankets for my sick boy. She told me that she must write to Captain Page first. Then I told her, must my little boy be perishing with the cold till you get a letter from Mr. Captain Page? …So my sick boy was dying…
>
> Caroline Morgan X[54]

The life of Mrs Morgan's son hung on a piece of paper. One of the many disturbing discoveries to emerge from archival research is the death-dealing (in)efficiency of colonial bureaucratic governance. Mrs Morgan's narrative reveals how white administrators used bureaucratic procedures in a way that jammed the governmental apparatus ostensibly designed to protect Aboriginal people's welfare. Established as a means of reliably implementing government policies on 'Aboriginal affairs', the various colonial protection agencies established in the 19th century seem often to have lost sight of any benevolent goals they had initially been entrusted to achieve. Efficiency, economy and strict regulation of Indigenous people's lives became ends in themselves, as bureaucratic careers were built 'on the backs of the blacks'. Pen-wielding colonial officials inflicted racial violence by remote control. Without ever shooting or poisoning Aboriginal people, they condemned large numbers of children and adults to suffering and death by a thousand paper-cuts.

Generally speaking, Protection Board officials used writing to govern Aboriginal people by remote control. They used writing as a means of self-protective record-keeping, and a device for maintaining a physical and social distance between themselves and those they were governing. Writing was crucial in establishing and maintaining the multi-tiered hierarchical structures that insulated white decision-makers from the Aboriginal people who felt the impact of those decisions. From the time the Central Board to Watch over the Interests of the Aborigines in the Colony of Victoria was established in 1860, its members seldom if ever visited the missions and reserves they were responsible for overseeing — even though the Board's purpose was to advise on and implement government policy on Aboriginal affairs.[55] In their extensive correspondence, members of the Board wrote *about*, rather than *to*, the Aboriginal people they ostensibly protected. When the Board wished to convey a message to mission and reserve residents, it was usually communicated by letter to the relevant reserve manager(s), who informed the people orally of the letter's contents. If the message caused anger or upset among the residents, the manager could say it was futile to punish the messenger. The Board officials who wrote these letters were out of earshot, in their comfortable offices in faraway Melbourne.

While colonial officials used writing as a strategic mode of record-keeping[56] and a means of asserting control from a distance, Aboriginal people used the same tool to bridge the spatial and social distances between themselves and those who could help them. As Caroline Morgan's document illustrates by its very existence, Aboriginal people were appropriating the written medium for their own purposes. Aboriginal petitions and letters of protest caused a good amount of trouble and embarrassment for local managers and Protection Board officials because they carried Aboriginal people's views over their heads, directly to the Chief Secretary or to other parliamentarians and influential citizens. These letters and petitions flouted the orthodox channels of bureaucratic communication, causing great difficulty for those who were suddenly called to account by their superiors. Sometimes Aboriginal groups made their views known to the public via the press; occasionally, as mentioned earlier, they went right to the top, to Queen Victoria herself. Unlike colonial officials, Aboriginal writers in colonial times used writing to breach the barriers — social, physical and attitudinal — that separated them from their fellow human beings. Today, many Aboriginal authors continue this tradition, writing their way into white readers' minds to dissolve the ignorance and apathy that have long made white and black Australians strangers to each other.

Aboriginal women used writing to keep friends and relations close. One of the rare private letters that found its way into the government archives was written in 1881 by Kitty Brangy to her sister, Edith (Eda) Brangy, at Coranderrk. Kitty lived at Wahgunyah on the Victorian side of the Murray River. Her letter is quoted in full:

> My dear sister I write these few lines hoping you are quite well as it leaves us All at present. My dear sister I am very sorry that I could not write before. Now my dear sister I must tell you that I am living in Wahgunyah and it is such a poor place you can hardly get anything to eat.
>
> I should like to come down there very much but I can never get the money to go anywhere. My dear sister I wish that you would ask Mr Briggs to lend me one pound and I will soon come and see you All. My dear sister I must tell you that I have got such a nice Little Boy and he is called Willie. My dear sister will you tell Mrs Briggs that her Uncle is dead. Tommy Read is dead. Mary send her love to her aunty and says that she would like to see you very much. My dear sister I think that the drink must of killed him he died in Corowan. My dear sister I am with Tommy McCays[?] tribe and they all send their kind love to you and would All like to see you. My dear sister I have not seen our dear Father since last year. I know not where he has got to. I should like to know very much
>
> My dear sister I hope you will write as soon as you can for I might not be here long and then I should not get it. My dear sister I have no more to say at present but next time I hope that I will have some more to say next time. No more at present from your Loving and true sister
>
> Kitty Brangy   kisses to you my dear sister
> XXXXXXXXXXXXXXXXXXX
> XXXXXXXXXXXXXXXXXX
> XXXXXXXXXXXXXXXXXXX   Address Kitty
> XXX XXXXXXXXXXXXXX   Brangy Wahgunyah
> XXXXXXXX[57]   Post Office

The most striking feature of this letter is Kitty's repeated affirmation of kinship, the family bonds that hold strong despite physical separation. In this short letter, Kitty addresses Eda as 'my dear sister' no less than twelve times, and signs off with the words 'from your loving and true sister', followed by eighty-three kisses. Here the letter 'X' works not as a phonographic sign but as an icon that annuls the bodily distance between people, carrying Kitty's kisses from her own lips to her sister's cheeks. Kinship is also affirmed in several other ways in Kitty's letter. She writes to her sister about her children, announcing the arrival of her baby son, Willie, and informing Eda that her niece (Kitty's daughter) would like to see her aunty very much. Kitty also conveys the sad news of the death of Mrs Briggs' uncle, and tells her sister that she has lost touch with their father and wishes she knew where he was. When Kitty refers to her family she refers to them as 'All', dignifying the collective with a capital A.

This letter is an attempt to knit a family back together. Its subtext is the decimation and displacement of Aboriginal clans across Victoria. Many families had been torn apart. People often lost track of each other. This letter attempts to reweave part of a kinship network by repeatedly affirming family relationships and delivering news of the far-flung members of the family. The point to be highlighted here is that this reweaving works, like the listing of names on many Aboriginal petitions, in diametrical opposition to the dividing, compartmentalising, individualising effect of mission and reserve records. Two diametrically opposed visions of social order are encoded in the respective textual practices of Aboriginal women and white male bureaucrats.

How a personal letter such as Kitty's found its way into the BPA archives remains unclear. In any case, when it came into Captain Page's hands he sent it to the Wahgunyah police with a request to find out whether Kitty Brangy would like to visit or reside permanently at Coranderrk.[58] The Wahgunyah police constable informed Page that Kitty did indeed wish to make a home at Coranderrk, but went on to say that 'she is a drunkard and it would not be safe to give her money.'[59] His reference to Kitty *Brangy* as Kitty *Brandy* suggests perhaps that he might have been rather partial to alcohol himself.

○ ○ ○

Another of the rare personal communications housed in archival institutions is a series of twenty-two postcards written in the early 1900s by a young Diyari woman, Rebecca Maltilina (b. 1887), to a young white woman, Dorothea Ruediger (b. 1892), daughter of the head stockman at

Bethesda Lutheran Mission at Killalpaninna in South Australia.[60] As girls at Killalpaninna, Rebecca and Dorothea had become close friends, but at the age of seventeen Rebecca was separated from her family and her country when she accompanied Lutheran Pastor Loehe and his family to Natimuk, near Horsham in western Victoria. It was from there that Rebecca exchanged letters and postcards with her long-time friend.[61] Eight of these postcards are in the Diyari language, and have been translated by Peter Austin.[62] The two young women corresponded for over a decade, until Dorothea's marriage during or shortly after World War I.[63]

A crucial aspect of Rebecca Maltilina's postcards is that their meaning has very little to do with their verbal content. At first I thought those in the Diyari language might contain some dramatic events or subversive thoughts cloaked in the language. But no; Peter Austin's translation of the postcards into English reveals that, as with all the postcards, Rebecca offered only the scantest news to her dear friend Dori. Her days as a domestic servant appear largely eventless, except that on one occasion she reports winning one guinea as first prize in the local swimming carnival.[64] Rebecca devotes a significant portion of her limited space to writing about writing: thanking Dori for a recent letter, telling Dori that she will write her a letter soon, apologising for only writing a few words, and expressing her happiness at receiving a photograph ('*pepa mudla*' or 'paper face') of her brother.[65] Like Kitty Brangy, Rebecca Maltilina used writing as a tool for social bonding. The purpose of the postcards is less to communicate news than to reaffirm her continued relationship with Dori and, through that relationship, her ties to her traditional country where the rest of her family remains. For both women, writing brings people close. It works as a means of sending something of oneself back to one's traditional country. As a material object, the written document is a surrogate for the writer's body. Rebecca Maltilina couldn't physically return to her country, but her letter could.

The power of true stories

The correspondence of Kitty Brangy and Rebecca Maltilina is addressed to loved ones rather than government officials. Hence we might expect that they draw their addressee close. Some Aboriginal women, however, attempted to bring government officials close by narrating stories in ways that induced feelings of pathos and empathy in the reader. Lena Austin was one such woman. In March 1917 she wrote to Mr Macleod, Chief Secretary of Victoria, as follows:

8 ~ Early writings by Aboriginal women

Two of the postcards written by Rebecca Maltilina; one in English, the other in the Diyari language. **Courtesy State Library of South Australia.**

Dear sir

...I am thinking about my poor little girl winnie[;] she is longing to come home again to her own native part[;] you no Mr Macleod that it is quite natural for a child to come home to her own mother and relations[.] ...Mrs Galbraith is treating her very unkindly[;] she knocked her head up against the door and she struck her[;] ...she told us in her letter that if she is left there much longer she will die[;] dear sir if you could only see the letters that my poor little girl writes home it would bring the tears to your eyes to see how the way she pleads to come home it would make your heart ache; dear sir if you

> know what a fathers love is for his children consider a mothers love for her child[;] every mother loves her child and it is quite natural that every child should love there mother[.] ...Mr Mcleod I plead with you from the very depth of my poor heart just for sake of my little girl as she is breaking her heart to come home once again as Mrs Galbraith is over working her...[66]

In this letter, Lena Austin pleaded explicitly with Mr Macleod to imagine how she must feel as a mother. Her desperate attempt to inspire empathy failed, however. Macleod used standard bureaucratic protocols to re-establish the distance between Lena Austin and himself. First, he declined to reply to her letter himself, handing it over instead to Mr Ditchburn, Secretary of the BPA. Whether the letter sat on Macleod's desk or Ditchburn's we don't know, but there was no reply to Lena Austin's letter for two months, the long silence effectively keeping her at a distance. When Ditchburn did eventually reply, he did not engage explicitly with any of Lena Austin's allegations regarding her daughter's mistreatment and distress. His formal tone and formulaic wording signalled his white professional masculine immunity to this Aboriginal mother's emotional pleas for empathy.

> Memo
>
> I have to acknowledge the receipt of letters from Ada Austin and yourself addressed to the Hon the Chief Secretary, asking that Winnie be returned to your care from Lake Condah. In reply I am directed to inform you that the Chief Secretary cannot grant your request as he considers that the environment of Framlingham is not conducive to the best moral interests of Winnie.
>
> Secretary[67]

One way of bringing people close is by telling them true stories, letting them know what has happened, and how it has affected you. Implicit in such narratives is the question: how would you feel if this happened to you? Many of the early letters from Aboriginal women to government officials used narrative in such a manner, as did most of the Aboriginal witnesses who testified at the Stolen Generations inquiry in the 1990s. Conspicuously absent from the *Bringing them home* report were testimonies by mothers whose children had been taken away. The experience of these mothers was literally unspeakable. In the 19th and early 20th century, however, many mothers wrote to government officials regarding the custody and welfare of their children.[68]

These letters are immensely valuable in understanding Aboriginal women's lives. They also have a bearing on some important theoretical questions, including the unresolved debate between Stephen Muecke and Anne Brewster over the repressive hypothesis. The central issue in this debate is whether Indigenous women's life-writings are best understood through Muecke's Foucaultian framework, which sees colonial power eliciting or inducing the production of life-narratives, or whether Anne Brewster is correct in arguing that such a model takes insufficient account of Aboriginal women's agency.

What I've been trying to show here is that the institutions of government do indeed induce Aboriginal writing. A vast body of Aboriginal writing was undoubtedly called forth through the processes of bureaucratic governance, and some of that writing deploys European literary tropes and discourses. That said, however, it's crucial to highlight the signs of Aboriginal women's authorial agency, and their use of writing to reaffirm the kinship bonds and affiliations to country upon which Aboriginal identity is traditionally based. Within the institutional structure set up to regulate Aboriginal affairs, Indigenous women exercised their initiative. Not only did they frequently circumvent bureaucratic process, they decided for themselves what they were going to write about. Moreover, their use of narrative and heartrending appeals to the empathetic imagination amounted to a significant disruption — indeed a total reversal — of bureaucratic decorum. By writing to bring people close, and by stimulating empathetic feelings in the reader, Aboriginal women used the small space allotted to them in the bureaucratic system to develop what amounts to an anti-bureaucratic discourse. Induced it may have been by bureaucratic administrative procedure, but Aboriginal women's writing was a product of their agency. No one can take that away.

One woman who used writing in this way was Margaret Green, a Kerrupjmara woman who lived on Lake Condah Mission Station in south-western Victoria in the early 1880s, around the same time as Annie Rich was wrangling with Superintendent Stahle. Margaret Green was a widow with three daughters. Stahle took Margaret Green's daughters from her and lodged them in the mission dormitory. His paternalism infantilised her, and institutionalised the parenting of her children. Stahle alleged that he 'had to take [the children] from her' as she was 'a bad mother'.[69]

Some of what Stahle saw as 'bad mothering' may in fact have been 'good mothering' in Kerrupjmara terms. Stahl described to his superior, Captain Page, a time when Margaret Green 'dragged' her two older daughters about in 'the stones', a piece of apparently barren land annexed to the mission. Margaret had travelled around with her daughters in the stones, he said, 'for not less than three full weeks in order that she might have an opportunity of living a wild roaming life'.[70] It's likely that by taking her two older daughters to this area Margaret was endeavouring both to carry out her traditional motherly role and to maintain her own spiritual and cultural associations with significant sites. What Stahle called 'wild roaming' was probably not random wandering at all, but methodical movement to sites significant to girls who had reached a particular stage of maturity. Margaret may have taken her daughters to the ancient stone eel ponds for which countless generations of local Indigenous women had woven basketwork eel nets. Or perhaps she was showing them their conception sites, and teaching them about their spiritual relationship with places and ancestral beings of special significance to girls and young women. But Stahle saw in these actions only bad mothering, and removed all three of Margaret's daughters from her.

Some years after the girls were taken into the dormitory, Margaret married Captain Harrison from Ebenezer Mission Station in Wergaia country, in the Wimmera District some distance north of Lake Condah. When Aboriginal women married, they traditionally moved to their husband's country. Margaret's husband did not wish to leave his country, so Margaret made her home there with him and tried to get her daughters back to live with her at Ebenezer. She wrote to BPA Secretary Captain Page, asking: '... kindly let me have my children who are at Condah.'[71] She also persuaded the Superintendent of Ebenezer to write to Stahle, asking him to allow the girls to be returned to her care.[72]

Stahle saw no reason to return the girls to their mother. He argued that Margaret was a bad mother, and that the children were happy where they were in the Lake Condah dormitory. He also let slip that the girls were attracting much-needed church funding to the mission, funding that would be lost if the children were 'removed'.[73] Stahle maintained that when he first took the girls into the dormitory, they were 'almost beyond control' — something he attributed to Margaret's mothering rather than to the fact that they had been taken from her. Finally, he tried to retain custody of the girls by claiming that their father 'before his death had given them over to his care'.[74]

When Margaret Green wrote to the Secretary of the BPA asking for the return of her daughters, Page referred the matter down the line to Stahle.

Stahle's response was to ask the eldest of the girls, Edith Taylor, where she would prefer to live. He backed up his own argument that the girls should remain at Lake Condah by having Edith write the following letter directly to Captain Page:

> Mission Station
> Lake Condah
> Oct. 15th 1883
> Captain Page
>
> Dear Sir
> Mr Stahle told me that my mother has asked you to send us her children up to her to the Wimmera and he asked me also whether we would like to go, but I said no, for I would sooner that my mother & little brother would come down to Condah again, than that we would have to go there.
> We are all very happy and comfortable here, this is our home and we all have our friends here and everybody is kind to us, so please Sir let us stop here, and tell my mother to come down.
> I remain
> Yours respectfully
>
> Edith Taylor.[75]

This is the sort of letter that critics of the *Bringing them home* report would be more than happy to see. So we have to ask: why shouldn't this young girl's letter be taken at face value? Why shouldn't it be read as evidence that she was happier in the Condah dormitory than she would have been with her mother at Ebenezer? The reason such a reading is invalid is that Edith appears to have been presented with a false set of options when she wrote the letter. She seems to think she is being offered the choice of living *with her mother* at Lake Condah or living with her mother at Ebenezer. Although Margaret Green had at that time made no offer to return to Lake Condah, Edith wrote that she 'would sooner that my mother & little brother would come down to Condah again, than that we would have to go there'. Perhaps Stahle had led Edith to believe that she could have the best of both worlds: the familiarity and friends at Lake Condah *and* her mother.[76] When Edith wrote that she was happy at Lake Condah, she might not have realised that her letter would be read as a request *not* to live with her mother at all. Stahle, at any rate, got his way, and the girls remained for the time at Lake Condah.

While Stahle thought Margaret Green was not a good mother, the Ebenezer Superintendent, Reverend Kramer (writing after the date of Edith Taylor's letter), claimed that Margaret 'does not make a very good wife': '… if her children are not sent here I fear she will [leave her husband and] go to Condah again.'[77] Before Margaret could prove herself a 'bad wife', however, Edith fell ill and died. Margaret, distraught, pleaded desperately with Captain Page to let her two surviving daughters be returned to her care:

> Ebenezer
> Mission Station
> April 9th, 1884
> Mr
> Captain Page
>
> Dear Sir
> Please would you kindly allow me to have my two [remaining] girls with me here as [the other] one of them died and I have not see her before she died and I should like the other two to be with me to comfort me.
>   Please to not disappoint me for my heart is breaking to have them with me. Please to send them up here and I shall not leave this station.
>   Please to ask Mr Stahle to let them come.
>   I am yours obedient
>   Servant
>
> Margaret Harrison [Green][78]

Margaret Green's desperation and sense of powerlessness are clearly evident in this letter. Unlike William Barak, she wasn't writing as a clan-head. Unlike Thomas Brune or Walter George Arthur, she wasn't invoking biblical morality or writing as a protégé of colonial officials. She was writing as a mother, for herself and her daughters only, yet writing as abjectly as a child addressing that most patriarchal of colonial institutions, the Board for the Protection of Aborigines.

Margaret Green's struggle to regain custody of her two surviving daughters was nonetheless successful. In April 1884, Stahle reluctantly agreed to let the girls go and live with their mother.[79] Margaret Green's heartfelt expression of emotion had activated a different kind of power, the same kind of power generated by the stories in *Bringing them home*. This is the power of true stories about human love, loss, grief and fear, the kinds of stories that can inspire empathy, and cause people to change their minds.

9

A book by any other name...?

Books have often served as icons of Western civilisation; their fate has reflected the progress of empire — and the threats to it. While some Australian literary landscapes are dotted with bodies of lost explorers and ailing stockmen, others are littered with torn, rotting, coverless, broken-spined books. In the novels of canonical authors such as Patrick White, Randolph Stow and David Malouf, the wilderness is a place where books and papers are manifestly vulnerable, and where European cultures of writing and reading are difficult to sustain.[1] The explorer's exhaustion and disorientation are reflected in the deterioration of his journal. Violent rainstorms wash ink from paper and turn it back into pulp. Pages, whole or in shreds, flutter away in the searing wind or lie scattered in mouldy drifts on the floors of abandoned houses. The lonely settler's degeneration is manifest in acts of bibliocide that involve tearing the covers off once-cherished books to prop up wobbly furniture, or ripping out printed pages to light the fire or mop up spills. The literary motif of the damaged or annihilated book functions as part of a grand narrative of the dangers posed to Western civilisation by the ravages of a hostile environment, natural and social. Books are exposed to the devastating effects of wild wind and weather in regions inhabited by wild, bookless tribes.

The British settlers who came to Australia from 1788 onwards brought with them a firmly established sense of what a book was. The business of making and selling books had been going on long enough in England and Europe for people to have a clear sense of what kinds of objects could legitimately be called books. Many convicts and free settlers in Australia did not know how to read, and may not have been very familiar with the contents of books, but they knew a book when they saw one, and they saw nothing resembling books in Aboriginal cultures. Books were defined Eurocentrically in a manner that excluded the devices Aboriginal societies had developed to serve as sign carriers. To colonial European eyes, books were bound gatherings of writing(s), usually on paper, and the paradigm of writing was alphabetic script.[2] Non-Western peoples' textual objects that did not contain alphabetic script were therefore not categorised as books unless, like certain Mesoamerican 'books of the devil',[3] they bore a close physical resemblance to European book forms like the medieval codex or the Renaissance printed book.

That pre-contact Aboriginal societies were without European-style books and alphabetic writing was in itself a politically neutral fact of Indigenous cultural history. This historical fact became politically charged, however, by the symbolic values Europeans attached to books. Europeans viewed books and alphabetic writing as signs of their own cultural superiority over Indigenous societies, whom they deemed to be without history, without writing, without books. Books and alphabetic literacy were taken to be a sign of cultural advancement. They were one of the many material and cultural benefits that European philanthropists and missionaries believed Indigenous peoples needed in order to be 'raised up' to the level of Europeans.

These Eurocentric understandings of what a book was, how it might function and what its very existence said about its culture of origin remained largely undisturbed in Australia until the later decades of the 20th century, when Aboriginal stories and songs previously collected by anthropologists were incorporated into major poetry anthologies.[4] When Indigenous Australian oral narratives were thus assimilated into the national literary canon, it became possible for non-Indigenous Australians to understand that, in certain respects at least, Indigenous oral narratives and songs performed functions comparable with those of certain kinds of texts in Western print cultures. Such function-based understandings of Aboriginal oral narratives created the conditions under which the question of what counts as a book could be reopened.

By the late 1990s, some members of settler societies had begun to entertain the possibility that, far from being exclusively a European artefact, books were and had always been a cultural universal. In his 1998 Garnett Sedgewick Memorial Lecture, eminent Canadian poet Robert Bringhurst lamented literary historians who focused exclusively on books and writing in the narrow European sense. These historians were leaving out of account the rich tradition of Indigenous oral narratives preserved in the manuscripts and publications of anthropologists, and in the narrative practices of contemporary Indigenous communities. Every language, Bringhurst argued, has its own distinct literature, whether or not it is 'lettered' in the European sense. Nor do books necessarily have to exist in material form, he maintained. While acknowledging that the verbal dimension of these narratives remained intangible until anthropologists wrote the words down and published them, Bringhurst sought to add prestige to Indigenous oral texts by calling them 'books'. He urged that the Indigenous storytellers whose words Franz Boaz transcribed in the 1890s, for example, should be regarded not as native informants but rather as authors. Conversely, Boaz should be known not as the author of the book version of these stories, but rather as the scribe, translator and editor.[5]

Accommodating as it is, the view that books are a cultural universal substitutes one mode of Eurocentrism for another. The Eurocentric perspective remains, only now it works through a process of inclusion rather than one of exclusion. Like Bringhurst, Germaine Warkentin has urged that books be defined in terms of their functions rather than their physical characteristics. Arguing that Indigenous North American writing systems and sign carriers should come within the purview of book history, Warkentin shifted the focus away from the book as object: 'The choice is not between objects that are books and objects that are not; rather, it is the much more interesting difference between cultures that exhibit "bookishness" and those that don't.'[6] Warkentin warned against 'reduc[ing] a Native category to a European understanding of it'.[7] Concentrating on bookishness rather than books, however, does not necessarily solve the problem of understanding non-European cultures in terms of European paradigms and terms of reference. To define all artefacts that perform 'bookish' functions as variants of 'books' is to obscure material, cultural and historical differences between cultures.

Warkentin endeavours to stretch the meaning of the word 'book' by stress-ing that 'it is the individual culture that determines, inflects, and reinvents what it wishes to be its books... The question cannot be "What is a book?" but rather "How does a given culture define what a book is?"'[8] Some Indigenous communities, however, might not be concerned with the question of whether or not their traditional textual artefacts are, as we say in English, 'bookish' in form or function. They might not be entirely pleased to see their artefacts as 'inflections' or 'reinventions' of a European category. Despite the global incursions of capitalism in recent decades, and the many legal and other contexts where power and authority are highly centralised, it is still true to say that the world has many alternative centres of cultural authority. If members of traditional Aboriginal cultures were to address the question of how different sign carriers can be compared, they might well do so from their own distinctive directions; asking, for example, how a book compares to a message-stick, or to a ritually painted body, or to an elaborately prepared ceremonial ground. The question, then, would not be How is an Aboriginal message-stick bookish? but rather 'How is a book message-stick-ish? It might even be conceded that it is up to non-Aboriginal cultures to decide what they wish to be their message-sticks. Moreover, as well as seeing the prestige of books and writing as *leading to* a denigration of cultures that lacked these markers of 'advancement', one might also calculate the extent to which the prestige of books and writing *grew out of* an imperialist ideological need to construct European cultures as superior to the cultures of those whose lands they were usurping.

Faced with the multi-centredness of cultural authority, and a desire to move beyond a facile celebration of cultural relativity, Walter D Mignolo has argued for a philological and comparative approach to book history. He has stressed the need to consider the locus and politics of scholarly enunciation, a consideration that might begin by focusing on the word 'book' itself:

> *Book* is neither the universal name nor the universal concept associated with solid surfaces in which graphic signs are inscribed, preserved, and transmitted. It is only from the point of view of a culture capable of applying its regional concept to similar practices and objects of other cultures that [one] could see Middle East clay tablets and Egyptian papyrus [or other inscribed objects] as forerunners [or variants] of Western and Christian books.[9]

When practitioners of Western academic disciplines bring non-Western textual artefacts within the purview of a field called 'book history', they perpetuate colonial power relations by demonstrating a continued desire to understand non-European cultures in terms of European categories and concepts. And yet, when Indigenous peoples engage with (European) books and writing within their own terms of reference and protcocols of communication, they often demonstrate the degree to which they remain culturally unassimilated. Books, in other words, may cease to function as (European) books when they move across cultural boundaries. A book by any other name may no longer be a book. At the same time as book historians are assimilating non-European sign carriers into the category of the book, non-European cultures have reinvented and recontextualised books in a manner that transforms them into something not entirely bookish (in the European sense).

How might Indigenous Australians be included in histories of the book without being characterised (Eurocentrically) as a people traditionally without books, or (equally Eurocentrically) as a people whose traditional means of communication are bookish in function or form? Both forms of Eurocentrism — the exclusive, and the assimilative — are made possible by a tendency to imagine cultures as discrete, bounded domains located on an abstract, ahistorical plane. The historical reality of post-colonial societies is that Indigenous and non-Indigenous cultures have become entangled in complex ways.[10] To pretend otherwise is to perpetuate what Johannes Fabian has called the 'denial of coevalness',[11] and to practise a mode of book history that approaches questions of cultural difference in ahistorical terms. Without imagining that the biases and blind spots of my own language and locus of enunciation can be avoided, this chapter focuses on a series of moments in the history of this entanglement between Indigenous and non-Indigenous Australian cultures. These moments open up a range of questions such as: To what classes of objects did books (and pieces of books) correspond in the minds of Aboriginal people during the early contact period?[12] How might these correspondences have shaped Aboriginal people's engagement with books and writing, and their early negotiations of the social roles and relations that centre around books and writing? How have Aboriginal people developed their own book cultures today? How do the social relations within which they write, publish and read books differ from those that prevail in European book cultures? And finally, how have Aboriginal and non-Aboriginal people gone about the process of making books together?

White men's message-sticks and black men's letters

Henry Reynolds has ascertained that Aboriginal people living considerable distances beyond the outskirts of white settlement felt the impact of European presence in the form of biological pathogens, animals and material objects.[13] Those who survived the ravages of introduced diseases found uses for the settlers' goods and chattels, some of which were transported across vast distances via Aboriginal trade routes. Aboriginal people collected iron implements such as tomahawks, knives, pots and pans, as well as glass bottles, clothing, blankets, sewing implements, and, occasionally, written and printed texts. Among the diverse array of articles contained in an Aboriginal camp in Gippsland in 1841, for example, were two children's copybooks, a Bible, and newspapers from London, Glasgow and Aberdeen.[14] And, as we saw in Chapter 5, Pallawah people made use of a Christian prayer book in their ceremonial rites.

While books and writing were almost synonymous in the minds of Europeans, it is crucial to remember that Aboriginal people in the early contact years would have encountered alphabetic writing on a wide variety of European sign carriers in addition to books and papers. Writing and books may not have been bound so closely together in conceptual terms as they have been in post-Renaissance European cultures. As noted in Chapter 4, early Aboriginal inscriptions of alphabetic characters carved on wooden objects suggest that they were probably not copied from printed books, magazines or newspapers, but from surfaces other than paper; for example, carved, painted, stamped or stencilled objects such as milestones, coins, ships, packing crates, flour bags, barrels, china, and metal weapons, tools and utensils.[15] In comparison with these sign carriers, books and papers are fragile objects. If books came into Aboriginal hands in areas remote from white settlement, they are unlikely to have been in anything like mint condition.

As I suggested in Chapter 4, Aboriginal people who encountered alphabetic writing in frontier settings, where they did not practise literacy in European ways, would not necessarily have engaged with alphabetic characters as a phonographic code for (the English) language. Rather, from the little evidence that is available, Aboriginal people who had had no contact with European principles of literacy appear to have engaged with alphabetic characters according to how they resembled the shapes of their own traditional inscriptions. The same principle applied to Aboriginal engagements with European sign carriers such as papers and books (or pieces of books). At times, Aboriginal and settler societies assimilated each other's textual artefacts into their own cultural categories, and integrated them into their own structures of social relations.

There is evidence to suggest that Indigenous and non-Indigenous societies, left to their own devices, viewed each other's communication technologies as analogous to their own. For example, the popular white perception of Aboriginal message-sticks was that they were the 'blackfellows' letters', and there are some recorded cases where message-sticks were read as a series of sentences,[16] or where the recipients had been able to decipher the message without the aid of the messenger.[17] Ethnologists, however, saw the equation between message-sticks and letters as misleading. They maintained that message-sticks carried ideographic signs, the primary function of which was to aid the messenger's memory, not to preserve a script for a given set of words.[18] The message lived not in the message-stick but in the messenger's memory and voice. Unlike books, message-sticks were not the primary locus for a verbal text, but a means of recycling information from one oral context to another.

As well as serving as a memory aid, message-sticks also functioned as a type of 'passport'.[19] They were '*bona fides* of the bearer' and 'a guarantee of good faith to show that there was no gammon'.[20] James Dawson emphasised that 'As the office of messenger is of very great importance, the persons filling it are considered sacred while on duty; very much as an ambassador, herald, or bearer of a flag of truce is treated among civilized nations.'[21] When written documents initially came into Aboriginal people's hands, they were sometimes made to serve in this manner as passports, flags of truce or badges of office. Despite the disparity between the kinds of signs carried on message-sticks and written texts, *as objects* the two could be made to perform similar functions.

In the early 1840s George Augustus Robinson made extensive excursions throughout what is now the state of Victoria, having left Van Diemen's Land to take up the post of Chief Protector of Aborigines in the Port Phillip District. When contacting unfamiliar tribes for the first time, Robinson used known Aboriginal people from nearby areas as go-betweens or messengers. He issued the messengers with visiting cards something like those used in polite British and colonial social circles. Without these messengers and their paper message-sticks, Robinson would in all likelihood have been attacked by the 'wild natives' he wished to befriend and defend.[22]

Some of Robinson's visiting cards were signed by himself; others were signed by Governor La Trobe. Many were merely printed pro formas carrying no handwritten message at all. The words written or printed on the cards were of no consequence whatsoever, because the cards ceased to function as phonographically written texts as soon as they passed into Aboriginal hands. Although they called the cards 'letters',[23] the Aboriginal messengers and recipients engaged with the cards as alien *objects* that could serve the same functions as message-sticks in their own culture. As objects, Robinson's visiting cards were inserted into Aboriginal cultural categories, where they functioned not only like message-sticks but like the special spears, balls of clay, hairnets, feathered branches, body paintings and other tokens traditionally carried and/or worn by messengers to signify their special status, indicate the nature of their message, and guarantee them safe passage through foreign country.[24] In some areas, message-sticks were sent usually by men of some seniority. By sending out visiting cards, which Aboriginal people saw as white man's message-sticks, Robinson may have elevated himself to a high rank in the eyes of the Aboriginal groups he visited.

Robinson's practice of sending cards was imitated by Aboriginal groups. Aboriginal people living on Edward Stone Parker's station on the Loddon River near Mount Franklin received 'letters' from Aboriginal people living to the south, inviting them to visit Melbourne. Like Robinson's visiting cards, these 'letters' were written documents that were not deciphered phonographically, but rather were treated as badges of the messenger's office. The message was delivered orally by memory, not read verbatim off the paper.[25] What was written on the paper was in Aboriginal cultural terms completely unimportant. During the 1940s, Edward Stone Parker recorded in his journal that one such 'letter' was simply 'a dirty fragment from the log book of a ship. The natives however accepted it as a formal proposal for them to visit their Melbourne friends.'[26] Here the dismembered object had been transformed in its new cultural context into something radically other than a (European) book.

In parts of central and northern Australia, written texts functioned in a manner akin to message-sticks until well into the 20th century. Spencer and Gillen observed the use of *'paper yabber'* as a badge of office in the Northern Territory. Seeing 'two strange natives coming into our camp' carrying letters in a cleft stick, they noted that:

> Though the natives had come through strange tribes...yet so long as they carried this emblem of the fact that they were messengers, they were perfectly safe... Such messengers always carry a token of some kind — very often a sacred stick or bull-roarer. Their persons are always safe, and so the same safety is granted to natives carrying 'paper yabbers'...[27]

Books as instruments of power

For many Aboriginal Australians, the word 'book' is a foreign word, part of the language of those they call the *gubbas, migloos, balanda, kardiya* — white people.[28] Books have functioned historically as part of a harsh, externally imposed technology of power. For many, the meaning of 'book' in Aboriginal English carries the memory of oppression. Used as a noun or an adjective, the word 'book' is used in northern Australia to denote 'European law or laws, characteristically written down, as opposed to Aboriginal law which is contained in oral tradition.'[29] As JM Arthur notes, the word 'book' is used metonymically as 'the icon of literate culture, significant because it was from this written tradition that the laws used to control Aboriginal people are drawn'.[30] In the Northern Territory, for example, Hobbles Danayarri used the word 'book' to explain the position of Aboriginal trackers ordered to kill other Aboriginal people: 'They got that book all over from Captain Cook [the government].[31] You might see blackfellows anywhere longa this country, you'll have to get them together and if them too wild, and shoot [the] whole lot… Captain Cook got the order from book.'[32]

Secular book law was backed up by the 'Holy Book', invoked by missionaries and reserve managers as a source of Christian morality and a path to spiritual salvation. This book loomed so large in the lives of Arrernte people at Hermannsburg Mission in the Northern Territory that they referred to everything associated with Christianity — church buildings, church sermons and meetings, as well as the Bible — as *pepe* (paper).[33] This tendency not to discriminate between books and other textual forms is not confined to Central Australia. For instance, *bihbar* in Western Bundjalung, and *piipa* in Wangkumara refer to books, paper, letters or mail.[34]

Books were also part of the daily administrative apparatus of reserve life. Superintendents used books to carry out roll-calls; to record the distribution of food, clothing and tobacco rations; to keep track of the work carried out by the adults; and to record the children's attendance at school. Rations, monetary payments and certain privileges were dispensed or withheld on the basis of information recorded in books. If disputes arose, information contained in the record books was often used to settle the matter. Many discrepancies existed between Aboriginal people's recollections and the facts as recorded in the superintendents' books. Books were therefore regarded with suspicion and hostility. The information they contained was written, read and acted upon by white authorities. On the authority of book records, white officials denied the accuracy of Aboriginal memory, undermined the truth value of Aboriginal people's spoken words, and subverted the structures of authority that bound Aboriginal societies together.

A white man could make a book say whatever he wanted it to say. Sometimes the same book could say different things on different occasions of reading. Accordingly, a significant proportion of Aboriginal people attribute little authority to books. For example, Chips Mackinolty recalled having:

> ...explained to Wainburranga the non-Aboriginal account of Captain Cook. When Wainburranga relayed this account to the people back at Beswick, it was greeted with some hilarity. How did white people know about Captain Cook? Only through books, of course: books are notoriously changeable.[35]

Oral narratives, on the other hand, are more likely to be viewed as reliable and permanent, especially if they are lodged in the land. Wandjuk Marika says, 'Many are the stories I could tell you — *already there in the land*.'[36] Bill Neidjie likens the land to a reliable, indestructible book: 'Our story is in the land...it is written in those sacred places... Dreaming place...you can't change it, no matter who you are.'[37] Books that are based on oral narratives may be reliable, however, if they are produced in proper, lawful ways. Bill Neidje tells Stephen Davis: 'I give you this story. This proper, true story. People can listen. I'm telling this while you've got time...time for you to make something, you know...history...book.'[38]

Dangerous books

Why do stories 'already there in the land' need to be transferred into books? In books, this need is usually explained with the aid of framing narratives about the imminent extinction of fragile oral traditions, or the vulnerability of Aboriginal lands to destruction by white development. Yet books can intensify the dangers they were ostensibly created to alleviate. When given material existence and mass produced in book form, stories once lodged in one unique place are disseminated indiscriminately over large expanses of space and time. Books thus pose a potential threat to the differential rights to certain kinds of knowledge that pertain in Aboriginal cultures. How and by whom are decisions made about a book's contents in a culture where the transmission of information is restricted according to age, gender, kinship, mortuary restrictions and affiliations to country? What problems arise when oral narratives are transformed into books, when their cultures of origin observe strict laws governing how, where, when and by whom certain kinds of knowledge must, and must not, be transmitted? Can mainstream commercial book publishing, which involves mass reproduction and mass circulation, be adapted to the needs of Aboriginal communities whose way of life is grounded in specific places, and whose social fabric is bound together primarily through face-to-face social interactions? Aboriginal people are well aware that books have the potential to violate traditional ownership and inheritance laws. They know that books, by disseminating stories previously lodged in specific sites, can transform owned textual territories into a terra nullius that belongs to everyone and no one.

A number of books have been published that contain secret, sacred knowledge which should never have passed into the public sphere. Yolngu elder Wandjuk Marika, for example, recalled how upset he and his family were to see information they had divulged to anthropologists being broadcast indiscriminately in books.[39] On another occasion, Wandjuk, a gifted painter and senior spiritual leader, came across one of his sacred paintings printed on a tea-towel in a tourist shop. He was so aggrieved that he ceased painting for several years. When recording his own life story for publication in book form, then, Wandjuk Marika pointed out that he had been careful not to include any secret sacred knowledge. Unable to control the circulation of the book, he expunged everything that children, women, *balanda* and other unauthorised people could not lawfully see or know. 'I'm not going to say it,' he maintained. 'The book will spread out too far.'[40] In oral contexts of transmission, Wandjuk would have been able to adjust each story, ceremony and painting in accordance with the knowledge rights of each audience he addressed. In his posthumously published book, *Wandkjuk Marika: life story* (1996), his narratives of sacred events are merely 'one for the books'. In Standard English, something that is special, noteworthy, important, deserving of fame is said to be 'one for the books'. For Wandjuk Marika, however, 'one for the books' would mean something altogether different — a version of a story designed to keep certain kinds of information secret; an abridged, secular rendition of a larger, more powerful, potentially more dangerous story. When Wandjuk Marika passed away in 1989, the imminent publication of his book, edited by Jennifer Isaacs, was postponed for several years in accordance with traditional Yolngu mortuary laws against naming and looking at images of recently deceased people.

Books and social relations

Like other elements of material culture, books are a focal point around which social roles and relations are organised. These roles and relations change not only across time, but as books move from one cultural context to another. Yet, as Alison Ravenscroft has pointed out:

> Dominant western conceptions of the written text tend to assume that the book carries the same relations across cultures and indeed this is the assumption that commonly shapes the encounter between western publishing structures and Aboriginal writers. White readers, editors and publishers tend to apprehend Black writers' texts according to a singular notion of the book and its powers.[41]

Books, documents and written textual production processes were assimilated to varying degrees into Indigenous cultures in colonial Australia. What kinds of social roles and relations are forming today around books at different points on the spectrum of Aboriginal Australian cultures? To what extent do present-day Aboriginal textual production processes differ from those of the colonial period?

Looking first at the moment of writing, European and Aboriginal authorial practices are shaped by disparate cultural values, laws, and conceptions of the addressee. In today's Western book cultures, the qualifications for authorship and readership differ from those that determine whether an individual has the right to pass on or receive information in traditional Aboriginal cultures (among which, it's essential to remember, there is considerable variety). In Western cultures, any person who can find a publisher is potentially the author of a book on any topic. Any literate person is potentially a reader. In traditional Aboriginal societies, by contrast, a person's authority to divulge and receive certain kinds of information may be determined by their connections to paricular sections of country, their place in the kinship network, their gender, age, and/or level of initiation. By criteria such as these, the giving and receiving of information is regulated. Wandjuk Marika, for example, could lawfully speak about his country, culture and history in *Wandjuk Marika: life story*, even though the editorial services of Jennifer Isaacs were required to transform his story into a publishable written text.

In Western print cultures, book authorship is usually conceptualised as a solitary, individual activity, even though the process of producing a book involves editors, designers and many other people whose input affects the experience of the reader.[42] As I've argued elsewhere, this romantic individualist model is not appropriate to the circumstances under which many Aboriginal people have produced written texts, beginning with Bennelong's letter dictated in 1796.[43] During the colonial era, Aboriginal people participated in translation work, and divulged stories, songs and other cultural knowledge to ethnologists and linguists. If their role was acknowledged at all in the resulting publications, these Aboriginal collaborators were called 'native informants' rather than co-authors. This exclusion of Aboriginal people from the category of (co-)author continued into the middle decades of the 20th century. In 1962, Waipuldanya was not named as the author of his own autobiography, *I, the Aboriginal*.[44] Despite the book's title, and the fact that the narrative was written in the first person, the front cover and title page of *I the Aboriginal* named Anglo-Australian journalist Douglas Lockwood as the author. Douglas's role had in fact been to interview Waipuldanya and to transcribe and edit Waipuldanya's story for publication. In his own autobiography, Waipuldanya had been relegated to the traditional but now ethically obsolete role of native informant, rather than author or co-author.

Since the 1960s, a growing number of Aboriginal people have authored books of various kinds, some working alone, others in collaborative relationships either with non-Aboriginal people, members of their own families, or other Aboriginal associates. When today's Indigenous elders record their stories, either for their families or to be published for posterity, a significant proportion occupy essentially the same authorial and scribal roles as William Barak and Thomas Dunolly in 19th-century Victoria, or as Bennelong and his unknown scribe in 18th-century New South Wales. Co-writing practices devised within colonial patronage relationships and in 19th-century mission and reserve cultures still exist. The continuation of these co-writing practices today attests to the survival of both traditional Indigenous authority structures and colonial power relations.

Writers such as Walter George Arthur and Thomas Brune were literally writing for the governor's pleasure. Mudrooroo was right to see this writer–reader power relation as a metaphor that illustrates the political position of Indigenous authors today. Even as Indigenous authors produce texts in accordance with traditional customs, the economic imperatives of commercial publishing mean they must attract as large a readership as possible, which means, in effect, that they are writing for white eyes. In the 1830s and 1840s, Walter George Arthur and Thomas Brune were required to display their assimilation into colonial Christian culture. Today's Aboriginal authors are required by commercial publishers to articulate 'authentic', marketable forms of Aboriginality.

Black–white collaborations today are seen by some as a process that 'dilutes' the authentic Aboriginality of the resulting books,[45] and by others as a means through which an Aboriginal author can gain a greater degree of control over the final published text by in-sourcing part of the editorial process.[46] Depending on the book's intended readership or market, the role of the 'white hand' may either be obscured or highlighted. This decision is usually made by the publishing house. Books aimed at tourist and overseas markets tend to play down white involvement in an effort to appear 'authentically' Aboriginal. In academic and other markets, where cultural métissage is viewed as an asset, the collaborative production process may be partly what the book is about.

Black–white textual collaborations

If books structure social roles and relations differently in different cultures (and in different intracultural spheres), what kinds of relations develop between authors, co-authors, editors and readers in contexts where Indigenous and non-Indigenous people work together in the making of books? How do these relations shape the content and language of Aboriginal-authored books? Alison Ravenscroft has broached such questions in relation to her work on *Auntie Rita* (1994) with Rita Huggins and Jackie Huggins.[47] She suggests that, unlike most Western authors who address a readership of strangers, Rita Huggins was writing in large measure for an existing community of family members and friends. Her sense of readership was based 'largely in the face-to-face, in corporeality, and a shared life, rather than in technologically extended communications such as print, although of course Aboriginal communities use these technologies'.[48] Rita wrote the book with the assistance of her daughter Jackie Huggins and with Alison Ravenscroft as editor. Ravenscroft was inserted into the family by being 'asked to call Rita "Auntie", the customary term of respect for Aboriginal women elders.'[49]

Rita Huggins' sense of the people she was writing for, and the kind of work her book would do in *their* world, shaped both the form and content of *Auntie Rita*. As Alison Ravenscroft has noted, Rita addressed her readers in quiet, intimate tones, as a known, familiar 'you', as 'someone whom she knows and loves…someone who is standing close by'.[50] Because she wanted her book to entertain and give enjoyment to this readership, she left out some of her most disturbing experiences: 'Her Aboriginal readership already knew the painful and unexpurgated life. It was their own.'[51] When, at the launch of the book, Rita met members of her unknown white readership, she drew them into a relationship of community. She spoke with each person at length, and continued that 'conversation she had started in the flesh' by writing 'a veritable letter on the flyleaf' of each book as she signed it.[52] Each copy of the book she sent out into the world at the launch carried on it a tangible trace of her bodily presence.

While Rita Huggins' authorial practices were grounded in a paradigm of face-to-face communication with family and friends, those of her daughter Jackie Huggins were shaped by a print-based sense of the reader as a white stranger. Jackie Huggins saw the book as a political document that could open the eyes of white readers to unknown or misunderstood aspects of Australia's black history. For this reason, she wanted to include painful incidents that Rita herself wished to omit. While Jackie used a gentle, loving voice, and departed from Standard English when addressing her mother in the book, she addressed the reader-as-stranger in a more academic, public voice, providing background information that placed her mother's life in its historical context.[53]

Ruby Langford Ginibi's *Haunted by the past* (1999) was also produced through a process of collaboration between Aboriginal family members with white editorial assistance: Ruby and her son Nobby (the biographical subject), and myself.[54] Nobby began to write his story while in prison, but found the task too difficult, so Ruby decided to write Nobby's story herself. She did a good deal of writing while Nobby was still behind bars, but when he was released in March 1996 he was able to sit down with Ruby and record some of his early memories and later experiences on tape. Ruby and Nobby had been separated for years at a time by prison walls. Making the book together gave them both a chance to share certain parts of their lives for the first time.

In an important sense, *Haunted by the past* is a gift from Ruby to Nobby, an assertion of her enduring love, trust and faith in her son. It is also an attempt to both retrieve and change the meaning of Nobby's life as previously recorded in the police, court and prison records. The book is dedicated to Nobby and to 'every mother's son or daughter who has fallen foul of the Westminster system of justice that came with the first squatters and settlers in 1788'.[55] These people, like Rita Huggins' family and friends, are already familiar with the kinds difficulties Ruby and Nobby have lived through. Yet the content and tone of *Haunted by the past* are shaped by Ruby's desire to reveal to (mainly white) readers a dimension of life that most would not have experienced themselves. Ruby wanted to confront an unknown, unknowing readership of white Australians whose lives were unlikely to have been touched by racial prejudice or the legal justice system.

Although, like Jackie Huggins, Ruby addressed a readership of strangers, like Rita Huggins her primary paradigm of social relations was based in the face-to-face. Paradoxically, she wanted to have a stranger — or someone who could anticipate the needs of strangers — physically present to serve as a sounding board. This was one of my roles. Reading over her drafts, I would identify points in the narrative where Ruby needed to add extra information to make the story clearer. Like Alison Ravenscroft with Rita Huggins, and Jennifer Isaacs with Wandjuk Marika, I was privileged to be incorporated into Ruby's network of familial relations. She made me her 'tidda', or 'sister'. As well as being Ruby's tidda, however, I understood that as Ruby's editorial assistant, one of my roles was to be a surrogate stranger, a representative of the person who does not know Ruby's family history.

The question of Ruby's imagined reader was complicated by the fact that some, but by no means all, of those who would be reading *Haunted by the past* would have already read parts of Nobby's story in Ruby's autobiography, *Don't take your love to town*, a book that has been reprinted many times since 1988. As a story, *Haunted by the past* had to stand on its own; it had to be addressed to a reader presumed to have no prior knowledge of Ruby's family history. Whenever Ruby rewrote events already covered in the earlier book, she would acknowledge that this was the case, in order to avoid being accused of the cardinal literary sin of repetition. To complicate matters further, Ruby and Nobby were acutely aware that some of their potential readers were not strangers at all, but individuals involved in events recounted in the book. Their names had to be suppressed in order to avoid possible legal action or more direct reprisals.

As well as being a sounding board, I was asked by Ruby to tidy up aspects of the text, such as spelling and punctuation, but under no circumstances was I to sacrifice the sense of her voice speaking through the text. Ruby may have seen herself as addressing a readership of strangers, but she wanted them to be able to hear her voice in their mind's ear. She positioned herself imaginatively in the bodily proximity of readers, while also addressing them as strangers. This dialogic, face-to-face relation is reflected in Ruby's use of the word 'aye?', a word that reviewer Ian Henderson has described as 'a hand held out to the reader'.[56] Strangers they may have been, but Ruby's readers were also urged to be with her, standing by her, *at* her side and *on* her side.

Walter D Mignolo has argued that in colonial contexts writing has been used as an 'instrument to tame the voice'.[57] Part of my work with Ruby involved adding punctuation and paragraph breaks without detracting from the oral feel of the text. Ruby's first drafts included very few full stops. Sections contained long chains of sentences joined together with the word 'and'. If a sentence is a grammatical concept grounded in writing and print rather than in oral utterance, Ruby's sentenceless prose reflected an oral paradigm of enunciation. One of my jobs was to add full stops to Ruby's prose where appropriate. Yet when Ruby reads from her books, she usually puts the 'ands' back in. Her readings are a process of re-voicing, an implicit reclaiming of the voice's freedom to break out of the bounds of the sentence. The voice has primacy over the book as a source of authority. Although Ruby takes full political advantage of the book's ability to disseminate knowledge to strangers dispersed over time and space, the primary home of her story is perhaps not in the material artefact of the book, but in the face-to-face social contexts in which it is re-voiced. This re-voicing may be actual, as in the case of 'live' readings, or imaginary, as when readers 'hear' her voice carried to them through the medium of the book. In either case, the book is not the main locus of the story, but rather a means of recycling the text from one (real or imagined) oral context to another.

The challenge of historicity

In emphasising this oral paradigm, I do not essentialise Aboriginal cultures in the pre-contact oral tradition. The manifold shortcomings of the oral–literate binary are by now well established, and it is clear that parts of Indigenous Australian society are no more or less 'oral' than other sections of Australian society. It is possible, however, to see patterns of connection between early and more recent phases of Aboriginal book history; for example, in the pressure to write for a white readership, in the tendency to work collaboratively, in the wariness towards books and writing as technologies of an alien power, in the practice of textually positioning readers as physically present to the author, and in the use of books and writing as a means of carrying stories from one (actual or imagined) context of oral enunciation to another.

The obvious challenge to those concerned with book history in Aboriginal Australia is to retain a cultural materialist focus that distinguishes between books and other textual artefacts without dismissing Aboriginal cultures as inferior to European ones. If one can resist the twin temptations of equating booklessness with primitiveness, and of seeing books as a cultural universal, it is historically valid and politically neutral to say that Aboriginal book history begins with the arrival of European material culture on Australian shores. Like Nobby Langford's life, contemporary Aboriginal engagements with books are manifestly haunted by the past — not a cloudy universal past of human semiosis, but a finite history of entanglement between practitioners of specific cultures at specific moments in particular physical, social and political environments.

Conclusion

The past is not another country

Marshall McLuhan was spectacularly wrong when he proclaimed in 1967: 'The phonetic alphabet, alone, is the technology that has been the means of creating "civilized" man.'[1] There is no such thing as 'the phonetic alphabet alone', and no such thing as a bare, *intrinsically* meaningful sign. There is no single, generic skill called 'literacy', only various cultural practices of different kinds of literacy. Nor is there any Aboriginal community in Australia that exists beyond any neatly mappable spatial or racial frontier. Frontiers are everywhere and nowhere. All over remote, rural and urban Australia, Indigenous people's lives have been changed in diverse ways as a result of their engagements not only with writing and print, but with the telephone, radio and television, email and the internet. Given these manifold changes, we may well ask how relevant are the cultures of Indigenous literacy that developed in colonial Australia? What is gained by thinking about early Aboriginal literacy in terms of traditional cultural orientations, individual collaborations, and bureaucratic mission and reserve cultures?

With the passage of time, it may become increasingly difficult to identify tidy similarities between past and present cultures of Indigenous literacy. Nonetheless, for the moment, significant congruencies are clearly apparent. The three cultures of literacy explored here will, I hope, serve as useful touchstones in future attempts to understand the dynamics of recent Aboriginal reading and writing.

Today, some sections of Aboriginal society, particularly in central and northern communities, resemble the traditionally oriented Wiradjuri carvers in central New South Wales, in that they conceptualise and use alphabetic writing within their own local, traditional frames of reference.

Anthropologist Jennifer Biddle describes how the Warlpiri community at Lajamanu have used the names of the letters of the alphabet as a means of observing the traditional prohibition against saying the names of recently deceased people. Like many Aboriginal communities, the Warlpiri people of Lajamanu observe strict laws that avoid the presence of the recently deceased. Since a person's name is considered part of them, a manifestation of their presence, saying the name of a recently deceased person is considered a serious offence. To avoid naming the deceased, the Warlpiri use a special word, *kumanjayi*, which means 'no name'.

Under certain circumstances, however, such as in land claim genealogies, social security and other bureaucratic purposes, explicit identification of a recently deceased person may be required. At such times, literate members of the community may 'communicate the proscribed name by spelling it aloud or writing it down'.[2] The substitute name is formed by writing or sounding out the names of the alphabetic characters that are used to spell the deceased person's name, or alternatively the initials of the deceased person's name.[3] For example, 'William Quinn Japaljarri' (a made-up name) would be pronounced 'Double-you-Kyoo-Jay'. Biddle argues that this naming by initials effects 'a radical severance of the letter from its sound; a radical reappraisal, in short, of the very relationship which constitutes the alphabet's raison d'être'.[4] The names of the alphabetic characters that are the deceased person's initials become spoken words that substitute for the unsayable name of the deceased. Like the Kulin petitioners led by William Barak at Coranderrk, the Warlpiri people at Lajamanu are today assimilating the alphabet in ways that uphold their own customary laws.

Reading, writing and texts are wrapped up in distinct ideologies, socio-political relations, languages, cultural institutions and material life-worlds. 'The "same" object or practice — in this case, alphabetic writing — is conceived quite differently in different cultures.'[5] By studying the words and metaphors that Indigenous peoples have applied to what English speakers call 'writing', it is possible to gain some understanding of how they have conceptualised, evaluated and used alphabetic writing from within their respective life-worlds. These words provide a sense of the classes of objects and the types of activities that Indigenous communities use when forming their ideas about what writing is, and how it can be used.

For the sake of comparison, it's useful first to explore some associations of the English word 'write'. According to the *Oxford English dictionary*, it derives from a group of Old English, Old Norse and Old Saxon words that denote scratching, cutting or scoring with a sharp instrument. These words reflect the physical and technological aspects of the practice of writing on tough, unforgiving surfaces, in European cultural contexts where writing was considered a craft, a form of physical labour, rather than an art or an indicator of cultural advancement on the basis of its ability to encode spoken language.

What kinds of words do Indigenous Australians today apply to the activities and objects that in English are called 'writing'? What do their languages reveal about their own ideologies of writing, their thinking about what classes of objects and types of activities can legitimately be called writing, and how alphabetic writing can be used? The nitty-gritty of hybridity is manifest, for example, in the language of the Burarra and Gun-nartpa peoples of Arnhem Land, who use the word *jurra* to refer to tracks and footprints, as well as to books and marks made on paper.[6] For the Kayardild people, by contrast, the word *raaj* means to write, spear, sew or make by sewing.[7]

For the Yidinjdji people of the Cairns-Yarrabah region in north Queensland, the closest thing to the modern phonocentric European concept of writing is the term *gijaada gurrun*, which means 'language in marks'. *Gurruna* means 'speech', or the verb 'to speak'. However, the Yidinjdji also refer to writing using the word *manyjam*, a word that in addition denotes scars, marks on a tree and cracks in the ground.[8] The Yidinjdji term *gijar gunda* refers to a variety of activities, objects and inscriptions, such as making cicatrices during initiation ceremonies, painting, drawing and writing. A mark painted or drawn on a shield, or on a person, or on paper is called *gijar gunda*, as are the stripes on a policeman's sleeve, or any natural marks that look like drawing; for example, the stripes on a snake, or a spider's web, or a piece of paper with lines on it, including money. *Gijar gunda* can also refer to the object on which the marks are drawn. As a verb, *gijar gunda* means 'to place, make a mark, sign a name'. The Yidinjdji word *gurrun* means language, story, news, message, or a piece of lawyer vine bent in a certain way and sent as a message-stick. So the Yidinjdji people understand the Western idea that alphabetic writing works as a phonographic script, and the Western function of the written signature as an individual identifying mark, but they also associate writing with the ceremonial scarring that signifies a male's transition to manhood, as well as with graphic art, animal markings and natural features of the land. While anthropologists see message-sticks as mere aides-mémoir, the Yidinjdji people use the same word for message-stick and writing. They have adopted the conventional Western idea of alphabetic writing as a code for spoken language, but they have also added a whole other set of denotations and associations from their own physical environment and cultural practices.

The materiality of written and printed texts appears to be of paramount interest in some Indigenous Australian societies. Some have adapted the English word 'paper' and applied it to a range of objects, a number of which lie outside the realm of what Europeans would consider the material culture of writing. As mentioned in Chapter 9, the Wangkumara people use the word *piipa*,[9] and the Western Bundjalung people use *bihbar* to refer to paper, books, letters and mail.[10] The Arrernte people at Hermannsburg Mission in Central Australia use the word *pepe* to refer not only to paper but to everything associated with Christianity: church buildings, church sermons and meetings, as well as the Bible.[11] The Arrernte classify Western Christianity as a paper culture.

By looking at this small, random sample of words that Aboriginal communities apply to alphabetic script and literacy, it becomes possible to see how deeply embedded people's perceptions of writing are in their own respective cultures, social practices and ecosystems. This finding is consistent with what we saw in Chapter 6, where primary authority was assigned on the basis of William Barak's traditional responsibility as head of the clan on whose estate Coranderrk Reserve was established. This principle of reverse assimilation also emerged in Chapter 4, where the Wiradjuri carver(s) engaged with alphabetic characters *not* on the basis of the phonographic values that Europeans ascribed to them, but in accordance with the roman numerals' resemblance to the shapes of their own traditional inscriptions.[12]

Continuities between past and present are also manifest in the sociopolitical processes of reading and textual production. In the last two decades, collaborative modes of contemporary Indigenous life-writing have attracted intense academic scrutiny in Australia, North America and Europe. Co-writing is nothing new. It began in Australia in 1796, when Bennelong dictated his letter to Lord Sydney's steward, Mr Phillips, having been inculcated into British letter-writing culture by his *beanga*, Governor Arthur Phillip. The etiquette of written communication is imposed by the politically dominant group, either tacitly or through explicit teaching. To lay down norms or enforce adherence to conventions of writing or reading is to exercise a form of power. Deliberately flouting those rules amounts to a mode of political resistance.

For powerless groups, such resistance may simply be too dangerous to attempt. Out of necessity, they abide by the imposed rules of language, genre, textual production and so forth, conceding implicitly to be governed by those who police and benefit from the rules. As we saw in Chapter 5, for example, Walter George Arthur in 1846 meticulously observed the proper procedure to enlist the authorial services of Catechist Clarke, in order to write a properly worded petition against the return of the megalomaniacal Dr Jeanneret. Every aspect of Walter George Arthur's petition was calculated to avoid alienating or offending his addressees. Only by submitting to his readers' standards of propriety could he create even a chance of winning their assent to his request.

Today, Indigenous authors, if they are writing for commercial publication, may be similarly pressured to satisfy the tastes and expectations of the economically dominant readership, even if this means conforming to ignorant white mainstream conceptions of authentic Aboriginality. Only certain kinds of authentic Aboriginality are now a commodity. Only some kinds of difference are eminently marketable. If we examine the economic and political causes of black–white authorial collaborations today, we see power relations completely congruent with those that shaped Bennelong's sporadically obsequious manner of addressing Mr and Mrs Phillips and Lord Sydney in the late 18th century, and Walter George Arthur's enlistment of Catechist Clarke in the mid-19th century. Now, as in the past, individual textual collaborations are symptomatic of political and economic inequality.

Nineteenth-century missions and reserves also have their modern-day counterparts in the form of prisons, children's homes, some mainstream schools and other sites of institutionalised racism. In *Haunted by the past* (1999), Ruby Langford Ginibi writes of Australia as one big prison, asserting that 'we Kooris are an invaded people. We have always had to conform to other people's laws, rules and standards.'[13] Letters from missions and reserves in the colonial era describe hard, constrictive, dehumanising conditions similar to those in the late-20th century prison writings of Kevin Gilbert, Robert Walker and Jack Davis, and in the autobiographies of writers such as Glenyse Ward and Ruth Hegarty, who were removed from their families as children and raised in institutions. In oppressive colonial structures where surveillance and regulation were intensive, early Aboriginal writers such as Walter George Arthur, Thomas Dunolly and Bessie Flower Cameron used their writing skills to carry their people's views to the ears of governments and, through the newspapers, to the public at large. The social function of these early Indigenous writers — their role as spokespeople for those who would otherwise be voiceless — is comparable to Alexis Wright's role in the writing of *Grog war* (1997), Kevin Gilbert's role in publishing *Living black* (1977), and Oodgeroo Noonuccal's role in publishing her poetry. As Oodgeroo observed, she was 'putting their voices on paper, writing their things... I didn't consider it my book, it was the people.'[14] In terms of both the socio-political process of producing written texts, and the harsh institutional conditions under which Aboriginal literacy was acquired and used, striking similarities exist between the colonial period and recent contexts of Aboriginal writing.

Today, as in the past, a whole culture of Aboriginal literacy has developed in response to the requirements of government bureaucracy. In times gone by, Aboriginal people wrote to the Protection Board or sympathetic members of parliament; today, they have to do the paperwork required to obtain housing, welfare, special social services, community development employment program payments, and so on. Volumes of oral history have been generated in the form of evidence in land claims, legal attempts to recover stolen wages, and endeavours to obtain compensation for the suffering of people removed from their families as children. Today, as in the past, an immense volume of Aboriginal writing is elicited by bureaucratic procedures. These aren't the kinds of writing that literary scholars attend to; nonetheless, they are part of the everyday lives of many Indigenous Australians.

Nicholas Thomas rightly claims that 'if actions and events are to be understood politically, they need to be situated historically.'[15] This book is a first attempt to reconstruct the micro-historical circumstances in which Aboriginal people became involved in the colonists' cultures of literacy, and developed their own distinctive practices of reading and writing. Three cultures of Indigenous literacy emerged in the colonial era: traditionally oriented cultures, individual black–white collaborations, and mission and reserve cultures. The continuation of these cultures today tells us two things very clearly: first, that present-day Australia is residually colonialist and, second, that Indigenous traditions are extremely resilient.

It is often said that literacy is empowering. Literacy opens doors. By learning to read and write, people broaden their opportunities. There are many varieties of literacy, however, and not all are available to everyone. Nor does each type of literacy bring about the same benefits. It's easy to romanticise exotic Indigenous cultures of literacy. Academics in the field of Aboriginal Studies get excited when they discover that important elements of Indigenous cultures have survived. Choosing a mode of literacy, however, means choosing a place to belong. The danger today is that Indigenous Australians are becoming confined to a literacy ghetto. As long as they have to choose between belonging to their communities and attaining a 'better' life, Australia cannot be called a post-colonial nation. We still need to ask: Whose traditions open up what kinds of opportunities? Whose literacy rules? Whose literacy is clothed in what kinds of power?

Notes

Introduction

1. P White, *Voss*, Penguin, London, 1957, p. 220.
2. WB Spencer & FJ Gillen, *The Arunta: a study of a Stone Age people*, Macmillan, London, 1927, p. vii. I attribute this quote to Spencer, who was responsible for writing up the data gathered by Gillen.
3. J Beston, 'David Unaipon: the first Aboriginal writer (1873–1967)', *Southerly*, vol. 3, 1979, pp. 334–50.
4. Koori and Pallawah are regional terms that refer respectively to the Indigenous nations of south-east mainland Australia and Tasmania.

1. Encountering the alphabet

1. EB Tylor, *Anthropology*, Chapter 8, Macmillan, London, quoted in Roy Harris, *Rethinking writing*, Continuum, London & New York, 2000, p. 4.
2. T Griffiths, *Hunters and collectors*, Cambridge University Press, 1996, pp. 53–54; R & C Berndt, *The world of the first Australians*, 5th edn, Aboriginal Studies Press, Canberra, 1999 (1964), pp. 535–36; DJ Mulvaney, 'Gum leaves on the golden bough: Australia's Paleolithic survivals discovered', in JD Evans, B Cunliffe & C Renfrew (eds), *Antiquity and man*, Thames & Hudson, London, 1981, pp. 52–64.
3. J Collins & R Blot, *Literacy and literacies: texts, power and identity*, Cambridge University Press, 2003.
4. E Hill Boone, 'Introduction: writing and recording knowledge', in E Hill Boone & WD Mignolo (eds), *Writing without words: alternative literacies in Mesoamerica and the Andes*, Duke University Press, Durham and London, 1994, p. 4.
5. B Street, *Cross-cultural approaches to literacy*, Cambridge University Press, New York, 1993; R Finnegan, *Literacy and orality: studies in the technology of communication*, Blackwell, Oxford, 1988.
6. Collins & Blot, p. 65.

7. M Gale, *Dhangum Djorra'wuy Dhawu: the development of writing in Aboriginal languages*, Aboriginal Research Institute, University of South Australia, Underdale, 1997.
8. See Human Rights and Equal Opportunity Commission, *Bringing them home: report of the national inquiry into the separation of Aboriginal and Torres Strait Islander children from their families*, Canberra, 1997, pp. 280–83.
9. Jessie Lindsay to Mr Hamilton, Native Protector, 17 September 1896, South Australian Aborigines Department, Correspondence Received, South Australian Public Record Office, GRG 52/1, 1896, Item 38.
10. ES Parker, Report, 1 January 1842 to 31 August 1843, quoted in MF Christie, *Aborigines in colonial Victoria, 1835–1886*, Sydney University Press, 1979, p. 126.
11. Grace Power, South Australian Aborigines Department, Correspondence Received, South Australian Public Record Office, GRG 52/1, 1896, Item 287.
12. Published in J Harris, *One blood*, 2nd edn, Albatross Books, Sydney, 1994, pp. 342–43.
13. N Thomas, *Entangled objects*, Harvard University Press, Cambridge, MA, and London, 1991, p. 4.
14. A Gaur, *Literacy and the politics of writing*, Intellect, Bristol & Portland, 2000, p. 33.
15. WE Roth, 'The expression of ideas by manual signs: a sign-language', in DJ Umiker-Sebeok & TA Sebeok (eds), *Aboriginal sign languages of the Americas and Australia*, vol. 2., Plenum Press, New York & London, 1978, pp. 273–301; AW Howitt, 'Gesture language,' in Umiker-Sebeok & Sebeok, pp. 303–15.
16. Gaur, p. 92.

2. Sky gods and stolen children

1. Richard Johnson to Henry Fricker, 9 April 1790, in J Woolmington (ed.), *Aborigines in colonial society 1788–1850: a sourcebook*, University of New England Publishing Unit, Armidale, 1988 (1973), p. 21.
2. K Vincent Smith, *Bennelong: the coming in of the Eora, Sydney Cove 1788–1792*, Kangaroo Press, Sydney, 2001, p. 60–61.
3. D Collins, *An account of the English colony in New South Wales: with remarks on the dispositions, customs, manners, etc. of the native inhabitants of that country*, ed. B Fletcher, 2 vols, AH & W Reed, Sydney, 1975 (1798), p. 495.
4. P Clarke, *Where the ancestors walked: Australia as an Aboriginal landscape*, Allen & Unwin, Sydney, 2003, pp. 25–29.
5. Samuel Marsden to William Wilberforce, 1799, in Woolmington, p. 21.
6. JJ Fletcher, *Clean, clad and courteous: a history of Aboriginal education in New South Wales*, Southwood Press, Sydney, 1989, p. 15.
7. Fletcher, p. 15.
8. Fletcher, p. 16.
9. Richard Johnson to Henry Fricker, 9 April 1790, in Woolmington, p. 21.

10. William Dawes, in Peter Emmett (ed.), *Fleeting encounters: pictures and chronicles of the First Fleet*, Historic Houses Trust of New South Wales, Glebe, p. 111.
11. Fletcher, p. 15.
12. Quoted in J Brook & JL Kohen, *The Parramatta Native Institution and the Black Town: a history*, University of NSW Press, Sydney, 1991, p. 56.
13. Brook & Kohen, p. 65.
14. Brook and Kohen, p. 65-66.
15. Brook & Kohen, p. 67.
16. Brook & Kohen, p. 70.
17. *Sydney Gazette*, 4 January 1817.
18. Brook & Kohen, p. 77; RHW Reece, 'Feasts and blankets: the history of some early attempts to establish relations with the Aborigines of New South Wales, 1814–1846', *Archaeology and Physical Anthropology in Oceania*, vol. 2, no. 3, 1967, p. 194.
19. James Backhouse in N Gunson (ed.), *Australian reminiscences & papers of LE Threlkeld, missionary to the Aborigines 1824–1859*, vol. 1, Australian Institute of Aboriginal Studies, Canberra, 1974, p. 76, n. 72. For other examples of this sort of cultural dissemination, see Gunson, pp. 56 & 57.
20. Brook & Kohen, p. 85.
21. Peter Read, *A hundred years war: the Wiradjuri people and the state*, ANU Press/Pergamon Press, Sydney, 1988, p.11.
22. Macquarie to Bathurst, 24 March 1819, H.R.A., I, x, p. 95, in Woolmington, p. 25.
23. *Sydney Gazette*, 3 January 1818, in Woolmington, p. 24.
24. *Sydney Gazette*, 17 February 1819, in Woolmington, p. 25.
25. Quoted in Brook & Kohen, p. 87.
26. *Sydney Gazette*, 30 December 1820, in Woolmington, p. 26.
27. JT Bigge, *Report of the Commissioner of the Inquiry on the State of Agriculture and Trade in the Colony of New South Wales*, 1823, p. 73, quoted in Woolmington, p. 29.
28. Brook & Kohen, p. 228.
29. *Sydney Gazette*, 9 January 1830, in Woolmington, p. 32.
30. Charles PN Wilton, 'Reverend Charles PN Wilton's views on civilizing the Aboriginals', [1828], quoted in Gunson, vol. 2, pp. 349–50.
31. Vincent Smith, p. 104.
32. Vincent Smith, p. 104.
33. AW Howitt, *The native tribes of south east Australia*, Aboriginal Studies Press, Canberra, 1996 (1904), pp. 98–100 & 106, n.1.
34. John Ritchie, *Lachlan Macquarie, a biography*, Melbourne University Press, 1986, p. 186.
35. Joseph Banks, quoted in Johanna M Blows, *Eagle and Crow: an exploration of an Australian Aboriginal myth*, Garland, New York & London, 1995, p. 45.
36. John Matthew, *Eaglehawk and Crow: a study of the Australian Aborigines*, Melville, Mullins & Slade, Melbourne and David Nutt, London, 1899, p. 15.

Notes (Chapter 2)

37. R. Brough Smyth, *The Aborigines of Victoria*, George Robertson, Melbourne & Trüber & Co., London, 1878, pp. 423–24. On page 15 of *Eaglehawk and Crow* Matthew quotes this passage almost word for word from Brough Smyth; however, on page 102 he erroneously places the names in reverse order, so that Eaglehawk is called Kilpara and Crow is Mak-quarra. In *The world of the first Australians* [1964] (Aboriginal Studies Press, Canberra, 1999 (1964), p. 44), Ronald and Catherine Berndt perpetuate this error when using Matthew to explain the workings of the moiety system.
38. Blows, p. 47. According to Ronald and Catherine Berndt in *The world of the first Australians* (pp. 44–45), the moieties are social divisions formed for ceremonial and other social purposes, particularly the choosing of marriage partners. People cannot marry someone who belongs to the same moiety as they do. Some moieties are matrilineal, others patrilineal.
39. Within these classes, Eaglehawk and Crow are variously named as totemic figures as well. See Howitt, chapters 2 and 3.
40. See 'The eagle', story M37 in Blows, p. 97. This story was recorded in Victoria, and in Wilcannia on the Darling River in western New South Wales, according to Blows, pp. 97 & 210.
41. Blows, p. 97.
42. Matthew, p. 19.
43. See Matthew, pp. 80–82.
44. Brook & Kohen, p. 228.
45. Read, pp. 10–11; J Harris, p. 61.
46. See Handt's journal entry of 29 January 1835, quoted in Woolmington, p. 68, reporting that the Wellington Valley people fled the mission after hearing a rumour that soldiers were coming from Bathurst. See also, J Harris, p. 62.
47. Watson's journal, 29 August 1832, quoted in Woolmington, pp. 92–93.
48. Fletcher, p. 24.
49. Watson's journal, 1839, quoted in Woolmington, pp. 96–97.
50. Gunther to Cowper, 8 February 1840, quoted in Woolmington, p. 93.
51. Gunther's journal, 22 September 1837, quoted in Woolmington, 97.
52. Read, p. 16.
53. Read, p. 19.
54. Read, p. 19.
55. Read, p. 17.
56. Read, p. 18; J Harris, p. 69.
57. J Harris, p. 66; see also James Gunther's extensive records in 'The Wiradhuri dialect', published as part of the appendix to LE Threlkeld, *An Australian language as spoken by the Awabakal*, ed. John Fraser, Charles Potter, Government Printer, Sydney, 1892, pp. 56–120.
58. J Harris, p. 67; Woolmington, p. 91.
59. Quoted in J Harris, p. 76.
60. Read, p. 21.

61. T Swain, *A place for strangers: towards a history of Australian Aboriginal being*, Cambridge University Press, 1993, pp. 126–28 & 145–46.
62. Gunther, quoted in Swain, p. 127.
63. Gunther, 'The Wiradhuri dialect', in Threlkeld, *An Australian language*, p. 70.
64. Horatio Hale, quoted in Swain, p. 145.
65. Swain, p. 127.
66. For example, story M9 in Blows, p. 23.
67. E Durkheim, *The elementary forms of the religious life*, The Free Press, New York, 1915, pp. 330 ff.
68. Threlkeld, *An Australian language*, p. 50.
69. Gunson, p. 21.
70. Gunson, p. 187.
71. Threlkeld, Author's Preface to 'A key to the structure of the Aboriginal language' [1850], in Threlkeld, *An Australian language*, p. 87.
72. Gunson, p. 60.
73. Gunson, p. 50.
74. Gunson, p. 134.
75. Lancelot Threlkeld, *Annual reports of the mission to the Aborigines, Lake Macquarie, New South Wales*, quoted in Harris, p. 57.
76. Threlkeld, Author's Preface to 'A key to the structure of the Aboriginal language' [1850], in Threlkeld, *An Australian language*, p. 87.
77. Gunson, p. 46.
78. Gunson, p. 46.
79. Gunson, p. 46.
80. Threlkeld, 'Reminiscences of Biraban', in *An Australian language*, p. 88.
81. Gunson, Introduction, *Australian reminiscences*, p. 6.
82. Gunson, Introduction, *Australian reminiscences*, p. 31, n. 39; p. 76.
83. Cunningham, quoted in Gunson, vol. 1, p. 6.
84. N Gunson, 'Biraban (McGill)', in G Pike (ed.), *Australian dictionary of biography*, vol. 1, Melbourne University Press, Carlton, 1966, pp. 102–4.
85. Gunson, in Pike (ed.), *Australian dictionary of biography*, vol. 1, p. 103.
86. Threlkeld, 'Reminiscences of Biraban,' in *An Australian language*, p. 88.
87. Gunson, *Australian reminiscences*, p. 5.
88. Gunson, *Australian reminiscences*, p. 6.
89. Gunson, *Australian reminiscences*, p. 46.
90. Gunson, *Australian reminiscences*, p. 99.
91. Threlkeld to the Archdeacon Rev. T Scott, 18 July 1829, in *Australian Reminiscences*, p. 106.
92. Threlkeld to Samuel Marsden, 26 October 1829, *Australian Reminiscences*, p. 106.
93. Threlkeld to Messrs. Hankey and Orme, 23 April 1829, *Australian Reminiscences*, p. 107.
94. Threlkeld to Governor Darling, 26 October 1829, *Australian Reminiscences*, p. 107.

Notes (Chapter 2)

95. J Harris, p. 56.
96. John Fraser, Introduction to LE Threlkeld, *An Australian language*, p. xv.
97. Preface to the Gospel of Luke, 15 August 1857, *An Australian language*, p. 126.
98. J Harris, p. 59.
99. See Threlkeld, *An Australian language*, pp. 88–89.
100. Threlkeld, *An Australian language*, pp. 134–-35.
101. See, for example, *Australian reminiscences*, pp. 46 & 66; *An Australian language*, p. 88.
102. See Gunson, Introduction, *Australian reminiscences*, p. 30, n.14, for an analysis of the relationship between the Awabakal people and other tribal and clan groups in the region of Lake Macquarie and the Hunter Valley. Tindale's map of Aboriginal Australia shows Awakabal country as separate from Wonarrua country; however, Gunson maintains that this error was made because Threlkeld was unaware that the Awabakal were a clan group within the Wonarrua nation.
103. E Webby, Biographical Note, in *Eliza Hamilton Dunlop, The Aboriginal mother and other poems*, Mulini Press, Canberra, 1981, pp. 1–2.
104. Eliza Hamilton Dunlop, quoted in Gunson, *Australian reminiscences*, p. 76, n. 75.
105. Threlkeld to the Rt Rev. William Grant Broughton, Lord Bishop of Australia, *6th annual report of the mission to the Aborigines*, 31 December 1836, in *Australian reminiscences*, p. 134.
106. Wayne Brennan, lecture on the Eagle's Reach site, 5 February 2005, Uniting Church Hall, Blackheath.
107. John Clegg, conversation at Milbrodale site, 8 January 2004.
108. David R Moore notes that RH Mathews, in 'Rock paintings by the Aborigines on Bulgar Creek, near Singleton,' took the rock shelter to be a bora ground, and the figure to represent Baiami laid out on the ground, as in the earth figures made for initiation ceremonies. Moore, however, says that 'contrary to the interpretation proposed by Matthews, this figure has always appeared to me to be flying; this impression is enhanced by its position on the overhang of the shelter and the unusually elongated arms... The white stripes, which have puzzled most viewers, seem to be dangling from the arms like wingfeathers.' (320-1). See DR Moore, 'The hand stencil as symbol', in Peter J Ucko (ed.), *Form in Indigenous art: schematisation in the art of Aboriginal Australia and prehistoric Europe*, Australian Institute of Aboriginal Studies, Canberra, 1977, pp. 320–21; RH Mathews, 'Rock paintings by the Aborigines on Bulgar Creek, near Singleton', *Journal of the Royal Society of New South Wales*, vol. 27, 1893, pp. 353–58.
109. Kellie Austin et al., *Land of Awabakal*, Yarnteen Aboriginal and Torres Strait Islander Association, Hamilton, 1968, p. 19.
110. A significant proportion of Aboriginal rock art in the Wollombi region has not yet been documented. In the newly (re)discovered Eagle's Reach site, there are many birds and hybrid animal/human figures. From the images published

so far (e.g. James Woodford, 'Out of the past', *Sydney Morning Herald*, 4 July 2004, p. 11), there appears to be nothing that resembles the Milbrodale Baiami. For information about the Eagle's Reach site, my thanks go to Paul Taçon (public lecture, Australian Museum, Sydney, 28 August 2003), and Wayne Brennan and Shaun Hooper (public lecture, Uniting Church Hall, Blackheath, 5 February 2005).

111. *Australian Reminiscences*, p. 59.
112. Moore, pp. 320–21.
113. John Fraser, Introduction, *An Australian language*, p. xv.
114. Plaque at the Milbrodale site, transcribed by the author, 8 January 2004.
115. Durkheim, pp. 330 ff.
116. My thanks to archaeologist John Clegg for his observations on the Milbrodale Baiami.

3. Bennelong's letter

1. David Collins, quoted in J Troy, 'By slow degrees...we began to understand each other', in R Gibson (ed.), *Exchanges: cross-cultural encounters in Australia and the Pacific*, Historic Houses Trust of New South Wales, Sydney, 1996, p. 25.
2. Collins, quoted in Troy, p. 25.
3. Sydney Cove is now called Circular Quay; Port Jackson is Sydney Harbour.
4. Watkin Tench, quoted in J Kenny, *Bennelong: first notable Aboriginal*, Royal Australian Historical Society in assoc. with the Bank of NSW, Sydney, 1973, p. 37.
5. J Troy, *The Sydney language*, Australian Institute of Aboriginal and Torres Strait Islander Studies, Canberra, 1993.
6. The whereabouts of the original manuscript of Bennelong's dictated letter (if it still exists) are unknown. The National Library of Australia (NK 4048, MS 4005) holds a handwritten copy of the original transcript, which is reproduced here.
7. N Thomas, *Entangled objects: exchange, material culture and colonialism in the Pacific*, Harvard University Press, Cambridge, MA, and London, 1991, p. 34.
8. Bennelong's reference to 'the Governor' refers to John Hunter, who became governor in 1795.
9. I Brodsky, *Bennelong profile*, University Co-operative Bookshop, Sydney, 1973, p.18.
10. Quoted in K Vincent Smith, p.42.
11. For evidence that Phillip wrote his own reports and letters, see GR Tipping (ed.), 'The official account through Governor Phillip's letters to Lord Sydney', typescript, Garry Tipping, Sydney, 1988, pp. 3 & 110.
12. Quoted in Kenny, p 36.
13. Phillip's Botany Bay memo, n.d. [1788], in Tipping, p. 20.
14. Tipping, p. 12.
15. See Tipping, pp. 12, 79 & 80.

16. Some of these were addressed to Nepean's junior under-secretary, Lord Sydney's son Mr T Townshend.
17. Tipping, p. 16.
18. Tipping, p. 59 & Isabel McBryde, '"To establish a commerce of this sort": cross-cultural exchange at the Port Jackson settlement', in J Hardy & A Frost (eds), *Studies from Terra Australis to Australia*, Australian Academy of the Humanities, Canberra, 1989, p 170.
19. Hunter, in Kenny, p. 14. Depending on their kinship relationship with Bennelong, people called him by a number of different names: 'This native has no less than five names, viz. "Bannelon, Wollewarre, Boinba, Bunde-bunda, Wogé trowey", but he likes best to be called the second' (Hunter in Kenny, p. 13). Additional names of Bennelong are Ogultroyee and Vogeltroyé. For a full list of Bennelong's names and their variant spellings see Vincent Smith, pp. 159–60.
20. Vincent Smith, p. 42. Tipping (p. 42) lists Andrew Miller as the commissary. Smith (p.42) says the commissary was John Palmer who, according to Tipping (p. 17), was provost-martial.
21. Tony Swain, *A place for strangers: towards a history of Australian Aboriginal being*, Cambridge University Press, 1993, p. 123.
22. Quoted in Troy, p. 112.
23. Brodsky, p. 53.
24. For example, WHH Stanner in *White man got no dreaming* (ANU Press, Canberra, 1979) suggests a range of grievances which Bennelong might have had against Phillip.
25. Vincent Smith, pp. 55–59.
26. Vincent Smith, p. 58.
27. Kenny, pp. 53-54.
28. Vincent Smith, p. viii.
29. Yemmerrawanie's gravestone is in the churchyard of St John's at Eltham. McBryde, *Guests of the governor: Aboriginal residents of Government House*, The Friends of the First Government House Site, Sydney, 1989, p. 22.
30. McBryde, *Guests of the governor*, p. 23.
31. Geraldine O'Brien, 'Bennelong: murry good with language', *Sydney Morning Herald*, 22 October 1994, p. 10.
32. Tipping, p. 11.
33. Extracts from Phillip's early journals during his time in the Portuguese navy from 1775–1778 were found among Lord Sydney's personal papers in the United States (see Tipping, p. 11). See also Tipping, Title page & p. 12.
34. Tipping, p. 12.
35. Quoted in Troy, p. 114.
36. My thanks to Professor Paul Eggert for pointing out that the handwriting of the National Library copy dates it in the mid- to late 19th century, and that

37. Kenny, p. 58.
38. Kenny, p. 59.
39. McBryde, '"To establish a commerce...', pp. 173 & 176.
40. McBryde, '"To establish a commerce...', pp. 179–80.
41. McBryde, '"To establish a commerce...', p. 171.
42. McBryde, '"To establish a commerce...', p. 181.
43. Hunter, quoted in McBryde, '"To establish a commerce...', p. 181.
44. McBryde, '"To establish a commerce...', p. 180.
45. McBryde, *Guests of the Governor*, p. 27.
46. McBryde, *Guests of the Governor*, p. 26.
47. McBryde, '"To establish a commerce...', p. 178.
48. See Reynolds, *The other side of the frontier*, Penguin, Ringwood, Vic., 1982.
49. McBryde, '"To establish a commerce...', pp. 176–77.
50. Phillip to Lord Sydney, 10 July, 1788, and Phillip to Banks, n.d., in Tipping, pp. 80-82.
51. Quoted in McBryde, *Guests of the Governor*, p. 31.
52. Collins, *An account of the English colony*, p. 439.
53. Reproduced in McBryde, *Guests of the Governor*, p. 22, Plate 19.

4. Borderlands of Aboriginal writing

1. Quoted in Jacques Derrida, *Of grammatology*, tr. Gayatri Chakravorty Spivak, John Hopkins University Press, Baltimore, 1974, p. 3.
2. See, for example, R Harris, *Signs of writing*, Routledge, London & New York, 1995; D Olson, *The world on paper*, Cambridge University Press, 1994; D Olson, 'A critical notice on Aboriginal literacy', *Interchange*, vol. 25, no. 4, 1994, pp. 389–94; J McGann, *The textual condition*, Princeton University Press, 1991.
3. Olson, *The world on paper*, p. 391.
4. WJ Ong, *Orality and literacy: the technologization of the word*, Methuen, London, 1982, p. 84.
5. Ong, p. 84.
6. Ong, pp. 86 & 90.
7. Dr P Taçon, personal communication with the author, Australian Museum, 23 April 1999.
8. On Wiradjuri Club B, on page 77, the carver reproduces M with one arch too many. On Club A, he may have attempted an M but made one arch too few.
9. Dr P Taçon, personal communication with the author, Australian Museum, 23 April 1999.
10. P Taçon, 'Changing imagery for a changing world: art, material culture and change in south-east Indigenous Australia, 1860–1970', Compromising Post-Colonialisms Conference, University of Wollongong, 10–13 February 1999.
11. J McGann, *The textual condition*.

12. A Sayers, *Aboriginal artists of the nineteenth century*, Oxford University Press, Melbourne, in assoc. with the National Gallery of Australia, 1994, pp. 115 & 145 n.28.
13. Sayers, p. 115.
14. 'Dutigallar' was the name of the woman with whom Batman's party first made contact. Researchers disagree over which tribal groups owned the land to which the treaty deeds applied. Alistair Campbell, in *John Batman and the Aborigines* (Kibble Books, Malmsbury, Vic., 1987, pp. 101–2) states that the territories marked out on Batman's map were owned by at least five tribes: the Wathaurung, Kurung, Woiworung, Bunurong and Taungurong, and that the men who 'signed' the treaty were members of the Kurnaje-berring clan of the Woiworung. Diane Barwick, in *Rebellion at Coranderrk* (Aboriginal History Inc., Canberra, 1998), p. 24, states that these territories approximately match those of the Wurundjeri-balluk (a Woiworung clan), the Yalukit-willam (a Bunurong clan), and two Wathaurung clans in the Geelong region with whom they married. She does not include the Taungurong, nor the Kurung (whom she names as a Woiworung clan rather than a tribe). To avoid perpetuating Batman's mistake, I will refer to the Dutigallar as the Woiworung.
15. Barwick, p. 20.
16. S Wiencke, *When the wattles bloom again: the life and times of William Barak, last chief of the Yarra tribe*, Woori Yallock, 1984, p. 3.
17. J Bonwick, *John Batman: the founder of Victoria*, ed. CE Sayers, Wren, Melbourne, 1973 (1867), p. 92.
18. Quoted in J Bonwick, *Port Phillip Settlement*, Samson Low, Marston, Searle & Rivington, London, 1883, p. 187.
19. Quoted in Bonwick, *Port Phillip Settlement*, p. 187.
20. Quoted in Bonwick, *Port Phillip Settlement*, p. 187.
21. Quoted in Campbell, p. 105.
22. Quoted in CP Billot, *John Batman: the story of John Batman and the founding of Melbourne*, Hyland House, South Yarra, 1979, p. 108.
23. Dawson and his daughter Isabella, who learned the local Aboriginal languages from Aboriginal people working on their property, Kangatong, obtained their information about Indigenous cultures directly from Aboriginal informants rather than by the more usual late–19th century method of sending out written questionnaires to settlers, missionaries and government officials involved in the administration of Aboriginal affairs.
24. James Dawson, *Australian Aborigines: the languages and customs of several tribes of Aborigines in the Western District of Victoria, Australia*, Australian Institute of Aboriginal Studies, 1981 (1881), p.112.
25. Wiencke, p. 8.
26. Billot, p. 83; Andrew Garran (ed.), *Picturesque atlas of Australasia*, vol. 1, Picturesque Atlas Publishing Company, Sydney, 1886. The *Picturesque atlas* was reprinted as *Picturesque atlas of Australasia*, Ure Smith, Sydney, 1974; *Australia,*

the first hundred years, Summit Books, Sydney, 1978; and *Australia, the first hundred years*, Landsdowne Press, Sydney, 1982.

27. R Harcourt, 'The Batman treaties', *Victorian Historical Journal*, vol. 62, nos 3–4, 1991–92, pp. 85–97.
28. This description of the signature is based on facsimile copies included in Harcourt and Dawson.
29. Because Batman did not reveal the existence of the Geelong deed until some days after his return to Tasmania, it is possible that the three copies of the Geelong deed were not drawn up at the same time as the Melbourne deed on 6 and 7 June. See Harcourt, p. 90.
30. Campbell, p. 105.
31. Bonwick, *Port Phillip Settlement*, p. 196.
32. MT Clanchy, *From memory to written record: England 1066–1307*, 2nd edn, Oxford University Press, 1993, pp. 304–8.
33. Clanchy, p. 196.
34. Clanchy, pp. 38, 258–59.
35. R Etheridge, The dendroglyphs or 'carved trees' of New South Wales, Department of Mines, Sydney, 1918, pp. 89–90; C Cooper, 'Traditional visual culture in south-east Australia' in A Sayers, pp. 91–109.
36. Cooper, pp. 92 and 146 n.3.
37. Given the size of the parcels of land in question, this would have been physically impossible.
38. Quoted in Bonwick, *Port Phillip Settlement*, p. 31.
39. Quoted in D Horton (ed.), *Encyclopedia of Aboriginal Australia*, vol. 1, Aboriginal Studies Press/AIATSIS, Canberra, 1994, p. 110.
40. DF McKenzie, *Oral culture, literacy & print in early New Zealand: the Treaty of Waitangi*, Victoria University Press, Wellington, 1985.
41. A Appadurai, 'Commodities and the politics of value', in A Appadurai (ed.), *The social life of things*, Cambridge University Press, 1986; Thomas, *Entangled objects*.

5. Textual battlegrounds in Van Diemen's Land

1. MM Bakhtin, *The dialogic imagination*, ed. M Holquist, trs C Emerson & M Holquist, University of Texas Press, Austin, 1981; VN Volosinov, *Marxism and the philosophy of language*, trs L Matejka and IR Titunik, Seminar Press, New York & London, 1973.
2. WJ Ong, '*Maranatha*: death and life in the text of the book,' in WJ Ong, *Interfaces of the word*, Cornell University Press, Ithaca & London, 1977, pp. 230–71.
3. L Ryan, *The Aboriginal Tasmanians*, 2nd edn, Allen & Unwin, Sydney, 1996, p. 9.
4. Gilbert Robertson (1828), quoted in Ryan, p. 102.
5. Ryan, pp. 102–13.

6. GA Robinson, *Friendly mission: the Tasmanian journals of George Augustus Robinson 1829–1834*, ed. NJB Plomley, Tasmanian Historical Research Association, Hobart, 1966, p. 410.
7. Robinson, *Friendly mission*, p. 410.
8. HK Bhabha, 'Signs taken for wonders', *The location of culture*, Routledge, London & New York, 1994, pp.102 & 107.
9. P van Toorn, 'Mastering ceremonies: the politics of ritual and ceremony in Eleanor Dark, Rudy Wiebe and Mudrooroo', *Australian and New Zealand Studies in Canada* 12, December 1994, pp. 73–89.
10. Van Toorn, pp. 74–76.
11. Robinson, *Friendly mission*, p. 410.
12. Robinson, *Friendly mission*, p. 410.
13. Robinson, *Friendly mission*, p. 411.
14. Robinson, *Friendly mission*, p. 438.
15. V Rae-Ellis, *Black Robinson*, Melbourne University Press, 1988, p. 107.
16. Wilkinson, quoted in NJB Plomley, 'A history of the Flinders Island Aboriginal settlement', in NJB Plomley (ed.), *Weep in silence*, Blubber Head Press, Hobart, 1987, p. 69.
17. Wilkinson, quoted in Plomley, *Weep in silence*, p. 69.
18. Plomley, *Weep in silence*, p. 69.
19. Arthur, quoted in Robinson, *Friendly mission*, p. 941, n. 29.
20. Plomley, *Weep in silence*, p. 68–69.
21. Arthur, quoted in Robinson, *Friendly mission*, p. 941, n.29.
22. Plomley, *Weep in silence*, pp. 69–70.
23. Robinson, *Friendly mission*, p. 61.
24. Robinson, 'Flinders Island journal', 13 December 1835, in Plomley, *Weep in Silence*, p. 319.
25. Walter George Arthur's and Thomas Brune's Aboriginal names are not recorded in the written archive. I refer to Walter George Arthur by his first name rather than his last name in order to distinguish him from Governor Arthur, after whom he was presumably renamed.
26. Quoted in Plomley, *Weep in silence*, p. 68.
27. This rewriting of Genesis is not signed, but Walter George Arthur was the only functionally literate Aboriginal resident at Wybalenna in 1835. Thomas Brune, the other young literate Aboriginal man, appears not to have arrived on Flinders Island until June 1836. See Ryan, pp. 325 & 327.
28. Robinson Papers, Mitchell Library (hereafter ML), A7073, vol. 52, part 6, f. 51, 27 October 1835.
29. Robinson refers to Clark's 'old, greasy dirty fustian jacket which he had worn until, as Mrs Nickolls observed, [it] would make excellent soup if boiled' ('Flinders Island journal', 14 December 1835, in Plomley, *Weep in Silence*, p. 319).
30. Robinson Papers, ML A7073, vol. 52, part 4, f. 39, 24 October 1837. Thomas Brune also used biblical quotations to urge the people to keep the Sabbath

in his sermon of 21 Februray 1838. See ML A7073, vol. 52, part 6, f.133. All quotations retain the spelling and grammar used in the original manuscripts.
31. Robinson, 'Flinders Island journal', 12 December 1835, in Plomley, *Weep in silence*, p. 318.
32. Ryan, p. 135.
33. Robinson, 'Flinders Island journal', 6 December 1835, in Plomley, *Weep in silence*, p. 314.
34. Robinson, 'Flinders Island journal', 6 December 1835 & 13 December 1835, in Plomley, *Weep in silence*, pp. 314 & 319.
35. Ryan, p. 184.
36. The first issue of the Flinders Island Chronicle is dated 10 September 1836; however, Plomley has corrected this dating to 1837. See Plomley (ed.), *Weep in silence*, p. 1009.
37. See Plomley, *Weep in silence*, p. 851, where Drule.er.par is named as Walter's father; cf. Plomley, p. 843, where Walter is not recorded among Drule.er.par's children.
38. On 8 November 1837, for example, Thomas Brune recorded in the *Flinders Island Chronicle* that 'The Native men…were singing bout their own country song.' Ryan also states that 'They hoarded ochre and performed ceremonial rites in secret' (Ryan, p. 185).
39. Ryan, p. 15–16.
40. In an untitled and undated text written by Thomas Brune, he states, 'And when I came on Flinders Island I seen all my brethren and friends and were very glad to see them then when they saw me they were very glad' (Robinson Papers, ML A7073, vol. 52, part 6, f. 71). Trugernana, Wourraddy, and Wourraddy's sons David and Peter Brune were from Bruny Island but their relation to Thomas Brune is not specified in any of the name lists published in *Friendly mission* or *Weep in silence*, where only nuclear family ties are recorded.
41. Robinson, 'Flinders Island journal', 11 October 1837, in Plomley, *Weep in silence*; Robinson Papers, ML A7073, vol. 52, part 4, f. 31.
42. Walter George Arthur to George Augustus Robinson, 1 February 1847; Robinson Papers, ML A7073, vol. 52, part 9, ff. 1–4.
43. Robinson Papers, ML A7073, vol. 52, part 4, f. 23.
44. Robinson, 'Flinders Island journal', 17 October 1837, in Plomley, *Weep in silence*, p. 489.
45. Robinson Papers, ML A7073, vol. 52, part 6, ff. 19, 21, 23.
46. Robinson Papers, ML A7073, vol. 52, part 6, f. 129.
47. Robinson Papers, ML A7073, vol. 52, part 6, ff. 73, 91, 93.
48. Robinson, 'Flinders Island journal', 14 December 1835, in Plomley, *Weep in silence*, p. 319.
49. Robinson Papers, ML A7073, vol. 52, part 4, f. 27.
50. Robinson Papers, ML A7073, vol. 52, part 6, ff. 67, 75, 77, 93, 109, 113, 117, 131.
51. Sermon, 7 February 1838, Robinson Papers, ML A7073, vol. 52, part 6, f. 81.

Notes (Chapter 5)

52. Undated sermon, Robinson Papers, ML A7073, vol. 52, part 6, f. 93.
53. For example, in the *Flinders Island Chronicle*, 2 October 1837, Robinson Papers, ML A7073, vol. 52, part 4, f. 21.
54. Thomas Brune, sermon, 13 February 1838, Robinson Papers, ML A7073, vol. 52, part 6, f. 83.
55. Thomas Brune, sermon, 22 September 1837, Robinson Papers, ML A7073, vol. 52, part 6, f. 67.
56. 'The school to open and conclude with prayer. Dr Bell's system to be adopted, as far as practicable. The children to be taught the English language.' Robinson to Governor Arthur, 15 April 1829, in Robinson, *Friendly mission*, p. 56.
57. Andrew Bell, quoted in Robinson, *Friendly mission*, p. 102, n. 21.
58. See Plomley, 'A history of the Flinders Island Aboriginal settlement'; Ryan; and Rae-Ellis.
59. For example, H Bhabha, *The location of culture*, pp. 85–122.
60. For example, Anne McClintock, *Imperial leather*, Routledge, New York & London, 1995, pp. 63–64.
61. Robinson, 'Flinders Island journal', 20 January 1837, in Plomley, p. 417.
62. Robinson, 'Flinders Island journal', 19 January 1837, in Plomley, p. 417.
63. Robinson, 'Flinders Island journal', 23 February 1838, in Plomley, p. 535.
64. Robinson, 'Flinders Island journal', 1 August 1837, in Plomley, p. 467.
65. Robinson, 'Flinders Island journal', 5 October 1837, in Plomley, p. 483.
66. Robinson, 'Flinders Island journal', 14 November 1837, in Plomley, p. 496; Rae-Ellis, p. 126.
67. Robinson, 'Flinders Island journal', 4 December 1837, in Plomley, p. 507.
68. Robinson, 'Flinders Island journal', 2 December 1837, in Plomley, p. 506.
69. Robinson, 'Flinders Island journal', 16 March 1838, in Plomley, p. 543.
70. Robinson, 'Flinders Island journal', 26 January 1838, in Plomley, p. 526.
71. Robinson, 'Flinders Island journal', 22 February 1838, in Plomley, p. 535.
72. Thomas Brune, sermon, 20 April 1838, Robinson Papers, ML A7073, vol. 52, part 6, f. 135.
73. M Bakhtin, *The dialogic imagination*, p. 344.
74. George Augustus Robinson renamed almost all the Wybalenna Aboriginal people, giving them names from the Bible, Greek and Roman mythology, and British history.
75. Journal annotations, 10 March 1838, quoted in Plomley, p. 726, n. 1.
76. Journal annotations, 17 March 1838, quoted in Plomley, p. 728, n. 1.
77. Journal annotations, 22 February 1838, quoted in Plomley, p. 724, n. 2.
78. Journal annotations, 14 April 1838, quoted in Plomley, p. 733, n. 1.
79. Robinson, 'Flinders Island journal', 20 October 1837, quoted in Plomley, p. 491.
80. Journal annotations, 24 February 1838, quoted in Plomley, p. 724, n. 1.
81. Journal annotations, 14 April 1838, quoted in Plomley, p. 733, n. 1.
82. See Robinson's sermon, 31 May 1829, in the Bruny Island language, where he translates 'Parlerwar' as 'native', in *Weep in silence*, p. 61.

83. Journal annotations, 14 April 1838, quoted in Plomley, p. 733, n. 1.
84. Bakhtin, *The dialogic imagination*, pp. 345–46.
85. See CW Grant, 'The gospel and culture: an Aboriginal perspective', in A Pattel-Gray (ed.), *Martung Upah: black Australians seeking a partnership*, HarperCollins, Sydney, 1996, pp. 162–86. See also J Harris, *One blood*, Albatross Books, Sydney, 1990, Ch. 13; T Swain & D Rose, *Aboriginal Australians and Christian missions*, Australian Association for the Study of Religions, Adelaide, 1988; and the Rainbow Spirit Elders, *Rainbow Spirit theology: towards an Australian Aboriginal theology*, HarperCollins, Blackburn, Vic., 1997.
86. Djiniyini Gondarra, *Let my people go*, Bethyl Presbytery, Darwin, 1986, pp. 13–14.
87. Djiniyini Gondarra, qtd. in A Pattel-Gray, 'Aboriginal spirituality and the gospel: Introduction', in A Pattel-Gray (ed.), *Aboriginal spirituality: past, present and future*, HarperCollins, Sydney, 1996, p. 49.
88. *Flinders Island Chronicle*, 7 December 1837, in Michael Rose (ed.), *For the record: 160 years of Aboriginal print journalism*, Allen & Unwin, Sydney, 1996, p. 18.
89. Rose, p. 17.
90. Rose, p. 208, n. 2.
91. 'Petition to Her Majesty Queen Victoria, 17 February 1846, in B Attwood & A Marcus (eds), *The struggle for Aboriginal rights*, Allen & Unwin, Sydney, 1999, pp. 38–39.
92. B Harlow, *Resistance literature*, Methuen, New York & London, 1987; C Kaplin, 'Resisting autobiography: out-law genres and transnational feminist subjects', in S Smith & J Watson (eds), *Decolonising the subject: the politics of gender in women's autobiography*, University of Minnesota Press, Minneapolis, 1992, pp. 115–38.
93. JC Scott, *Domination and the arts of resistance*, Yale University Press, Newhaven & London, 1990, p. 24.
94. Walter George Arthur to Colonial Secretary, 15 July 1946, in Attwood & Marcus (eds), p. 40.
95. H Reynolds, *Fate of a free people: a radical re-examination of the Tasmanian wars*, Penguin, Ringwood, Vic., 1995, p. 12.
96. Attwood & Marcus, p. 31.
97. Reynolds, pp. 7 & 15.

6. Literacy, land and power: the Coranderrk petitions

1. A Sayers, *Aboriginal artists of the nineteenth century*, Oxford University Press, Melbourne, in assoc. with the National Gallery of Australia, 1994, p. 13; S Wiencke, *When the wattles bloom again: the life and times of William Barak, last chief of the Yarra tribe*, Woori Yallock, 1984, p. v.
2. John Harris, *One blood: 200 years of Aboriginal encounter with Christianity*, 2nd edn, Albatross Books, Sydney, 1994 (1990), p. 153.

Notes (Chapter 6)

3. For additional details about the Port Phillip Protectorate and government policy in subsequent years, see D Barwick, *Rebellion at Coranderrk*, eds Laura E Barwick & Richard E Barwick, Aboriginal History Inc., Canberra, 1998, Ch. 2; MF Christie, *Aborigines in colonial Victoria 1835–86*, Sydney University Press, 1979; and E Foxcroft, *Australian Native policy*, Melbourne University Press, 1941.
4. For further background on this policy, see B Attwood, *The making of the Aborigines* Allen & Unwin, Sydney, 1989, pp. 81 ff., and Barwick, p. 38.
5. Barwick, p. 46.
6. Barwick, p. 49.
7. Barwick, p. 66.
8. Barwick, p. 66.
9. Barwick, p. 8.
10. In *The making of the Aborigines*, Bain Attwood argues that as white racial ideas and attitudes were translated into government policies, they shaped the ways in which Indigenous peoples' constructed and reconstructed their own identity. His approach contrasts with that of Diane Barwick who, in *Rebellion at Coranderrk* and 'A little more than kin: regional affiliation and group identity among Aboriginal migrants in Melbourne' (PhD thesis, ANU, 1963), highlights the continuity of traditional kin- and land-based modes of identification, and the longstanding social cohesiveness that resulted from intermarriage and other ties between the peoples of the Kulin confederacy.
11. Barwick, p. 278.
12. I use Barwick's adaptation of Tindale in naming these groups. See Barwick's map, p. 11.
13. Barak identified these alliances to ethnologist William Howitt in the 1880s.
14. Barwick, p. 13.
15. Thomas Bamfield was also known as Birdarak, Thomas Banfield, Thomas Mickie, and Punch.
16. Barwick, p. 187.
17. Barwick, p. 55, notes that Barak's second wife, Lizzie, was acquired in a sister-exchange with the Brataualung clan of the Kurnai. Barak's sister Borat (c. 1838–1871) moved to Port Albert to live with her Kurnai husband, Andrew (Pondy-yaweet). Through Borat, their children would have had rights under Indigenous law, but not colonial law, to reside at Coranderrk.
18. Barwick, p. 7.
19. Goodall was said to favour those of mixed descent at the expense of those of full descent, and for this reason was not universally liked by the Coranderrk residents. See Barwick, pp. 277–80.
20. Barwick, p. 122.
21. WJ Ong, *Orality and literacy: the technologizing of the word*, Methuen, London & New York, 1982.
22. Barwick, p. 9.
23. Barak, quoted in Barwick, p. 9.

24. Barak, quoted in Barwick, p. 9.
25. Barwick, p. 9.
26. PROV, VA 475 Chief Secretary's Department, VPRS 1226 Supplementary Inward Registered Correspondence, Unit 4, Y6176, 'Minutes of evidence taken before the board appointed to enquire into the condition of the Aboriginal station at Coranderrk', p. 98. Copies of documents authored by the Aboriginal residents of Coranderrk have been lodged with the Koori Heritage Trust, and with members of the families of the Coranderrk residents now living in the Healesville area. For their valuable advice and assistance in this research, my sincere thanks go to Victor Briggs, Kerry Paton and Gayle Harradine at the Koori Heritage Trust, Melbourne; Jim Wandin, Joy Murphy (nee Wandin) and Judy Wilson at Healesville; Margaret Briggs Wirrpunda and Zeta Thomson at Worawa Aboriginal College, Healesville; Irene Swindle at the Koori Coop, Healesville; and Jeannette Crew and Steve Ross in Sydney.
27. Barwick, p. 67.
28. Barwick, p. 67.
29. John Green, quoted in Barwick, p. 67.
30. Green, quoted in Barwick, p. 68.
31. Green, quoted in Barwick, p. 89.
32. In 1869, the *Aboriginal Protection Act* was passed, and the Central Board to Watch over the Interests of the Aborigines in the Colony of Victoria was renamed the Board for the Protection of the Aborigines (BPA). Its membership remained the same.
33. Barwick, p. 91.
34. Barwick, p. 102.
35. Barwick, p. 79.
36. See Sayers, Chapter 1.
37. In the 1880s, ethnographer AW Howitt transcribed a good deal of information provided by Barak about his culture. This was included in Howitt's *The native tribes of south-east Australia* (1904). At some point between 1883 and 1907, the period in which Mr Shaw was manager of Coranderrk, Barak dictated a brief account of his life to a young man, William Edmonds. The transcript is reproduced in Wiencke, p. 3, and correlates with other records of historical events at the time.
38. Barwick, p. 109.
39. Barwick, p. 105.
40. Barwick, p. 113.
41. Barwick, p. 254.
42. PROV, VA 475 Chief Secretary's Department, VPRS 3991 Inward Registered Correspondence II, Unit 834, 75/12439.
43. Barwick, p. 107.
44. Barwick, p. 127.
45. Barwick, p. 133 & 120. See also ME Hoare, '"The half-mad bureaucrat": Robert Brough Smyth (1830–1889)', *Records of the Australian Academy of Science* 4/2 (1974), pp. 25–40.

46. Ogilvie, quoted in Barwick, p. 133.
47. Testimony before the 1881 parliamentary inquiry, in 'Report of the board to enquire into and report upon the present condition and management of Coranderrk Aboriginal station, together with the minutes of evidence', papers presented to both houses of parliament, Victoria, session 1882–83, vol. 2, no. 5, p. 116.
48. EM Curr, Testimony before the Royal Commission on the Aborigines of Victoria, 1877, in 'Report of the commissioners…together with minutes of evidence and appendices', Victorian Legislative Assembly, *Votes and Proceedings* 1877–78, vol. 3, p. 78.
49. EM Curr, Testimony before the 1881 parliamentary inquiry, in 'Report of the board…', 1882–83, vol. 2, no. 5, p. 120.
50. PROVIC, VA 475 Chief Secretary's Department, VPRS 3991/P0000 Inward Registered Correspondence II, Unit 1104, part III, K 9992, Halliday to Ogilvie, 11 September 1876.
51. There appear to have been no minutes recorded at this meeting.
52. William Barak et al. to EH Cameron, 'Minutes of evidence taken before the board appointed to enquire into the condition of the Aboriginal station at Coranderrk', p. 60.
53. Thomas Dunolly to EH Cameron, 'Minutes of evidence', p. 60.
54. Barwick, p. 166.
55. National Archives of Australia (NAA), Melbourne: series B313/1, item 198.
56. Barwick, p. 9.
57. Quoted in Barwick, p. 125.
58. Barwick, p. 74.
59. Barwick, pp. 279–80.
60. NAA: series B313/1, item 213, folio 30.
61. For further details of the conflict between Goodall and Jeannie Rowan and Annie Manton, see Barwick, pp. 275–80.
62. Barwick, p. 279.
63. All but nine signatories appear to have signed their own names; those who didn't have wavering, tentative crosses after their names. There is also a list of firm, confident crosses before the names of all but six people (including those who signed for themselves). These firm crosses suggest that someone was checking off the signatories' names against a list, thereby monitoring who was loyal to whom.
64. Central Board for the Protection of Aborigines, *6th report*, 1869, p. 19, quoted in Attwood, p. 84.
65. Quoted in Attwood, p. 91.
66. See Attwood, pp. 84–103 for background on and analysis of the changes in racial ideology underlying the 1886 amendments to the Aboriginal Protection Act.
67. P Read, Introduction, *The lost children*, eds C Edwards & P Read, Doubleday, Sydney, p. xii.

68. Barwick, p. 302–3.
69. Barwick, p. 303.
70. Barwick, p. 303.
71. Barwick, p. 310.

7. Hidden transcripts at Lake Condah Mission Station

1. Stahle to Ogilvie, 19 June 1876, National Archives of Australia, Melbourne, series B313/1, item 106.
2. In ordinary usage, a 'transcript' is a written copy; however, James C Scott uses the word 'transcript' to refer to speech, writing and non-verbal actions.
3. JC Scott, *Domination and the arts of resistance: hidden transcripts*, Yale University Press, Newhaven, 1990, p. xii.
4. Scott, p. 96.
5. Scott, Epigraph.
6. S During, 'Post-colonialism', in *Beyond the disciplines: the new humanities*, ed. KK Ruthven, Australian Academy of the Humanities, Canberra, 1992, p. 95.
7. Ranajit Guha, *Dominance without hegemony: history and power in colonial India*, Harvard University Press, Cambridge, MA, 1997, pp. xii, 24.
8. Scott, p. 18.
9. Scott, p. 19.
10. John Sutton Jr to Captain Page, September [n.d.] 1877, NAA: B313/1, item 110.
11. Stahle to Page, 14 September 1877, NAA: B313/1, item 110.
12. Stahle to Page, 4 October 1877, NAA: B313/1, item 110.
13. Stahle to Page, 18 October 1877, NAA: B 131/1, item 110.
14. Stahle to Page, 6 November 1880, NAA: B313/1, item 115.
15. Stahle to Page, 6 November 1880, NAA: B313/1, item 115.
16. The precise extent of these forms of personal correspondence is unknown. Few personal letters have survived in the government files, but more may exist in private collections.
17. Scott, pp. 223–24.
18. Obviously no relation to James C Scott of Yale.
19. Stahle to Page, 12 November 1880, NAA: B313/1, item 115.
20. Quoted in J Critchett, *Untold stories: memories and lives of Victorian Kooris*, Melbourne University Press, 1999, p. 154.
21. Critchett, p. 154.
22. My thanks to Victor Briggs at the Koori Heritage Trust, Museum of Victoria, for this information.
23. F Elmore for J Sutton, W Gorrie and T Green to Page, July [n.d.] 1880, NAA: B313/1, item 115.
24. This is not to say that the issues they addressed did not have relevance for the wider Condah community.
25. Ernest Mobourne was first reported to the Board for the Protection of Aborigines for disobedience in 1892. My main source of biographical infor-

mation about Maggie and Ernest Mobourne is Jan Critchett's *Untold stories*, Chapter 9.
26. Maggie Mobourne to the Editor, *Hamilton Spectator*, (n.d.), quoted in Critchett, p. 160.
27. From facsimile copy of Maggie Mobourne to DN McLeod, MLA, 27 February 1900, NAA, series B337, item 507, in Critchett, p. 242.
28. The relatives I have been able to identify were Ernest Mobourne, Robert Turner (Maggie's father) and Bella Mobourne (her sister-in-law).
29. Italics added.
30. For example, Peter Hewitt et al. to the Hon Members of the Cabinet, 2 July 1907 (penned by Ernest Mobourne), PROV, VPRS 3992, Unit 1056, A5318.
31. Peter Hewitt et al, PROV, VPRS 3992, Unit 1056, A5318.
32. Peter Hewitt et al, PROV, VPRS 3992, Unit 1056, A5318.
33. L Gandhi, *Postcolonial theory*, Allen & Unwin, Sydney, 1998, p. 172.
34. Guha, p. 24.

8. Early writings by Aboriginal women

1. D Barwick, *Rebellion at Coranderrk*, eds LE Barwick & RE Barwick, Aboriginal History Inc., Canberra, 1998, p. 217. See also p. 193.
2. These are the main headings in *Letters from Aboriginal women of Victoria, 1867–1926*, eds E Nelson, S Smith & P Grimshaw, Department of History Monograph Series, University of Melbourne, 2002.
3. See examples in D Coleman, *Romantic colonization and British anti-slavery*, Cambridge University Press, 2005, pp. 187–97, and in GA Robinson, *Friendly mission: the Tasmanian journals of George Augustus Robinson 1829–1834*, Tasmanian Historical Research Association, Hobart, 1966, and *Weep in silence*, Blubber Head Press, Hobart, 1987, both edited by NJB Plomley.
4. This letter was separate from the one the Kulin delegation sent to the Queen, mentioned in Chapter 6.
5. Barwick, pp. 66–67.
6. Jeanneret had been Superintendent at Wybalenna from June 1842 to early 1844, when he was dismissed. He appealed successfully to the Home Office against his dismissal, and was reinstated and given financial compensation (S Dammery, *Walter George Arthur: A free Tasmanian*, Monash Publications in History, Melbourne, 2001, p. 28).
7. Quoted in Reynolds, *Fate of a free people: a radical re-examination of the Tasmanian wars*, Penguin Books, Ringwood, Vic., 1995, p. 21.
8. Quoted in Reynolds, p. 21.
9. See Chapter 6.
10. Dammery, *Walter George Arthur*, p. 13.
11. Dammery, p. 15.
12. Quoted in Reynolds, p. 14.
13. National Archives of Australia, Victorian Office: B313/1, item 221.

Notes (Chapter 8)

14. Information about Annie Rich's life was kindly given by her granddaughter, Mrs Dawn Lee, to whom I express my sincere gratitude.
15. Stahle to Page, 31 July 1882, NAA: B313/1, item 118.
16. Author's personal communications with Dawn Lee, 19 January 2000, 12 June 2003 and 6 December 2004.
17. Mary Stahle to Page, 11 November 1882, NAA: B313/1, item 118.
18. Stahle to Page, 3 November 1882, NAA: B313/1, item 118.
19. Harcourt to Page, 29 March 1882, NAA: B313/1, item 117.
20. Annie Rich to Captain Page, 5 April 1882, NAA: B313/1, item 117.
21. Harcourt, cover letter to Captain Page, 13 April 1882, NAA: B313/1, item 117.
22. Stahle to Page, 31 July 1882, NAA: B313/1, item 118.
23. Stahle to Page, 31 July 1882, NAA: B313/1, item 118.
24. Stahle to Page, 31 July 1882, NAA: B313/1, item 118.
25. My thanks to Dawn Lee for this information.
26. Rev. Brown, editorial, 'The Aborigines in Western Australia', *Church of England Newspaper*, 1 February 1868; Bessie Flower, Letters, La Trobe Collection, State Library of Victoria, MS 12117.
27. Biographical information about Bessie Flower Cameron's life is taken from B Attwood, '"…in the name of all my coloured brethren and sisters…", a biography of Bessie Cameron', *Hecate*, vol. 12, nos 1–2, 1986, pp. 9–53; B Attwood, *The making of the Aborigines*, Allen & Unwin, Sydney, 1989; and Nelson, Smith & Grimshaw, *Letters from Aboriginal women of Victoria, 1867–1926*.
28. Attwood, '…a biography of Bessie Cameron', p. 14.
29. Flower to Camfield, 24 July 1867, Flower Letters, folio 13.
30. Anne Camfield, quoted in Attwood, '…a biography of Bessie Cameron', p. 14.
31. Attwood, '…a biography of Bessie Cameron', p. 14.
32. Attwood, '…a biography of Bessie Cameron', p. 14.
33. Attwood, '…a biography of Bessie Cameron', p. 18.
34. Bessie Flower to Anne Camfield, n.d., Flower Letters, folio 15; Bessie Flower to Anne Camfield, 24 July 1867, Flower Letters, folio 13.
35. Bessie Flower to Anne Camfield, 12 June 1867, Flower Letters, folio 5.
36. Attwood, '…a biography of Bessie Cameron', pp. 20 & 21.
37. Attwood, '…a biography of Bessie Cameron', p. 21.
38. Quoted in Attwood, '…a biography of Bessie Cameron', p. 21.
39. Quoted in Attwood, '…a biography of Bessie Cameron', p. 22.
40. Quoted in Attwood, '…a biography of Bessie Cameron', p. 29.
41. Attwood, '…a biography of Bessie Cameron', p. 29.
42. Bessie Cameron to R Brough Smyth, NAA: B313/1, item 163.
43. Attwood, '…a biography of Bessie Cameron', p. 33.
44. Quoted in Attwood, '…a biography of Bessie Cameron', p. 33.

45. See Janice Radway, *Reading the romance: women, patriarchy and popular literature* (University of North Carolina, 1984), on the gender politics of reading popular women's romance.
46. Hagenauer to Page, 24 August 1879, NAA: B313/1, item 173.
47. Quoted in Attwood, '…a biography of Bessie Cameron', p. 36.
48. Quoted in Attwood, '…a biography of Bessie Cameron', p. 37.
49. Quoted in Attwood, '…a biography of Bessie Cameron', p. 38.
50. Quoted in Attwood, '…a biography of Bessie Cameron', p. 40.
51. Bessie Cameron, the *Argus*, 5 April 1886, p. 7, quoted in Attwood, '…a biography of Bessie Cameron', pp. 41–42.
52. Attwood, '…a biography of Bessie Cameron', p. 45.
53. Noelene Brasche, 'Leaving country without leaving the country: Aboriginal life-writing as a discourse of diaspora', PhD thesis, Department of English, University of Sydney, 2003.
54. 'Minutes of evidence taken before the board appointed to enquire into the condition of the Aboriginal station at Coranderrk', p. 67, Victorian Public Record Series (VPRS) 1226, Box 4, Public Record Office Victoria.
55. From 1869 to 1957, when it was abolished, this body was called the Board for the Protection of Aborigines.
56. See Barwick, p. 7.
57. Kitty Brangy to Eda Brangy, n.d., NAA: B313/1, item 42.
58. Page to sergeant of police, Wahgunyah, 19 May 1881.
59. James Percy to AMA Page, 21 May 1881, NAA: B313/1, item 42.
60. The postcards were given to the Mortlock Library in Adelaide in 1985. C Cane & N Gunson, 'Postcards: a source for Aboriginal biography', *Aboriginal History*, vol. 10, no. 2, 1986, pp. 171–74.
61. The letters are mentioned in some of the postcards, but their fate is unknown.
62. Peter Austin, 'Diyari language postcards and Diyari literacy', *Aboriginal History*, vol. 10, no. 2, 1986, pp. 175–92.
63. Cane & Gunson, p. 174.
64. See facsimile copy of postcard dated 1 April (no year is included), in Austin, p. 191.
65. My remarks apply to Austin's translations of Rebecca's postcards in 'Diyari language postcards and Diyari literacy', pp. 180–88.
66. Lena Austin, Purnim, to Mr Macleod, Chief Secretary of the BPA, 29 March 1917, in Nelson, Smith & Grimshaw, p. 114.
67. Mr Ditchburn, Secretary of the BPA, to Lena Austin, 18 June 1917, in Nelson, Smith & Grimshaw, p. 115.
68. In Nelson, Smith & Grimshaw (eds), a hundred pages are devoted to letters regarding children and family, see pp. 25–124.
69. Stahle to Page, 10 October 1883, NAA: B313/1, item 121.
70. Stahle to Page, 10 October 1883, NAA: B313/1, item 121.

71. Margaret Green to Captain Page, 20 September 1883, NAA: B313/1, item 121.
72. Kramer to Page, 22 October 1883, NAA: B313/1, item 121.
73. Stahle to Page, 10 October 1833, NAA: B313/1, item 121.
74. Stahle as paraphrased in Kramer to Page, 22 October 1883, NAA: B 313/1, item 121.
75. Edith Taylor to Page, 15 October 1883, NAA: B313/1, item 121.
76. My thanks to Ian Henderson for this insight.
77. Kramer to Page, 22 October 1883, NAA: B 313/1, item 121.
78. Margaret Harrison [Green] to Page, 9 April 1884, NAA: B313/1, item 122.
79. Stahle to Page, 28 April 1884, NAA: B313/1, item 122.

9. A book by any other name...?

1. The following images are taken from Patrick White's *Voss* (1957), Randolph Stow's *Tourmaline* (1963) and David Malouf's *Remembering Babylon* (1993).
2. WD Mignolo, *The darker side of the Renaissance: literacy, terratoriality and colonization*, University of Michigan Press, Ann Arbor, MI, 1995, p. 76.
3. Mignolo, p. 83
4. See, for example, R Hall (ed.), *The Collins book of Australian poetry* (1981); L Kramer (ed.), *My country: Australian poetry and short stories* (1985); L Murray (ed.), *New Oxford book of Australian poetry*, and K Goodwin & A Lawson (eds), *The Macmillan anthology of Australian literature* (1990).
5. R Bringhurst, 'Native American oral literatures and the unity of the humanities', Garnett Sedgewick Memorial Lecture, University of British Columbia, Vancouver, 17 July 1998.
6. G Warkentin, 'In search of "The word of the other": Aboriginal sign systems and the history of the book in Canada', *Book History*, vol. 2, (1999), eds E Greenspan & J Rose, Penn State University Press, 1999, p. 18.
7. Warkentin, p. 20.
8. Warkentin, p. 18.
9. Mignolo, p. 119.
10. The concept of 'entanglement' is developed in N Thomas, *Entangled objects*, Harvard University Press, Cambridge, MA, and London, 1991.
11. J Fabian, *Time and the other: how anthropology makes its object*, Columbia University Press, New York, 1983.
12. Regular contact between Aboriginal and settler societies occurred at different times in different parts of Australia, beginning at Sydney Cove in 1788 (and spreading west after 1813); in Tasmania in 1803; in Victoria, South Australia and the south-west of Western Australia in the 1830s; and in central and northern Australia in the second half of the 19th century and the early decades of the 20th century.
13. H Reynolds, *The other side of the frontier*, Penguin, Ringwood, Vic., 1981, Chapter 1.

14. Reynolds, p. 49.
15. P van Toorn, 'Transactions on the borderlands of Aboriginal writing', *Social Semiotics*, vol. 11, no. 2, August 2001, pp. 209–27.
16. FN Bucknell, 'Message sticks and their meanings', the *Australian Anthropological Journal*, 27 February 1897, p. 10.
17. R Hamlyn-Harris, 'On messages and "message sticks" employed among the Queensland Aborigines', *Memoirs of the Queensland Museum*, vol. 6, 1918, pp. 15, 30–31.
18. Hamlyn-Harris, pp. 13, 15; WW Thorpe, 'Aboriginal message sticks', the *Australian Museum Magazine*, vol. 2, no. 12, 1926, p. 423; CP Mountford, 'Aboriginal message sticks from the Nullabor Plains', *Transactions of the Royal Society of South Australia*, vol. 62, no. 1, 22 July 1938, p. 126.
19. Mountford, p. 126.
20. Thorpe, p. 423.
21. J Dawson, *Australian Aborigines*, George Robertson, Melbourne, 1881, p. 74.
22. J Critchett, *A distant field of murder: Western District frontiers 1834–1848*, Melbourne University Press, 1990, pp. 9–10.
23. Critchett, p. 10.
24. AW Howitt, *The native tribes of south-east Australia*, Aboriginal Studies Press, Canberra, 1996 (1904), pp. 678–710.
25. Critchett, p. 37.
26. E Morrison, *Early days on the Loddon Valley: memoirs of Edward Stone Parker 1802–1865*, n.p. (Daylesford, Vic.), c.1966, p. 55.
27. Quoted in Thorpe, p. 425.
28. These words are used by Aboriginal people in different regions to refer to white people: *gubbas* in south-eastern Australia, *migloos* in Queensland, *balanda* in northern Australia, *kardiya* in central and western Australia.
29. JM Arthur, *Aboriginal English: a cultural study*, Oxford University Press, Melbourne, 1996, p. 137.
30. Arthur, p. 137.
31. Here 'Captain Cook' refers metonymically to the government; cf. Paddy Fordham Wainburranga in the film *Too many Captain Cooks*, dir. Penny McDonald, Australian Film and Television School, Sydney, 1988.
32. Hobbles Danayarri in D Bird Rose, *Hidden histories: black stories from Victoria River Downs, Humbert River and Wave Hill Stations*, Aboriginal Studies Press, Canberra, 1991, p. 72.
33. D Austin-Broos, unpublished lecture, 16 March 2000, University of Sydney.
34. M Sharpe, *Dictionary of Western Bundjalung*, 2nd edn, Linguistics Department, University of New England, 1995; C Robertson, *Wangkumara grammar and dictionary*, n.p., n.d.
35. C Mackinolty & P Wainburranga, 'Too many Captain Cooks', in T Swain & D Bird Rose (eds), *Aboriginal Australians and Christian missions*, Australian Association for the Study of Religions, Sydney, 1988, p. 360.

36. Wandjuk Marika, *Wandjuk Marika: life story*, as told to Jennifer Isaacs, University of Queensland Press, St Lucia, 1995, p. 22.
37. B Neidjie, S Davis & A Fox, *Kakadu man*, Mybrood, NSW, 1985, pp. 47, 48.
38. Neidje, Davis & Fox, p. 33.
39. Wandjuk Marika, p. 14.
40. Wandjuk Marika, p. 40.
41. A Ravenscroft, 'Strange and sanguine relations: Aboriginal writing and Western book culture,' *Meridian*, vol. 16, no. 2, October 1997, p. 261.
42. See J Stillinger, *Multiple authorship and the myth of solitary genius*, Oxford University Press, New York, 1991.
43. P van Toorn, 'Early Aboriginal writing and the discipline of literary studies', *Meanjin*, vol. 55, no. 4, 1996, pp. 754–65; 'Authors, scribes and owners', *Continuum*, vol. 13, no. 3, 1999, pp. 333–43.
44. Douglas Lockwood, *I, the Aboriginal*, Rigby, Adelaide, 1962.
45. See, for example, Mudrooroo, *Milli Milli Wangka*, Hyland House, Melbourne, 1997, pp. 184–85.
46. P van Toorn, 'Indigenous texts and narratives', *Cambridge companion to Australian literature*, ed. Elizabeth Webby, Cambridge University Press, 2000, pp. 19–49.
47. Ravenscroft, pp. 261–69.
48. Ravenscroft, p. 263.
49. Ravenscroft, p. 265.
50. Ravenscroft, p. 263.
51. Ravenscroft, p. 266.
52. Ravenscroft, p. 264.
53. Ravenscroft, p. 267–68.
54. I am not aware of the precise nature of Alison Ravenscroft's editorial work with Rita and Jackie Huggins. The following account of my work with Ruby Langford Ginibi should not be taken as indicative of the nature of Alison Ravenscroft's work.
55. R Langford Ginibi, *Haunted by the past*, Allen & Unwin, Sydney, 1999, p. v.
56. The more orthodox spelling is 'eh'. Ian Henderson, personal communication to Penny van Toorn, 26 July 1999.
57. Mignolo, p. 43.

Conclusion

1. M McLuhan, *Understanding media: the extension of man*, Sphere Books, London, 1967, pp. 93–94.
2. Quoted in J Biddle, 'Writing without ink', in A Lee & C Poynton (eds), *Culture and text: discourse and methodology in social research and cultural studies*, Allen & Unwin, Sydney, 2000, p. 180.
3. Biddle, p. 181.
4. Biddle, p. 182.

5. WG Mignolo, *The darker side of the Renaissance: literacy, territoriality, and colonization*, University of Michigan Press, Ann Arbor, MI, 1995, p. 23.
6. K Glasgow (comp.), *Burarra–Gun-nartpa dictionary*, Summer Institute of Linguistics, Berrimah, NT, 1994.
7. N Evans, *Kayardild dictionary & thesaurus*, Dept of Linguistic & Language Studies, University of Melbourne, 1992.
8. RMW Dixon (comp. & ed.), *Words of our country: stories, place names and vocabulary in Yidiny [Yidinjdji], the Aboriginal language of the Cairns-Yarrabah region*, University of Queensland Press, St Lucia, 1991.
9. C Robertson, *Wangkumara grammar and dictionary*, n.p., n.d.
10. M Sharpe, *Dictionary of Western Bundjalung*, 2nd edn, Linguistics Department, University of New England, 1995.
11. D Austin-Broos, unpublished lecture, 16 March 2000, University of Sydney.
12. P van Toorn, 'Transactions on the borderlands of Aboriginal writing', *Social Semiotics*, vol. 11, no. 2, 2001, pp. 209–27.
13. R Langford Ginibi, *Haunted by the past*, Allen & Unwin, Sydney, 1999, p. v.
14. Oodgeroo Noonuccal, Interview, *Meanjin*, vol. 36, no. 4, 1977, p. 429.
15. N Thomas, *Entangled objects*, Harvard University Press, Cambridge, MA, and London, 1991, p. 9.

Index

Aboriginal Christianity, 118–19
Aboriginal economy: destruction of in Victoria, 123
Aboriginal graphic tradition, 20; and writing, 2
Aboriginal languages: early colonial interest in, 53; translations into, 37–8; words for 'book' in, 214; *see also* Awabakal people and language; Ben Lomond people and language; Big River people and language; Bruny Island people and language; Diyari people and language; Northern people and language; Wangkumara people and language; Western Bundjalung people and language; Western people and language; Wiradjuri people and language
Aboriginal nationalism: beginnings of, 117, 118
Aboriginal Protection Act 1869 (Vic.): 1886 amendments to people of mixed descent, 149–50, 181, 191
Aboriginal resistance, 173; consequences of, 156, 158; dangerous wanderers and, 164–5, 169
Aboriginal women: authorial agency of, 201; colonialism and, 6, 176; letters by *see under* letters; literacy and language skills of, 177; translators of speeches by men, 116, 117, 176; between two patriarchies, 178; Woiworung, 127; writing by *see* writing by Aboriginal women

Aboriginality: black–white authorial collaborations and, 219; as commodity, 218, 228; literacy and, 18
'Aboriginals' Narrative', 159–62, 163–4
The Aborigines of Victoria (R Brough Smyth), 32
Account of the English colony in New South Wales (David Collins): portrait of Bennelong in, 69
Acheron Reserve, 123–4, 147
Albert, Henry, 170
Albert, Herbert, 157–8
alphabet: assimilation of to customary law, 225
alphabetic literacy: at Coranderrk Reserve, 6, 129; and ideological contexts, 13–14; and 'oral' societies, 3–4; traditionally based Indigenous practices of, 11; *see also* non-alphabetic graphic systems
alphabetic script: Aboriginal non-phonographic use of, 74–9, 91, 92, 211, 227; Aboriginal uses of on borderland between cultures, 73–4, 92; and books, 207, 211; and entanglement of orality and literacy, 140; variety of, 74–5; on variety of sign carriers, 211
Arabanoo, 57
archival research: and silences of archives, 173
Arrernte people, 214, 227
Arthur, Governor Sir George: and observance of Sabbath, 101–2; and translation of Bible into Aboriginal

Index

languages, 100–1, 117; and war against Aboriginal people of Van Diemen's Land, 95–6

Arthur, Mary Anne (*nee* Cochrane): and emerging culture of Pallawah literacy, 178–9; letter of to Queen Victoria re Dr Henry Jeanneret on behalf of whole Coranderrk community, 178–9, 179

Arthur, Walter George, 114, 204, 218; authority of, 105, 106, 130, 149; and black–white authorial collaboration, 121, 122, 228; Robert Clark and, 108, 121, 122; and colonial authority, 104–5, 106; and etiquette of written comm-unication, 228; formulaic repetition in writings and sermons of, 108–9; and institutional conditions of Indigenous literacy, 228; and mediation of Bible in assimilationist ways, 101; and obser-vance of Sabbath, 102–3; and petition against reinstatement of Dr Henry Jeanneret, 119, 121, 177–8; George Augustus Robinson and, 104, 111–12, 130; and use of Bible for political instruction, 107; use of pers-onal pronouns in and ambiguity of social positioning and audience in writings and sermons of, 111–12; writings and sermons of, 104, 106, 107–8, 110, 118

assimilation: amendments to *Aboriginal Protection Act 1869* (Vic.) re people of mixed descent and, 150; Bible and, 95, 100, 101, 102, 103; literacy and, 12–13, 18; and removal of children, 15; *see also* hegemonic control

Attwood, Bain: on Bessie Cameron (*nee* Flower), 193

Auntie Rita (Rita Huggins and Jackie Huggins), 219–20

Austin, Lena: letter by, 198–200

Australian Aborigines (James Dawson), 84

Australian reminiscences and papers (Lancelot Threlkeld), 43, 46

authorial practices: denial of authorship to Aboriginal people, 208, 218; European and Aboriginal, 217–18; of Jackie Huggins, 220; of Rita Huggins, 220

authority structures *see* Indigenous land-based and kin-based authority structures

autonomous model of literacy, 8–9, 11–12, 23; and government policy, 12–13

Awabakal people and language, 4, 39; literacy in language of, 40; translations into, 40

Baiami, 38–9; *see also* Milbrodale Baiami

Bains, Robert, 140

Bakhtin, Mikhail, 97; on monologic and dialogic reading practices, 94

Bamfield, Betsy: as scribe, 179, 181

Bamfield, Thomas, 127, 143, 146, 147, 149, 151, 181

Barak, William, 123, 128, 134, 147, 204, 225; authority of, 105, 149, 227; and Coranderrk Reserve, 124, 127; and John Batman's treaty, 82, 84, 123, 143; as *ngurungaeta*, 125, 130, 146; as painter, 133; and petitions, 130, 131–2, 134, 140, 141, 143, 144, 145, 146, 179, 181; and scribes, 133–4, 134, 179, 181; and traditional Indigenous law, 126; and written 'loyal address' to Queen Victoria re land for Coranderrk Reserve, 125

Barker, James [Jemmy], 139

Barwick, Diane, 126, 127

Batman, John *see* Batman treaty with Woiworung people

Batman treating with the Blacks (engraving by GR Ashton), 84, 85, 86

Batman treaty with Woiworung people, 5, 82, 92, 123, 124; declared void, 91; as forgery, 83, 84, 87, 90–1; signatures on, 83, 84, 86–9; use of non-writing and, 91; versions of, 82–3, 85–6

Bell, Dr Andrew: educational method of, 112

Ben Lomond people and language, 104, 105, 177; translation of Bible into language of, 100; translations into, 100

Bennelong, 4–5, 14, 19; adoption of Governor Arthur Phillip into kinship network, 59–61, 62, 63; and black–white authorial collaboration, 228; in

258

England, 61, 62, 69; as exotic exhibit, 69; letter of *see* Bennelong's letter; and letters as means of asking for things, 67–8; and letters as tradable objects, 56, 67, 70; as mimic, 5, 56, 57, 64; and Governor Arthur Phillip, 5, 14, 56–8; and Mr and Mrs Phillips, 61, 62, 64, 67, 69–70; and scribe, 54, 227, 228; and trade, 5, 66–7, 70

Bennelong's letter, 4, 5, 53, 54–5, 61–2, 64, 65, 69–70, 217; and etiquette of written communication, 55–6, 227; and genres of colonial bureaucratic writing, 56; as intercultural entanglement, 54, 56; and patterns of gift exchange, 56, 62–3, 67–8; Governor Arthur Phillip's correspondence as models for, 5, 58–9

Berry, Graham, 181

Bhabha, Homi: on potential ambivalence of the book, 97

Bible: in Aboriginal ritual and Christian liturgy, 5; and assimilation, 95, 100, 101, 102, 103; and Biraban's dream, 48; and 'civilisation', 23; in colonial contexts, 93–4; decolonisation of, 95; as 'Holy Book', 214; interpretation of, 22; monologic and dialogic reading practices and, 94–5; monologic reading of, 99; older men's rearticulation of, 115–18; Roman Catholic and Protestant readings of, 93; teaching of from direct knowledge, 110; teaching of only in English, 99, 101, 117; translation of *see* translation of Bible; and use of for political instruction, 107; George Van Dieman's assimilation of to recent historical experience of Aboriginal people, 100; Wiradjuri assimilation of to traditional understanding of universe, 38

Big River people and language, 104, 116

Bigge, JT, 29–30

Billibillary, 123

Billie Blue, 40

Biraban, 4, 14, 19, 22, 42–3; as author, 44–6; as Awabakal clan-head, 43; and biblical translation and linguistic work with Lancelot Threlkeld, 39, 42, 43–6, 48; dream of, 47–8; and Eaglehawk, 42, 43, 46; and Milbrodale Baiami, 48–52; spiritual leadership of, 47

black–white authorial collaborations, 122, 218–19; and Aboriginality, 219; Walter George Arthur and Robert Clark, 121, 122, 228; Bennelong and scribe, 54, 227, 228; Biraban and Lancelot Threlkeld, 44–5, 47–8

black–white textual collaborations, 219–22

Blot, Richard *see* Collins, James, and Richard Blot

Blows, Johanna M: on Eaglehawk and Crow, 33

Board for the Protection of Aborigines (BPA), 155; and struggles over Coranderrk Reserve, 127–8, 133; *see also* Page, Captain

Boaz, Franz, 208

Bon, Ann, 128, 147, 149, 175

Bonwick, James: on Mary Anne Arthur, 178

the book and books: Aboriginal words for 'book', 214; authored by Aboriginal people, 218; connotations of word 'book' for Aboriginal people, 213–15; and cultural evolution, 207, 209, 223; defined Eurocentrically, 206–7, 208, 210; and entanglement between Indigenous and non-Indigenous Australian cultures, 210; as function, 208; Indigenous oral cultural traditions and, 215; as instruments of power, 213–16; and message-sticks, 209; and non-European sign-carriers, 209–10; parts of used in ritual, 68, 96–9, 211; physical form of, 207; potential ambivalence of, 97; production of by Indigenous and non-Indigenous people *see* black–white textual collaborations; and readership of strangers, 219, 220, 221–2; reinvention and recontextualisation of by non-European cultures, 209–10; and reserve life, 214; and social relations, 216–19; as threat to differential rights Aboriginal knowledges, 215–16; as tradable objects rather than sign carriers, 210–11; transformations of by Aboriginal

people, 6; in wilderness, 206; *see also* black–white authorial collaborations
book history, 208, 209–10; Aboriginal, 222–3
Book of common prayer, 97; pages of used in Aboriginal ritual, 96–9, 211
Boorong, 24–5, 26, 176
borderland writings, 5
Bourke, Governor Richard: and John Batman's treaty, 91
Brangy, Edith (Eda), 196, 197
Brangy, Kitty: letter to sister Edith, 196–7, 198
Briggs, John, 140
Briggs, Louisa, 140
Brindle, Emily (*nee* Peters), 190
Bringhurst, Robert: on books and oral texts, 207–8
Bringing them home: report of the national inquiry into the separation of Aboriginal and Torres Strait Islander children from their families, 15–16, 24, 200, 203, 204
Brisbane, Governor Sir Thomas: and war against Wiradjuri people, 34
Brough Smyth, R: on Eaglehawk and Crow, 32
Brune, Thomas, 204, 218; authority of, 105–6, 110, 130, 149; and Bible, 106–7; Robert Clark and, 106–7, 108; and colonial authority, 104–5, 106; formulaic repetition in writings and sermons of, 108–9; and mediation of Bible in assimilationist ways, 101; George Augustus Robinson and, 104, 111–12, 119, 130; and use of Bible for political instruction, 107; use of personal pronouns in and ambiguity of social positioning and audience in writings and sermons of, 111–12; writings and sermons of, 104, 106–7, 107–8, 109–10, 115, 118, 119
Bruny Island people and language, 96, 101, 104, 105, 116, 117
Bungett, 90
Bunurong people, 126
Burapper people, 127, 139–40, 140
bureaucratic governance: and Aboriginal writing, 21, 22, 125, 135, 201, 229; and Bennelong's letter, 56; and writing as governance of Aboriginal people by remote control, 194–5; and writing to keep Aboriginal people at a distance, 200
Burrara people: associations of their word for writing, 226

Cameron, Bessie (*nee* Flower), 179, 186–94; as immigrant, 194; and institutional conditions of Indigenous literacy, 228; letters of, 187–8, 189, 191, 192–3; petition by, 189, 190; as self-authorising woman, 193–4; writing and reading abilities of, 186, 188, 190, 193; writing and reading abilities of as evidence of success of missions, 186, 188, 189–90
Cameron, Boyd, 190
Cameron, Donald, 188, 189, 190, 191
Camfield, Anne, 186, 187
Camfield, Martie, 187
catechetical question-and-answer, 109, 115
Central Board to Watch over the Interests of the Aborigines, 124, 195
Charles, John, 139
child removal *see* stolen generations
Christian, Samuel, 25
Clark, Robert: and Walter George Arthur and Thomas Brune, 106–7, 108, 121, 122; and black–white authorial collaboration, 121, 122, 228; preaching by in pidgin English, 101, 103
clubs, carved wooden: in Wiradjuri country *see* Wiradjuri clubs
Cochrane, 36
coercion and ideological controls, 173; and Aboriginal people, 154–5, 173–4; *see also* hegemonic control
Colby, 29, 57, 65
Collins, David, 69
Collins, James, and Richard Blot: on literacy, 10
colonialism: and Aboriginal women, 6, 176; and coercion, 152, 154, 170; writing and, 23; *see also* gendered power structure of colonial society
commercial publication: and etiquette of written communication, 228

context: ideological and cultural contexts of sign systems, 72–3; literacy and *see* literacy in context; perceptions of writing and, 227

Coranderrk petitions, 6, 130; September 1874, 133–4; October 1875, 134–7; September 1876, 137–40; September 1881, 141–2; late 1881, 131–2; 21 January 1884, 147–9; October 1893, 179–81; authenticity of as formal record of spoken words, 140; author, scribe and owner of, 146; and entanglement or orality and literacy, 140–4; face-to-face representations in support of, 134, 141, 143–4; and messengers and mediators, 137; questioning of authenticity of, 137, 138, 139, 143, 144–6; 'speakers' and, 146; written evidence and, 141, 142

Coranderrk Reserve, 22, 124, 132; closure of, 151; Green years, 132–3; identification of community at with original country, 127; Indigenous land-based and kin-based authority structures at, 125–6; inquiry into, 194; land-based and kin-based authority structures at, 130; letter to *Argus* (1882) re restrictions at, 144–5; and literacy, 129, 133; and literacy and traditional gendered gerontocracy, 130; paper wars with Board for the Protection of Aborigines over, 127–8, 133; petitions *see under* petitions; social composition of community at, 126

co-writing *see* black–white authorial collaborations

cross-cultural exchange of goods, 65–6, 68–9

Crow: and Daramulun, 39; in Eora language, 31; Kulin nation and, 126

Crow and Eaglehawk: in Aboriginal mythology, 31, 32, 33, 34; narratives of and stolen children, 4, 33; and traditional marriage customs, 32

cultural authority: multi-centredness of, 209

cultures of literacy *see under* literacy

Curr, Edward, 128, 138

dangerous wanderers, 162; and transmission of hidden transcripts between isolated cells of oppressed group, 163; *see also* Scott, James

Daramulun (son of Eaglehawk), 39

Davis, Jack, 228

Dawes, Lieutenant William: and recording of Aboriginal languages, 53

Dawson, James, 84

Deans, James, 138, 140

deceased persons: use of names of alphabetical letters and traditional prohibition on saying names of, 225

dendroglyphs, 89, 90; signatures, 84, 86; signatures and John Batman's treaty, 83, 84, 86, 87, 89, 90

Dharug people, 4, 62, 64

dialogic reading practices: and monologic reading practices, 94–5

dissent: Aboriginal people and, 6; *see also* open dissent and resistance

Ditchburn, Mr, 200

Diyari people and language, 197, 198

Djadjawurung people, 127, 139, 140, 146, 177

Djiniyini Gondarra, 118–19

Domination and the arts of resistance (James C Scott), 152

Don't take your love to town (Ruby Langford Ginibi), 221

Dow.wring.gi ('Leonidas', also named 'David'): rearticulation of Bible by, 116

drawings of writings of Charlie Flannigan, 5

Drine.ne ('Neptune'): rearticulation of Bible by, 116

Drue.mer.ter.pun.ner ('Alexander'): rearticulation of Bible by, 116

Duffit, Mr, 166, 167

Dunlop, Eliza Hamilton, 46–7

Dunolly, Thomas, 146–9, 150–1, 181, 218; and Coranderrk Reserve land, 127; and institutional conditions of Indigenous literacy, 228; letter of rebutting evidence of BAP officials, 242; and Caroline Morgan's petition, 194; and penning of Coranderrk petitions, 144, 146, 147,

149; and petition of 21 January 1884, 147; as scribe of William Barak, 146, 147, 149, 150, 218

Eagle and Crow (Johanna M Blows), 33
'The eagle chief' (Eliza Hamilton Dunlop), 46
Eaglehawk: and Biraban, 42, 43, 46; and Daramulun, 39; and Jehovah, 47, 48, 49–50, 51, 52; *see also* Milbrodale Baiami; Kulin nation and, 126; similarities of words for in Aboriginal languages with Macquarie's name, 31–2, 34; and Reverend William Watson, 36–7
Eaglehawk and Crow: in Aboriginal mythology, 31, 32, 33, 34, 37; narratives of and stolen children, 4, 33; and traditional marriage customs, 32
Eaglehawk and Crow (John Matthew), 32
Eastern Kulin-speaking societies, 126
Ebenezer Mission Station, 40, 43, 49, 165, 188, 191, 202, 204
Edgar, James, 140
Ellen, 177, 179
Elmore, F, 160, 162
Embling, Dr Thomas, 147
English language: and literacy, 14; phonetical similarities with words in Aboriginal languages, 30–1
Eora people, 31
Essai sur l'origine des langues (J-J Rousseau), 71
etiquette of written communication: and petitions and power relations, 120–2; and power relations, 155–6, 227–8
Eurocentrism: autonomous model of literacy and, 9, 12; and the book, 206–7, 208, 210; and literacy and cultural evolution, 71–2, 207
European manuscript cultures, 79
European patronage systems: and Aboriginal kinship networks, 63

Fawkner, John Pascoe: and John Batman's treaty, 82, 84
Finnegan, Ruth: on orality and literacy, 10

Flannigan, Charlie, 79–80; drawing writing of, 5, 74, 79, 80–1, 91, 92
Flinders Island *see* Wybalenna settlement on Flinders Island
Flinders Island Chronicle, 103, 104, 106, 116, 119, 122
Flower, Ada, 187, 190
formulaic repetition: Walter George Arthur and Thomas Brune and, 108–9
Franklin, Governor Sir John, 114
Fraser, Jackie, 158

Geelong deed, 85, 86, 87
gendered gerontocracy *see* traditional gendered gerontocracy
gendered literacy and language use: patterns of, 177
gendered power structure of colonial society, 175
gerontocracy *see* traditional gendered gerontocracy
gift exchange: and Aboriginal kinship systems, 62; Bennelong's letter and, 56, 62–3, 67–8
Gilbert, Kevin, 228, 229
Ginibi, Ruby Langford, 220–2, 228
Glenelg, Lord: and John Batman's treaty, 91
God: Baiami and, 39; *see also* Jehovah
Goodall, William, 128, 145–6, 147
Gorrie, Billy, 158, 160
government policy: and literacy, 12, 13; *see also* bureaucratic governance
Gramscian model of hegemony: hidden transcripts and, 152–3
Green, Reverend John, 124, 128, 133, 134, 147; and Kulin people, 132
Green, Margaret *see* Harrison, Margaret (*nee* Green)
Green, Mary, 124, 132, 133, 134, 147
Green, Thomas, 158, 160
Grog war (Alexis Wright), 229
group awareness: lack of in Maggie Mobourne's letters and petitions, 167, 169; transmission of hidden transcripts between isolated cells of oppressed group and, 163

Guha, Ranjit: on differences between colonialism, 154, 170
Gunnartpa people: associations of their word for writing, 226
Gunther, Reverend James, 35–6, 37, 38

Hagenauer, Reverend FA, 150, 187; and Bessie Cameron (*nee* Flower), 188, 190
half-castes *see* people of mixed descent
Halliday, Hugh, 137, 138, 140, 144
Handt, Reverend Johann CS, 30, 34–5
Harker, George, 134, 135
Harrison, Captain, 202
Harrison, Margaret (*nee* Green), 201–5; letters by, 202, 204
Haunted by the past (Ruby Langford Ginibi), 220–1, 228
Hegarty, Ruth, 228
hegemonic control: and fiction of Aboriginal consent, 174; hidden transcripts and, 152–4; at Lake Condah Mission Station, 173–4; varieties of, 173; *see also* assimilation
Hewitt, Peter, 170
hidden expressions of anger and resentment, 156; *see also* open dissent
hidden transcripts, 152–4; and articulating silences, 173; and public transcripts, 161, 162; of Robert Sutton's court case, 157–8; transmission of between isolated cells of oppressed group, 163
Hobbles Danayarri, 214
Howitt, Alfred W, 189, 190
Huggins, Jackie, 219, 220, 221
Huggins, Rita, 219–20, 221

I, the Aboriginal (Waipuldanya [Douglas Lockwood]), 218
ideographic scripts, 5, 71, 72, 73, 89, 91, 92
ideographic signs, 212
ideological context of literacy, 13–14, 16–18
ideological controls and coercion, 173; and Aboriginal people, 154–5, 173–4; *see also* hegemonic control
ideological model of literacy, 9–11

imperialism: writing and, 23
Indigenous land-based and kin-based authority structures, 125; at Coranderrk Reserve, 125–6, 130; and writing at Coranderrk Reserve, 131; *see also* traditional gendered gerontocracy
Indigenous oral cultural traditions: and books, 215; and European print cultures, 207–8; Ruby Langford Ginibi's *Haunted by the past*, 221–2; and land, 215; and literacy, 11, 12–13, 16, 18; loss of, 11; *see also* orality
Indigenous patriarchal practice *see* traditional gendered gerontocracy
individual black–white collaboration: and Indigenous literacy, 19
Infant System, 35
institutional context of literacy, 14–15
intergenerational collaboration of speaking and writing: amendments to *Aboriginal Protection Act 1869* (Vic.) re people of mixed descent and, 150
Isaacs, Jennifer, 216, 217, 221

Jajowrong people, 126, 179, 194
James, John Stanley, 191
Jeanneret, Dr Henry: letter of Mary Anne Arthur to Queen Victoria re, 178–9; petition against reinstatement of, 119–22, 177–8
Jeffrey, Alexander (aka Andrew Jackson): and Annie McDonald (*nee* Rich), 184, 185–6; and Annie McDonald (*nee* Rich), 183
Jehovah: Eaglehawk and, 47, 48, 49–50, 51, 52; *see also* Baiami; God; Milbrodale Baiami
Jupagilwournditch people, 188

Kaurna people, 17
Kayardild people: associations of their word for writing, 226
Kerrupjmara people, 165, 183, 201
kinship networks: adoption of Governor Arthur Phillip into Bennelong's, 59–61, 62, 63; and European patronage systems, 63; and obligation of exchange of gifts, 62

Kneale, Captain: George Augustus Robinson on, 99–100
Kramer, Carl, 188
Kramer, Reverend, 204
Kulin nation/confederacy, 140; Reverend John Green and, 132; languages, social customs and religious beliefs of, 126–7; and literacy, 129, 149; writings of, 3, 127, 131; *see also* Coranderrk Reserve
Kurnai people, 127, 187, 190, 192

Lake Condah Mission Station, 6, 152, 155; coercion, hegemonic control and pretended submission at, 173–4; proposed closure of, 170
Lake Macquarie Mission, 39
Lake Tyers Mission Station, 187, 188, 190, 191, 192
land: Indigenous oral cultural traditions and, 215; written documents and struggle for, 124
Langford, Nobby, 220, 223
Langford, Ruby *see* Ginibi, Ruby Langford
learning by imitation, copying, repetition, 112–13; deficiencies of, 113–14, 115; subversive potential of, 112, 113–14
Lee. Dawn, 183
Leichhardt, Ludwig, 1
letters: from Aboriginal women *see* letters from Aboriginal women; to *Argus* (1882) re restrictions at Coranderrk Reserve, 144–5, 146; Bennelong's *see under* Bennelong; as means of asking for things, 67–8; and message-sticks, 67; Maggie Mobourne, 166–9, 170; as tradable objects, 56, 67, 70; writing of by Aboriginal people, 3, 21; *see also* etiquette of written communication
letters from Aboriginal women: Mary Anne Arthur, 178–9; Lena Austin, 198–200; Kitty Brangy, 196–7, 198; Bessie Cameron (*nee* Flower), 187–8, 189, 191, 192–3; elicited by colonial bureaucracy, 201; Ellen, 177, 179; Margaret Harrison (*nee* Green), 202, 204; Annie McDonald (*nee* Rich), 184–5; Edith Taylor, 203; to Queen Victoria, 195–6
Letters from Aboriginal women of Victoria, 1867–1926, 175
letters to Queen Victoria, 195–6; Mary Anne Arthur, 178–9; Ellen, 177, 179; seen as 'women's business', 177
Lindsay, Jessie, 16, 17
linguistic context of literacy, 14
literacies: and empowerment, 7
literacy: and Aboriginality, 18; and agency, 22–3; and assimilation, 11, 12–13, 18; bureaucratic governance and, 21, 22, 125, 135, 229; and construction of 'the helpless', 183, 185; in context *see* literacy in context; Coranderrk petitions and entanglement of and orality, 140–4; and cultural evolution, 9, 12, 71–2, 207; cultures of, 3, 6, 18–22, 224, 229; *see also* mission and reserve cultures of Indigenous literacy; traditionally oriented cultures of Indigenous literacy; individual black–white collaboration; gendered literacy and language use, 177; government policy and, 13; history of Indigenous, 2–3; ideological model of, 9; Indigenous, 4, 12, 18; and Indigenous oral cultural traditions, 11, 12–13, 16, 18; institutional conditions of, 228–9; in language of Awabakal people, 40; in language of Wiradjuri people, 37; of Annie McDonald (*nee* Rich), 183–4, 185; micro-historical context of, 18, 229; and orality *see* orality and literacy; Pallawah, 178; and prisons, 228; settler ideology and, 1–2; and stolen generations, 4, 15–18, 24, 25, 29, 35; and struggle for Aboriginal land, 124; in Wiradjuri language, 37; of women *see* literacy of women; writing before, 74; of young people *see* literacy of young people; *see also* alphabetic literacy; autonomous model of literacy; ideological model of literacy; literacies; writing
literacy in context, 2, 3, 4, 9–10; ideological, 13–14, 16–18; institutional, 14–15; linguistic, 14; material, 14;

Index

semantic, 14; socio-political, 14
literacy of women, 177; and construction of 'the helpless', 183–6; men's attitudes to, 181, 183; white vested interests in, 186–94
literacy of young people: at Coranderrk Reserve, 129, 133; and traditional gendered gerontocracy, 105, 109, 113, 129, 130, 149
literary works: Aboriginal people and, 3
Living black (Kevin Gilbert), 229
Loehe, Pastor, 198

McDonald, Alf, 184
McDonald, Annie (*nee* Rich), 181, 183–6; and Alexander Jeffrey (aka Andrew Jackson), 184, 185–6; as immigrant, 194; letter of to Captain Page, 184–5; literacy of, 183–4, 185
McDonald, Euphemia, 184
MacDonald, Reverend Murdoch, 190
McLeod, DN, 166, 167, 168, 169
McLeod, JN, 161
Macleod, Mr, 198, 200
Macpherson, JA, 134
Macquarie, Governor Lachlan: annual 'meetings of the tribes', 27–9, 31, 34, 39, 43; phonetic similarities of his name with words in Aboriginal languages, 30–1, 34; and stolen children, 4, 27–8, 34
Male and Female Orphan Schools, 30
Maltilina, Rebecca: postcards written by, 197–8, 199
Maria (Colby's daughter), 29
marriage *see* traditional marriage customs
Marsden, Samuel, 25–6
Marxism: hidden transcripts and, 152, 154
material context of literacy, 14
materiality of writing, 14
Matthew, John: on Eaglehawk and Crow, 32, 33–4
Meananger (Benang) people, 186
Melbourne deed, 85, 86, 87
message-sticks: and books, 209; letters and, 67, 211–12; and messenger's memory, 212; and George Augustus Robinson's visiting cards, 212–13; written texts used as, 213
messengers and mediators: and message-sticks, 212; and petitions and letters, 137
Mignolo, Walter D: on book history, 209; on writing as taming of the voice, 222
Milbrodale Baiami, 48–52; *see also* Biraban
Milligan, Dr Joseph, 121
mission and reserve cultures of Indigenous literacy, 5–6, 19, 20–1, 23; *see also* prisons
missions and reserves: and books, 214; coercion and ideological controls and, 154–5; pretence of benevolence by administrators of, 155, 194–5
Mobourne, Ernest, 166, 169, 170; petition penned by, 167, 170, 171–2
Mobourne, Maggie, 170; letters and petitions by, 166–9, 170
Mohican Station, 124, 147
monologic reading practices: Bible and, 99; and dialogic reading practices, 94–5; sermons of Thomas Brune and, 110
Morgan, Caroline: petition of, 194, 195
Mukwara *see* Eaglehawk

Nanbaree, 25
National School at Windsor, 30
nationalism *see* Aboriginal nationalism
Native Institution *see* Parramatta Native Institution
Native Legends (David Unaipon), 2
Neidje, Bill, 215
Ngurai-illam-wurrung people, 126
ngurungaeta, 125, 130, 146, 147
Noemy (Mar.wer.reek): rearticulation of Bible by, 116–17
non-alphabetic graphic systems, 18, 20
Northern people and language, 116
Nuenonne band, 105
Nyoongah people, 187, 188

Officer, Charles, 179–80
Ogilvie, Christian, 137, 138
Ong, Walter J: on formulaic repetitions, 109; on writing and non-writing, 71–2, 73

Oodgeroo Noonuccal, 229
open dissent and resistance: consequences of, 156, 158; dangerous wanderers and, 164–5, 169; *see also* hidden expressions of anger and resentment
'oral' societies: and alphabetic literacy, 3–4; *see also* Indigenous oral cultural traditions
orality and literacy, 10, 18, 222; Coranderrk petitions and entanglement of, 140–4

Page, Captain, 128; and 'Aboriginal' Narrative', 160, 162, 163, 164; and Kitty Brangy, 197; and Bessie Cameron (*nee* Flower), 191; and Coranderrk petition (September 1881), 142; and 'grateful Aborigines' petition, 158; and Margaret Harrison (*nee* Green), 201, 202, 204; and letter to *Argus* (1882), 145; and Annie McDonald (*nee* Rich), 184; and Edith Taylor, 203
Pallawah peoples, 99, 117, 130, 140, 176, 177, 211; position of women, 178; reading and writing by, 2–3
Pangerang people, 127, 140
paper: associations of in Aboriginal languages, 214, 227
paper yabber, 213
Parker, Edward Stone, 213
Parker, ES, 16
Parramatta Native Institution, 26–7, 29
patriarchal practice *see* traditional gendered gerontocracy
patrilineal moiety system: of Kulin nation, 126; *see also* traditional marriage customs
patronage *see* European patronage systems
people of mixed descent: 1886 amendments to *Aboriginal Protection Act 1869* (Vic.) and, 149–50, 181, 191; at Coranderrk Reserve, 126, 181
petitions: by Walter George Arthur, 228; by Bessie Cameron (*nee* Flower), 189, 190; Coranderrk Reserve *see* Coranderrk petitions; gender categorisation of, 179; by Ernest Mobourne, 167, 170, 171–2; by Maggie Mobourne, 166–9, 170; by Reverend John Heinrich Stahle against

'disruptive' Sutton group ('grateful Aborigines' petition), 158–9, 159; to Queen Victoria by Pallawah people against reinstatement of Dr Henry Jeanneret, 119–22, 177–8; *see also* etiquette of written communication; signatures
Phillip, Governor Arthur: and Bennelong, 5, 14, 56–8, 69; and Bennelong's kinship network, 59–61, 62, 63; and cross-cultural exchange of goods, 68–9; as exotic exhibit, 69; and recording of Aboriginal languages and culture, 53
Phillips, Mr and Mrs: and Bennelong, 61, 62, 64, 67, 69–70
phonographic scripts, 5, 71, 72, 73, 92
pictographic scripts, 5, 71, 72, 73, 92
Picturesque atlas of Australasia, 84
Pie.yen.kome.yen.ner ('Wild Mary'), 117
Pignaburg ('Bessy'), 117
Plunkett, Pol, 36
postcards: by Rebecca Maltilina, 197–8, 199
Power, Grace, 17
pretence of benevolence: by administrators of missions and reserves, 155, 194–5
pretence of submission, 153, 154, 155–6, 158, 159, 173; reserve superintendents and, 155
prisons: and modern Indigenous literacy, 228
protectionism: construction of 'the helpless' (illiterate) and, 183–6; lack of open attack on, 169; open attack on, 165; *see also Aboriginal Protection Act 1869* (Vic.); Board for the Protection of Aborigines (BPA)
public transcripts, 152, 155–6, 157; and hidden transcripts, 161, 162

Queen Victoria: letters to *see* letters to Queen Victoria; petition by Pallawah people against reinstatement of Dr Henry Jeanneret, 119–22, 177–8; written 'loyal address' to re land for Coranderrk Reserve, 125

Ramahyuck Mission Station, 165, 179, 187, 188, 190, 191, 192, 193
Ravenscroft, Alison, 219–20, 221
reading practices: monologic and dialogic, 94
Rebellion at Coranderrk (Diane Barwick), 127
red ochre: in Aboriginal ritual, 98
refraction *see* ventriloquism and refraction
Reid's Mistake mission, 40, 43
removal of children *see* stolen generations
Report on the literacy progress of the Aboriginal children in the Native Asylum, Parramatta (Elizabeth Shelley), 29
repressive hypothesis, 201
reserve culture *see* mission and reserve cultures of Indigenous literacy
reserves *see* missions and reserves
resistance: hidden forms of *see* hidden transcripts *see* Aboriginal resistance
Rich, Annie *see* McDonald, Annie (*nee* Rich)
ritual: parts of books and written documents used in, 68, 96–9, 211
Robinson, George Augustus: and Mary Anne Arthur, 178; and Walter George Arthur and Thomas Brune, 104, 111–12, 119, 130; and gathering of Aboriginal people in Van Dieman's Land, 96; and pages of *Book of common prayer* used in Aboriginal ritual, 96–9; and protection of Aboriginal people, 107, 123; and schooling on Flinders Island, 112, 113–15; and visit of Governor Sir John Franklin to Flinders Island, 114; and visiting cards issued to messengers, 212–13; way of dealing with Aboriginal people, 104; and Wybalenna settlement, 101, 103
Rousseau, J-J, 71
Ruediger, Dorothea, 197–8

Sabbath: Aboriginal contextually determined views of, 103; observance of and assimilation, 101–3
schooling: and removal of children, 15–16

Scott, James: and 'Aboriginals' Narrative', 163–4; and open rejection of hegemonic public discourse of protectionism, 164–5, 169
Scott, James C: on hidden and public transcripts, 152–4
scribes: and author and owner of written documents, 146; William Barak and, 133–4, 134, 146, 149, 150, 179, 181; Bennelong and, 54, 227, 228; European anthropologists as, 208; gender of, 179, 181
semantic context of literacy, 14
settler ideology: and fiction of Aboriginal consent, 174; and Indigenous literacy, 1–2
Shelley, Elizabeth, 26, 27, 29
Shelley, William, 26–7
sign carriers: in Aboriginal societies, 207, 209; alphabetic writing on variety of, 211; non-European and books, 209–10
sign systems: and ideological and cultural contexts, 72–3
signatures, 89; of Aboriginal men on petition by Reverend John Heinrich Stahle against 'disruptive' Sutton group, 159; concept of, 146; on John Batman's treaty, 83, 84, 86–9; order of on petitions, 132, 140, 170; questioning of on Coranderrk petitions, 144–6
signum, 89
silences: articulating, 173–4
Simpson, Martin, 140
Smyth, Robert Brough, 133, 137, 189
Snodgrass, Peter, 124
socio-political context of literacy, 14
speakers, 146–7
Spenser, WB: on Aboriginal people, 2, 72
Stahle, Reverend John Heinrich, 155; and Aboriginal women at Lake Condah Mission Station, 165, 166, 183, 201–4; and 'Aboriginals' Narrative', 161–2, 164; ambiguous power position of in official hierarchy, 160–1; beating of boys by, 157–8, 160; charge of assault against, 152, 156–7; and Coranderrk

petitions, 133–4; and Margaret Green, 201–2; inaction of over allegations of sexual misconduct, 160; and Annie McDonald (*nee* Rich), 183, 184, 185; and Mobournes, 166, 169, 170; petition by against 'disruptive' Sutton group, 158–9

Stahle, Mary, 164

stolen children *see* stolen generations

stolen generations: in early colonial period, 24–30, 34–6; literacy and, 4, 15–18, 24, 25, 29, 35; narratives of Eaglehawk and Crow and, 4; return of to own community to marry, 26–7, 30, 34

strategic performances: by oppressors and oppressed, 155; *see also* pretence of benevolence; pretence of submission

Strickland, Frederick, 128, 142, 144

Sutton, John Jr: indirect accusation in letter by, 157–8

Sutton, John Sr, 158, 165; and 'Aboriginals' Narrative', 159–60

Sutton, Robert: and charge of assault against Reverend John Heinrich Stahle, 152, 156–7

Sydney, Lord, 63–4; and Bennelong's letter, 58, 62, 68

Tanderrum ceremony: and John Batman's treaty, 82, 123, 151

Ta.ne.e.ber.rick ('Clara'), 117

Tasmania *see* Van Dieman's Land

Taungurong people, 123, 124, 126, 127, 139, 146, 149, 181

Taylor, Edith, 204; letter by, 203

Tench, Watkin, 53, 54–5

Thomas, William, 124; and Coranderrk Reserve, 124

Threlkeld, Launcelot, 4, 14, 22; and biblical translation and linguistic work, 40–1, 93; and biblical translation and linguistic work with Biraban, 39, 42, 43–6, 48; and intellectual astuteness of Awabakal people, 40

tradable objects: European goods, 210; letters as, 56, 67, 70; written and printed texts, 210–11

trade: Aboriginal networks, 66–7; written documents and, 2, 5, 68; *see also* cross-cultural exchange of goods

traditional gendered gerontocracy, 129; amendments to *Aboriginal Protection Act 1869* (Vic.) re people of mixed descent and, 150; literacy of young people and, 129, 130, 149; literacy of young people and inversion of, 105, 109, 113, 129, 130, 149; and order of signatures on petitions, 132, 170; and women's writing, 179; *see also* Indigenous land-based and kin-based authority structures

traditional marriage customs: Eaglehawk and Crow and, 32; of Kulin nation, 126; of Kurnai people, 187; stolen generations in colonial period and, 26–7, 30; *see also* patrilineal moiety system

traditionally based Indigenous practices of alphabetic literacy, 11

traditionally oriented cultures of Indigenous literacy, 19–20, 224–5

translation of Bible, 3, 4, 37–8; into Awabakal language, 39, 40, 44–5; on Flinders Island, 117–18; into language of Ben Lomond people, 100; and recontextualisation of, 118–19; into Wiradjuri language, 37, 38

Tristan, 25–6

true stories: bringing people closer together, 198–205

Truganini, 176

Tylor, Edward Burnett: on writing and civilisation, 8–9, 72

Unaipon, David, 2

Van Dieman, George, 99–100

Van Dieman's Land: war against Aboriginal people of, 95–6, 117; *see also* Pallawah peoples

ventriloquism and refraction: political dynamics of, 5–6

Victoria: destruction of Aboriginal economy in, 123; establishment of Aboriginal reserves in, 123; *see also*

Batman treaty with Woiworung people
visiting cards: Aboriginal use of fragment of text as, 213; George Augustus Robinson's, 212–13
Volosinov, V N: on monologic and dialogic reading practices, 94
Voss (Patrick White), 1

Waipuldanya, 218
Walker, Robert, 228
Walter *see* Arthur, Walter George
Wandin, Jemima Burns, 150, 151
Wandin, Joy Murphy, 151
Wandin, Robert, 147, 151, 181
Wandjuk Marika, 216, 217, 221
Wandjuk Marika: life story, 216, 217
Wangkumara people and language, 214, 227
Ward, Glenyse, 228
Warkentin, Germaine: on the book as function, 208
Warlpiri community at Lajamanu: and use of names of alphabetical letters and traditional prohibition on saying names of deceased persons, 225
Wathaurung people, 126
Watson, Reverend William, 30, 34–5, 36, 37; as eaglehawk, 36–7; and use of Wiradjuri language, 37, 38
Wave Hill Station, 80, 81
Weapons of the weak (James C Scott), 152
Wellington Valley Mission, 30, 34–6, 38–9
Western Bundjalung people: associations of 'paper' in their language, 227
Western Bundjalung people and language, 214
Western Kulin-speaking societies, 126
Western people and language, 104, 116, 117
White, Patrick: and Aboriginal people and written documents, 1
Wilkinson, Thomas, 101; and translation of Bible, 100
Willemering, 60–1
Windradyne, 28, 34
Wiradjuri carver(s), 224–5
Wiradjuri clubs: club A, 75–8; club B, 77, 78; use of alphabetic characters in accordance with traditional inscriptions, 74–9, 91, 92, 211, 227
Wiradjuri people, 5, 28; and assimilation of Bible to traditional understanding of universe, 38; Baiami ceremonies of, 38–9; literacy in language of, 37; removal of children of, 34–7; and war with colonists, 34
Wiradjuri people and language: translations into, 37
Woiworung people, 124, 139, 140, 146, 181; treaty with John Batman *see* Batman treaty with Woiworung people; women, 127
women *see* Aboriginal women
Wonga, Simon, 123; and Coranderrk Reserve, 124, 127; as *ngurungaeta*, 125; and traditional Indigenous law, 126; and written 'loyal address' to Queen Victoria re land for Coranderrk Reserve, 125
Wonnarua country, 48, 49
Worgan *see* Crow
Worgan, George, 31
Wourraddy ('Doctor'/'Count Alpha'): rearticulation of Bible by, 117–18
Wright, Alexis, 229
writing: by Aboriginal people as means to bridge spatial and social distances, 195–7, 198; adaptation of to traditional protocols of communication, 3, 6, 22, 211, 213; associations of English and Aboriginal words for, 225–7; and biological and cultural advancement of humankind, 8–9; bureaucratic governance and, 21; by colonial bureaucrats as governance of Aboriginal people by remote control, 194–5, 197; and communication with world outside mission/reserve, 161; and English language, 14; history of reading, 2–3; ideologies of, 225–6; and Indigenous land-based and kin-based authority structures at Coranderrk Reserve, 131; before literacy, 74; materiality of, 14; materiality of and

associations of in Aboriginal languages with reference to 'paper', 227; and meaning, 14; and non-writing, 72, 73, 91, 92; perceptions of and cultural contexts, 227; as performative medium, 6; and power and status, 57; and talking back about abuse of power, 142; true stories, 198–205; *see also* intergenerational collaboration of speaking and writing; letters; literacy; petitions; postcards

writing by Aboriginal women, 6; authority to write, 179; on behalf of community, 179–83, 189; letters and petitions, 165–72, 175–6, 177–9, 184–5; literacy and language skills, 177; men's attitudes to, 181, 183; as scribes, 179–81

written documents: author, scribe and owner of, 146; and struggle for Aboriginal land, 124; as tradable artefacts, 2, 5, 68; used in ritual, 68; Patrick White on Aboriginal people and, 1; *see also* the book and books

Wurul. Wurulbadyaou, 26

Wurundjeri clan, 82, 125, 126

Wurundjeri-willam clan, 125

Wybalenna settlement on Flinders Island, 100; heterogeneity of Aboriginal languages in, 116; heterogeneity of Aboriginal peoples in, 104, 105; inversion of traditional gerontocracy in, 105, 109, 149; older men's rearticulation of Bible in, 115–18; scriptural education in, 109, 112–15; traditional ceremonial practices and power structures in, 105; visit of Governor Sir John Franklin to, 114

Yemmerrawanie, 61

Yidinjdji people: associations of their word for writing, 226–7

Yolngu people, 216